I KNOW WHO YOU ARE

I KNOW WHO YOU ARE

HOW AN AMATEUR
DNA SLEUTH UNMASKED
THE GOLDEN STATE KILLER
AND CHANGED CRIME
FIGHTING FOREVER

BARBARA RAE-VENTER

BALLANTINE BOOKS
NEW YORK

Published in the United States by Ballantine Books, an imprint of Random House, a division of Penguin Random House LLC, New York.

BALLANTINE is a registered trademark and the colophon is a trademark of Penguin Random House LLC.

Hardback ISBN 978-0-593-35889-4
Ebook ISBN 978-0-593-35890-0

PRINTED IN THE UNITED STATES OF AMERICA ON ACID-FREE PAPER

randomhousebooks.com

9 8 7 6 5 4 3 2 1

First Edition

Illustration by polesnoy/stock.adobe.com

DEDICATED

To all the survivors of the many crimes
related in this book, and to the memories
of all the victims. The DNA spoke for you.
You are not forgotten.

And to my number one (and only) son,
Christopher Emrys Rae Venter,
who encouraged me to rescind my request
for anonymity and go public with my role
in identifying the Golden State Killer.
Without that encouragement we would not
have this book.

PREFACE

No human walks this world without leaving a trace. The earth measures our presence through the imprints and remnants of our time here, some subtle or microscopic, some as striking as the buildings we build or the mountains we move. We are not a stealthy species; we boldly or blindly mark where we have been. Some traces may never be examined or even known to another living being. But others *will* be searched for and uncovered, and from them, much can be extracted: ancient histories, family ties, illness patterns, heredities and behaviors, guilt or innocence.

We have over time become more and more proficient at analyzing these traces, to the point where bones buried for millennia can unlock the deepest mysteries and a single drop of dried blood can reveal the most fearsome monster. At this moment we are living through a forensic revolution linked to how we understand and read the human genome.

Improbably, at least to me, I am part of this revolution.

In March 2017 a man named Paul Holes called me at my home in Northern California. He identified himself as a cold-case investigator for the Contra Costa County Sheriff's Office.

At the time, I was retired after a long career as a patent attorney, and I had no training in criminal investigations or anything like that. In what began as a postretirement hobby, I was volunteering as a genetic genealogist—a "search angel" who uses DNA matches to build family trees and help solve unknown parentage issues. Often I worked with adoptees who were searching for their biological families.

In March 2015, I had begun working on a project to identify a woman who had been abducted as an infant and did not know her name or history or parentage, and I had successfully used her DNA to uncover her identity—solving a mystery that had baffled both the woman and detectives for decades. Now, two years later, Paul Holes had heard about my work on the case from an FBI lawyer and called me.

"I have a cold case I need help with," Paul said. "Would you be willing to work with me in identifying a criminal suspect?"

I did not ask about the crime or the case. I just said that I would be willing to help. Eventually Paul told me who we were hunting for:

The Golden State Killer.

What happened over the next few months changed the field of criminology. As *Time* magazine put it, the work I performed on the Golden State Killer case "provided law enforcement with its most revolutionary tool since the advent of forensic DNA testing in the 1980s."

This book is about some of the cases I worked on during a brief but extraordinary window of opportunity—from roughly 2015 to 2018—that may one day be seen as the golden age of investigative genetic genealogy (IGG). During this remarkable time, crimes long considered unsolvable were solved with relatively stunning speed, and criminals who had long avoided not just capture but even identification were suddenly named and held to account. Cold case files long buried in dusty cabinets were pulled out into the light and finally, satisfyingly, closed. The impossible, suddenly, was possible. Aside from the beginnings of forensic fingerprinting in the late nineteenth century and the start of DNA profiling in the 1980s, there have been precious few moments when detectives, FBI agents, and other crime fighters gained such a powerful edge over the criminals they hunt.

And then, almost as suddenly as it opened, this extraordinary window of opportunity was very nearly shut.

The full story of how this breakthrough came to pass—of how a small band of us applied startling technological advancements to active criminal cold cases—has never truly been told before. I am telling it now. The pages that follow offer an up-close, firsthand account of the cold cases that pushed the boundaries and changed the rules, as well as an exploration of what these cases reveal about human nature—about us.

A parallel story describes how someone with no background in law enforcement and both feet planted firmly in retirement could, somehow, end up front and center in the one criminal cold case that most moved the needle, that generated thousands of headlines around the world, and that triggered perhaps the most significant ethical debate of our time: the case of the Golden State Killer.

I learned about the Golden State Killer through his victims.

There was Patrice, a nurse and newlywed, friendly and full of life, murdered brutally in her home in 1975. Patrice was twenty-seven years old in 1975, the same age I was that year. There was Jane, a young mother bound and raped repeatedly in the home she shared with her three-year-old son, who was in the house and tied up when the horrors occurred. There was Charlene, an interior decorator, discovered on her bed by her stepson, her skull crushed by a fireplace log.

And many more—dozens of them—most about the same age I was during the rape-and-killing spree that spanned the twelve years between 1974 and 1986. After the last known crime in the spree, the killer vanished into anonymity, and the case went cold—so cold it remained unsolved, and seemingly unsolvable, for more than thirty years.

But then, in 2017, his victims began to speak out to me through the pages of old newspapers that described the terrible crimes against them but only guessed at the nature of their unknown assailant: a lurking, stalking monster who hid behind bushes and crept through unlocked doors and windows, crouching, noiseless, quick to pounce, and now, so many years later, still only a shadow in the dark, still taunting and haunting those who survived his mayhem.

I had no experience with, or even knowledge of, the existence of such evil in our world, and I sensed that joining in the pursuit of this man would take me to some very dark places, darker than anywhere I had been before. But I also knew that I wanted to help identify him.

I was acting on an instinct ingrained deeply within me and reflected in so many pivotal moments in my life: the need to know what I do not know.

When I was young and growing up in New Zealand my mother referred to this instinct as my "grasshopper mind," a restless, jumpy inquisitiveness, a tendency to examine issues from seemingly strange angles until I found a novel way to resolve them. This way of learning helped me succeed in my career as a patent attorney, and it has helped me solve cases in the nascent field of investigative genetic genealogy— including some of the most infamous, bloody, and baffling cold cases of all time.

My personal traits and history are what brought me to this historic case at just that time, but I believe that all of us are to some degree natural puzzle solvers, curious about what we do not know and excited to unearth secret connections—investigators of our own lives.

Some of you reading this may share my interest in genetic genealogy and researching family histories, driven to crack the mysteries of your own ancestors and ultimately of yourselves. Some of you may be professional or passionate amateur genetic genealogists, helping others on their journeys of self-discovery. And some of you may be true-crime enthusiasts, drawn to the procedural nuts and bolts—and the undeniable visceral thrill—of solving a long-cold murder case.

Whatever it is that has brought you to this story, it is my hope that you find it not only informative and exciting but also inspiring in how it describes the brave and worthwhile journeys of discovery we all must undertake at some point in our lives. Because behind the story of this pivotal moment in history, beyond the case of the Golden State Killer and other long-cold crimes I helped solve, lies something strong and shared and primal:

The desire to uncover that which is hidden from us.

CONTENTS

PART ONE

LISA JENSEN
MARCH 2015

1

On March 3, 2015, a volunteer genealogist at a not-for-profit organization called DNAAdoption opened the following email:

SUBJECT: Unknown Person Search

MESSAGE: I work for the San Bernardino County Sheriff's Department. I am working a cold case involving a kidnapping of a child when she was approx. age 2; she was recovered at approx. age 5. We do not know her real name, date of birth, etc. She is now grown in her '30s and the only known survivor of the suspect. As we back track the suspect for other victims we are attempting to tell her who she is. We have already signed up with Ancestry DNA and gotten a hit on a second cousin. I have been reading your site and would like to ask if you had any other advice given the uniqueness of our search.

The person who sent the email was Deputy Peter Headley of the San Bernardino County Sheriff's Department Crimes Against Children Detail. The volunteer was me.

It was only a few months earlier that I had signed up as a search angel with DNAAdoption, a group that teaches adoptees how to identify biological relatives using autosomal DNA. Nearly all of the emails that I opened were from adoptees hoping to learn how to identify their birth parents, and I did my best to answer their questions. But this email was different. I was intrigued, so I immediately called Deputy Headley to learn more.

He told me the story of a girl who had been abducted and was now part of a long-cold case. Her name was Lisa Jensen, and her story—at least the part of it that was known to law enforcement—began in 1986, when Lisa was around five years old and living at the Santa Cruz Ranch RV Resort. It was an unremarkable trailer park tucked around the redwood trees of California's Santa Cruz Mountains, on the site of a bygone theme park called Santa's Village.

That year, Lisa befriended a woman named Kathy Decker, who lived in a mobile home at the park. Kathy came to know Lisa as a friendly and chatty child, outwardly normal in most ways. But Lisa was also alarmingly skinny, and she had bruises on her body and stains on her clothes. She had no toys of her own, and she came over to play with Kathy's young grandson nearly every day, as if she had nowhere else to go. Kathy noticed that Lisa and her father—a widower named Gordon Jensen, who worked at the park as a handyman—slept in an open camper shell in the back of a pickup truck, even on nights when it was freezing.

"Lisa was tattered and torn," Kathy later said. "She was a little ragamuffin."

Just as Lisa looked to Kathy's grandson for company, Lisa's father, Gordon, turned to Kathy for emotional support. He confided in her about how much he missed his late wife, who he said had died of cancer when Lisa was just an infant. Kathy watched him break down in tears as he remembered her. Jensen also complained about how hard it was to be a single father to Lisa.

When Kathy mentioned that her own daughter and son-in-law were eager to have a child but had not been able to conceive, it was Gordon Jensen who suggested that Kathy's daughter take little Lisa to live with her in Chico Hills, California, for three weeks—a trial run before, perhaps, he would grant them permission to legally adopt her.

Lisa was excited by the idea. When Kathy bought new shoes for her for the trip to Chico Hills, Lisa wore them to bed.

It was an odd arrangement, to be sure, but for a while it worked out well. Lisa loved her new home with Kathy's daughter and husband, and they in turn loved the little girl.

Then, one day, young Lisa began describing the ways her father had abused her. Her stories were shocking and sickening—one police officer later said Lisa had been "severely molested and tortured." Kathy's daughter quickly called the police.

Officers from the San Bernardino County Sheriff's Department soon arrived at the trailer park, but by the time they got there Gordon Jensen was gone. He had packed up and disappeared, leaving Lisa behind with Kathy's family.

Investigator Cliff Harris of the San Bernardino County Sheriff's Department searched the Santa Cruz Ranch RV Resort and pulled a single fingerprint off video equipment that Jensen had installed in the park's community area. It appeared that Jensen had wiped off the equipment before leaving but had overlooked a single incriminating print. Harris ran the fingerprint and learned that Jensen, under the alias Curtis Kimball, had been arrested a year earlier, in 1985, after driving drunk and crashing a car with his young daughter, Lisa, in it. That year, a district attorney charged Jensen with driving under the influence and endangering the welfare of a child.

But Jensen failed to show up at court on those charges, and then he fell off the radar. Law enforcement picked up his trail one year later when Kathy Decker's daughter called police about him.

And now, yet again, Jensen had slipped away. A full year passed, then another. Meanwhile, because Gordon Jensen had fled before signing any adoption papers, and because Lisa was not related to Kathy's daughter and had a living father, she was taken away from Kathy's family and placed in the custody of the state.

For Kathy Decker and her daughter, the perfect ending never happened.

For Lisa, her escape from Gordon Jensen led her into foster care and created a lasting uncertainty about her identity. She had no knowledge of her mother, no birth certificate—no documents at all—and the name she knew her father by was, police had learned, an alias.

But that was not all. Some years later, in 2003, a DNA test revealed that Gordon Jensen was *not* Lisa's biological father. He was her abductor.

Which meant that Lisa Jensen was, in technical terms, a "living Jane Doe"—a female whose name and identity are unknown.

In November 1988, police finally caught up with Gordon Jensen. Officers pulled over a car in San Luis Obispo on suspicion that it was stolen. The driver identified himself as Gerry Mockerman and produced documents with that name on them. He was poised and sure of himself. The driver's fingerprints, however, revealed that the man was actually Gordon Jensen. He was arrested for driving a stolen vehicle, and an investigation connected him to the abandonment of Lisa Jensen in 1986. "He would steal people's identities, and he had all their names stored up in his head," says Deputy Headley of Gordon Jensen. "He had an incredible memory and he was a very smart guy. He spoke several languages fluently."

For the crime of abandoning Lisa, a judge sentenced Jensen to three years in prison.

Jensen served only a small part of that stretch before being paroled in 1990. He then did what he had done many times before in his criminal career: he vanished, again, leaving no trace, this time for twelve long years.

In late 2012, Lisa Jensen's long-unsolved Jane Doe case was taken over by San Bernardino deputy Peter Headley. (San Bernardino is a large county just east of Los Angeles.)

A Southern California native who got his start in law enforcement conducting mountain search-and-rescue missions, Headley was working the Crimes Against Children Detail when he picked up Lisa's case. Lisa was now in her thirties and had children of her own. She insisted on living a quiet, private life, but she was also determined to uncover her biological identity. Despite the trauma of her early years, Lisa was a vibrant, beautiful woman who embraced life, taught dance classes, and was fiercely protective of her family.

For years Lisa and Deputy Headley worked together to find enough bits of information to pin down her real name and establish her identity, but, sadly, they made little progress.

"It was a cold case going way, way back, and people who knew about it had died, or they could not remember," Headley told me. And as for police interviews of Jensen, "he never gave us anything. He said he couldn't even remember Lisa."

Neither Lisa nor Headley gave up. One day, Lisa watched the genealogy TV show *Who Do You Think You Are?*, which follows celebrities as they trace their family trees to learn more about their personal histories. After watching the show, Lisa called Deputy Headley.

"Do you think DNA could work for me?" she asked.

Analyzing DNA to find potential relatives and even potential criminal suspects was not a new concept for Headley. Years earlier he had read up on the emerging technology and looked into a new consumer-genealogy website called AncestryDNA, which encouraged people to submit their DNA for testing and build their own family trees. "But back then," says Headley, "the databases were still very small"—meaning too few people had joined the site to create a big enough pool of potential relatives who might "match" Lisa's DNA. Investigative genetic genealogy is a numbers game, and Headley had to wait for the numbers to build up.

In 2014, when the AncestryDNA database and other similar databases were more robust, Deputy Headley opened an account for Lisa Jensen there and Lisa submitted a saliva sample. Lisa's DNA test produced several hundred genetic matches. Looking at the long list of names, Deputy Headley realized he had no idea what to do with the information.

This was the point when he decided he needed some help. "It was still relatively new technology to me," he says. "A lot of the time I was stumbling in the dark."

I was moved by Lisa's story and her struggle for identity, and I agreed to help in any way I could. Deputy Headley offered me the chance to take the lead on the DNA side of the case, and on March 3, 2015, I joined the team working on what became known as the Lisa Jensen Project.

I was a volunteer genealogist with precisely no law enforcement experience, yet suddenly I was front and center in an open criminal cold case. How in the world had this happened?

2

When I opened Deputy Headley's email in 2015 I was, technically, a retiree.

Several years earlier I had finished a long career as a patent attorney. My specialty had been biotechnology innovations—that is, helping inventors patent genetically modified organisms and the tools to modify them. For example, I worked on a well-known case involving a genetically modified tomato called the Flavr Savr, and I opened my own law firm. I was a patent attorney for two decades before my retirement, which, frankly, I was quite enjoying.

Back then, the same as now, I lived in a house along the Northern California coast, not far from the ocean, in an area that reminded me of the rugged splendor of my native New Zealand. In retirement I had more time to spend with my son, Christopher, and to tend to the little garden I kept behind my home, where I grew potatoes, tomatoes, runner beans, and kale—a sweet echo of the garden I kept when I was ten and my mother paid me market value for radishes, tomatoes, and chard. I played tennis with friends and filled my home with orchids from a local nursery, and I traveled to China and Europe and New Zealand. My cats, Bijou and Emrys, were always afoot, dragging in birds and mice and leaving them for me in my bathroom as gifts.

I also finally had the time to research the history of my family, tracing both my maternal and paternal lines as far back as I could—which was difficult on my father's side because New Zealand does not release any census data to the public. I was basically learning research methods as I went. But as can happen once you get into the thickets of your family history, the "hobby" of genealogy became increasingly consuming for me, to the point where I was spending the better part of most days neck-deep in one family mystery or another.

I had the good fortune of retiring just as direct-to-consumer DNA testing services were taking off. This new kind of deep-dive, DNA-based research—the use of DNA tests to identify biological relatives—appealed to me right from the start, and I was one of the earliest people to use DNA for family history research. The astonishing scope of it—ancient ancestral origins, great waves of human migration, genetic markers traveling through the centuries, the vast kaleidoscopic history of us all—was fascinating, but so was the nitty-gritty of analyzing DNA matches pulled from hundreds of thousands of points of DNA data.

All around me, the field grew with exponential speed. In 2000, FamilyTreeDNA issued the first direct-to-consumer test kit, which allowed users to identify and connect with relatives they might not have known about, and to verify family history they had dug up through traditional methods. New DNA profiles constantly flowed into many new online sites—MyHeritage, FamilyTreeDNA, 23andMe—creating massive databases of potential DNA matches. In 2015 fewer than one million people in the United States had submitted samples for genetic testing to AncestryDNA. Today, that number is well over thirty million across all the U.S. genealogical sites.

Because of my background working in biotechnology, and because I have a PhD in biology, I understood the science of DNA and how it worked in relation to ancestry. I understood the nature of chromosomes and how autosomal DNA was replicated and passed from one generation to the next, and what that means in the grand scheme of ancestral research—a conceptual challenge that many amateur genetic genealogists, and some fairly seasoned ones, continue to face. In the course of my research I discovered that I was able to quickly see connections that might take others much longer to puzzle out.

Still, when I began researching my family roots I knew very little about genealogy research itself, and I immediately set out to learn everything I could.

I signed up for a four-semester family history class offered online by Monterey Peninsula College. It was designed and taught by Karen Clifford, one of the leading genealogical researchers in the world and a pioneer in the field who had authored textbooks and guidebooks on the subject. Karen's class—which was purely about genealogy, or family history research—was the beginning of my immersion in the field.

I learned about sources and methods for researching ancestors back to 1850, and more advanced strategies for before then. I learned how to pore over all kinds of records, including census, tax, probate, land, property, military, and more; how to extend a family line past U.S. borders to ancestral countries; how to decipher the handwriting on documents dating back to the seventeenth century; how to poke around the dustiest nooks of genealogical research, from benefit records from the Spanish-American War to eighteenth-century slave schedules and enumeration rolls.

Karen Clifford's class was a dazzling introduction to all that is possible in a genealogical search—and all that can confound you if you miss a step. In the span of less than a quarter century, enormous technological strides (e.g., scanning and digitalization, indexing of records) had been made, opening the field of genealogy to just about everyone and making it far less taxing and time-consuming.

For much of the twentieth century, the only way to construct a solid family tree was to physically visit archives and halls of records and collect birth and death certificates, marriage licenses, and other paper evidence. Add in trips to graveyards to glean information from headstones and family stories passed down through the years, and you would have an approximation of your family's history for two hundred years or so.

I have a cousin in New Zealand who did just that, traveling to

England over the decades to research our family history and secure precious family documents. I have looked through her massive folders full of original birth certificates and other milestone records, and I have marveled at her diligence. She collected everything in those folders herself, and I can only imagine the hundreds of hours of legwork involved. It was a stunning achievement, and over many years she succeeded in assembling a truly beautiful family history.

But times have changed. Today it would not take several years to assemble such a history. Someone with mostly northern or western European ancestry could possibly create a similar family history in just a few weeks.

One of the first things I did in my family history research was something my New Zealand cousin had not been able to do: I used DNA to confirm, augment, or disprove all the work I was doing on that shared branch of my family tree. To do this I had to persuade as many of my relatives as I could to take DNA tests, including my New Zealand cousin's father.

My cousin's father's test immediately revealed a family mystery that I set out to solve.

As far back as I can remember, I was told a branch of my family was related to the Yorkshire Rowntrees, a well-known nineteenth-century Quaker family from northern England, near the Scottish border. However, when I tested my cousin's father's Y-DNA (which tracks the paternal line), I was surprised to see he did not match *any* Rowntrees.

He did, however, match literally hundreds of men in Clan Irwin, a less well known family from Dumfries in the south of Scotland.

What did this mean?

To find the answer, I had to go back to the Middle Ages.

I tested more-distant direct-line male Rowntree relatives and eventually tested a relative whose shared ancestors with me were from a time in history when the border between Scotland and England was a lawless and predatory stretch of land, prone to blood feuds, wanton theft, and frequent maiming and murdering. Border Country, as it was known, had its own laws, written and unwritten, which were enforced by various clans on either side. These laws gave rise to bandits known as Border Reivers: men who roamed across the border stealing herds of cattle and perhaps a wife before crossing back over the border with seeming impunity.

Here was the likely explanation for the Rowntree/Irwin mystery—some long-ago Clan Irwin lad from Dumfries had crossed the Border Country and raped a Rowntree wife while in Sunderland, creating a child with the Rowntree name who was, in the male line, genetically an Irwin. Instead of being related to the gentle, peace-loving Quakers of the Yorkshire Rowntree family, we actually traced our lineage back to a daring little reiver clamoring across the lawless border.

To encounter this odd family mystery, and then to solve it through genetic genealogy—at least to the point of knowing what most likely had happened and when—was exhilarating. There was something stirring about being transported back in time by the DNA and allowing the DNA to guide me through the actual twists and turns of my lineage. The DNA was powerful, precise, and determinative—a truly remarkable tool.

This may have been the moment when I first became addicted to the rewarding payoff of genetic genealogy: the thrill of discovery.

Early on in my adventures in genetic genealogy, I was contacted by a man named David Abbott. David had been at his home in Kent in the United Kingdom, not far from the Strait of Dover in the English Channel, when, one ordinary day in 2014, he watched the same genealogy TV show, *Who Do You Think You Are?*, that Lisa Jensen had seen. David was intrigued enough to visit the genealogy site FamilyTreeDNA.

"They were offering free kits," he recalls, "so I decided to have a go, just for something to do."

The DNA test, and David's dive into his family history, unearthed a startling secret. The man he believed was his father was *not* a biological relative; in fact, David discovered that he was born in a home for orphans, and the line on his birth certificate reserved for his father's identity was blank.

"I had all these questions I needed answered," says David, "but there was no one left to ask." Tragically, his mother had died just three days before he learned the truth about his father, and his mother's sister told him his biological father had been a Canadian airman stationed in the United Kingdom—but that was all she could tell him.

That single detail, though, resonated with David. "I remember having three model airplanes when I was young," he says. "I didn't know where they came from, but I still have one. I've also always had this old photograph of a dog in an airfield somewhere. I just didn't know what these things meant."

David's 2014 FamilyTreeDNA test produced a long list of people who shared some small fraction of DNA with him. The most closely related one was a possible third cousin—someone who, with any luck at all, might be able to help David identify his biological father.

I was David's possible third cousin.

David reached out to me in the early stages of my dalliance with DNA. He said he was desperately hoping to discover his father's identity and asked for my help. I was intrigued by my connection to his tangled family history, and I agreed to do whatever I could.

In order to properly help David, I felt I needed to learn more. I searched for classes that focused on emerging techniques in the field of genetic genealogy—the use of DNA to identify biological relatives. (Karen Clifford's class, by contrast, was about traditional family history research and did not touch on DNA.) One of the groups I researched was DNAAdoption. Launched in 2012, the not-for-profit organization started as (and continues to be) a collection of unpaid volunteers from all sorts of disciplines: genealogists, scientists, computer specialists, accountants, geneticists, and even hobbyists who had become skilled sleuths. The group focused its work on connecting adoptees with birth relatives. They offered an intensive six-week online DNA analysis course that was not too expensive and seemed quite comprehensive. I signed up right away. This was the first time I learned how to build family trees with the new science of DNA and use that information to identify the biological parents of an adoptee.

My biology background, it turned out, helped me identify some scientific errors in DNAAdoption's online lessons. I brought these errors to the group's attention, and its members were completely gracious about it and even asked me to rework the lessons. I was pleased to see that these pioneers in the field of genetic genealogy saw themselves not as unapproachable experts but, much as I did, as perpetual students, always learning, always evolving, open to new information and techniques. If something was not working, all they cared about was finding a way to fix it.

At the end of six weeks I did not quite feel like an expert, but I certainly felt like I had learned enough to at least try to help David identify his biological father. This was my first time helping another person explore their family roots. It would not be the last. I came to understand that there were many, many people like my cousin David—people desperate for help in unraveling their tangled family histories. I saw how badly these people needed answers to their many questions. And the thought I had was:

I would like to know how to help these people.

And so, in 2014, I joined DNAAdoption as a volunteer search angel.

Karin Corbeil, who took up genetic genealogy after a long career in international accounting, was one of the people who welcomed me into DNAAdoption. Along with her fellow co-founders Rob Warthen, Diane Harman-Hoog, and Gaye Tannenbaum, Karin developed and refined a revolutionary search technique they called the Methodology. I learned the technique in their six-week course, and I want to take a moment to explain it. Even after many years, it still serves as the basis of my work with both adoptees and forensic cases.

The Methodology basically changed the field of genetic genealogy by establishing a formal way to build out family trees using DNA matches. The Methodology is based on a scientific breakthrough: the introduction of autosomal DNA testing in 2007. These tests provided new ways to match DNA and larger sets of relatives who could not previously be identified. (For more on autosomal DNA testing, see the Glossary, page 247). For the first time there was a reliable method for identifying people whose identities were not known.

The breakthrough development of the Methodology, or DNA segment triangulation, was the realization that if three people all match one another on the same segment of DNA—and if we find a common ancestor of two of them—then the third person *must also be* a descendant of that common ancestor.

In other words, if the DNA of Person A (who is of unknown parentage) matches the DNA of Persons B and C at a second-cousin level, and if Persons B and C are also second cousins and share a set of great-grandparents, we can be sure that Person A is *also* a descendant of this set of great-grandparents.

To identify who Person A is, you first identify the most *recent* common ancestor (MRCA) of Persons B and C—the set of great-grandparents. Then you identify every descendant of this MRCA all the way down to the generation in which Person A was born. Among all those descendants, you look for someone who matches up with information that you have about Person A, such as their age, where they lived, any known physical characteristics, etc. Ultimately, you will uncover the identity of Person A.

The identification of all the descendants is called building *down* a descendant line: moving chronologically *forward* in time through more and more recent generations, as opposed to the traditional way of building a family tree—starting, say, with yourself and building *up* to find more and more distant relatives.

I recognized immediately that this was an exciting tool to use. It could involve a significant amount of work, especially if the most recent common ancestor had multiple children and I had to identify dozens or even hundreds of descendants to find the person of interest. But I now had a clear path to help people find their biological relatives—once I had identified the most recent common ancestor, I could be sure that the answer was there. Hidden, perhaps, and hard to locate, but there, somewhere, waiting for me to find it.

At DNAAdoption Karin Corbeil and I went through all the emails we received from people eager to find biological relatives. If a case seemed like it might require a particular brand of expertise, we funneled it to the search angel best equipped to help. Karin and I would also personally take on cases that seemed especially difficult or time sensitive.

Early on, I took on a case involving a ninety-eight-year-old woman named Ellen Law. Ellen was eighty-five when she discovered that she had been adopted, and she wanted to know the identity of her birth parents before she died. Her case is a good example of the type of work I was doing with DNAAdoption.

The email requesting help was from Ellen's granddaughter, Tonya. With Tonya's assistance, Ellen believed she had pieced together some of her family history over the years. She had, for instance, obtained a copy of her original birth certificate from Chicago. The names of the parents listed on the certificate were Maria Jensen and Claude Holt. She spent eight years looking for Maria and Claude but was never able to find them.

Ellen's test results from 23andMe produced quite a few matches, many encouragingly close. With Ellen's permission I contacted some of these matches, including a woman named Marilyn, through the 23andMe messaging system. People often take weeks to respond to such messages, if they respond at all, but I was lucky. Marilyn responded within twenty minutes and sent me a family tree. In Marilyn's profile, she listed her mother's maiden name as Jensen—the same surname as on Ellen's birth certificate. This was exciting. Two other matches also responded quickly and sent me their family trees.

I began working with the information on all these trees and discovered someone named Anna Maria Jensen, who was Marilyn's great-aunt. This woman fit the age profile for Ellen Law's mother.

But there was a problem: Anna Maria Jensen lived in Minnesota and Ellen was born in *Chicago*.

I kept digging. The two additional matches who responded were related closely enough that I was able to combine their two trees into one. When I did that, I made a huge discovery: the grandfather of one of the matches was named Claude. When I dug further and located the most recent common ancestor on the combined tree, I saw that that the MRCA's name was also Claude. They were the same man: our paternal most recent common ancestor.

My other key discovery was that Claude had been married to a woman named Anna Maria Jensen, the woman who was the right age to be Ellen's mother. The names Maria and Claude appeared on Ellen's Chicago birth certificate, but they did not precisely match the full names of our two discoveries, Claude Henry Allen and Anna Maria Jensen. And there was still the geographical issue: Ellen had been born in Chicago in November 1919, and from what I could tell both Claude and Anna lived in Minnesota at that time.

I reached out to Marilyn to see if she might have any other information about Claude and Anna that could help us figure out the discrepancies. Incredibly, she had *just* what I needed: a biography of Anna Maria that contained the following passage (italics added):

ANNA MARIA JENSEN Following her sister Laura's 1913 marriage to George Holst, she went to live with them while attending school. She later moved to Chicago where she joined her sisters Martha and Emma, working by day in a candy store and attending night school. When her sister Tillie fell ill, she went to Minneapolis to care for her and her children. Around 1917 she returned to Alden [Minnesota] to fill in at the bank for her brother Bill who had left for the war. *She worked there until 1919, and it is there that she met Claude. After returning to Chicago for two years, she again went to Minneapolis* to assist Tillie. Claude was studying in Minneapolis, and the two were reunited and then married.

There it was. The geographical riddle was solved. I had mapped out Ellen's maternal and paternal lines, and I had found the place where they converged: the marriage of Claude Henry Allen and Anna Maria Jensen, the biological parents of Ellen Law.

Ellen's surviving relatives were delighted she had found them. They planned a huge family reunion in Los Angeles, and they even invited me. At the reunion Ellen met the children of the full siblings she had never known about, who all looked almost exactly like her (sadly, her full sister had died just a few months earlier). The phrase that kept popping up in my mind as I watched them hug and laugh was *peas in a pod*. It was a deeply emotional moment for Ellen, and for everyone there, including me.

This kind of happy conclusion, in my opinion, happens a lot of the time. Maybe even 80 percent of the time. But it is not guaranteed. I have found that sometimes birth family members want nothing to do with found relatives, which can be devastating for the new relative. So when Ellen's reunion took place, and I was there to see firsthand how happy Ellen was to be among family, I did not take the moment for granted.

Beyond all the DNA and percentages and family trees, there are human beings, wonderful and flawed, searching for connection, for belonging, for love. To be able to help them find these things is a privilege and a blessing. What mattered most to me about Ellen's case was her pure joy, and the joy of her newfound relatives, and the opportunity I had to help all these lovely people, something for which I am forever grateful.

My adventures in genetic genealogy might have continued on this clement path, helping adoptees like Ellen Law find their biological families, had I not opened that 2015 email from Deputy Peter Headley.

3

Deputy Headley was working with the San Bernardino County Sheriff Department's Crimes Against Children Detail when I called him after receiving his email.

His first question was "Can the methods you use be applied to identify a living Doe?"

In other words, could the Methodology help identify someone with no name or identity or history at all? Someone who was a complete blank in terms of public records and other identifiers? Someone like Lisa Jensen?

I told him I believed it could.

Deputy Headley's passion for the case came through in our call. It was one of those cases he simply could not let go of, and solving it had become a priority. Over the years he had forged a real bond with Lisa, someone who had endured unspeakable torment and was now trying to piece together some missing part of herself. He was fond of her and protective of her privacy.

"At one point the National Center for Missing and Exploited Children [NCMEC] wanted to put Lisa on a national show to see if anyone remembered her," Headley recalls. "She was almost ready to do it, but then she called me back and said, 'I was in the grocery store with my kids, and what if someone recognizes me from the show and says something about it in front of my kids?' So in the end she said, 'No, not going to happen.' "

Lisa had been let down by life many times—robbed of a childhood, robbed of her parents, her innocence shattered at an impossibly early age—and Deputy Headley did not want to let her down again. So he made her case personal to him. "I kept in contact with her and gave her updates on what was happening, even though most of the time I felt like I was beating my head against a wall trying to determine who she was," Headley says. "But I wasn't going to give up. At some point that just became the bottom line: I am not giving up."

His passion was contagious, and I understood that he was not asking me to merely help with a case—he was asking me to help a human being solve the central mystery of her identity and find some measure of peace in her life. This felt like serious, meaningful work, and work that came with responsibilities, all of which inspired me and made me want to be a part of it. I discussed Deputy Headley's request with Karin Corbeil and others at DNAAdoption, and they encouraged me to take on the case myself.

So it was that on the sun-filled spring morning of March 3, 2015, I began working on my first criminal case.

I set my MacBook Pro laptop on the round glass table in my family room. Next to it, I set my iPad in its external keyboard case. The family room is painted yellow (my entire house is painted in various shades of yellow, a color I love). There is a plaited ficus made up of three separate trees in a planter against the stairs and, on a table by the window, another planter box filled with purple and white live orchids (which I also love). I brewed a café Americano in my espresso machine and poured it into my favorite bone-china mug, which I had picked up in a sundry store in Grantown-on-Spey in the Scottish Highlands. It is yellow, too, and decorated with five stylized sheep. I sat down in the green-cushioned chair that matches the pedestal of the table and turned on my laptop and iPad. An unimaginably sprawling world of information—obscure, arcane, complex, dark, and mysterious—was mine for the searching.

Now I was ready to find out who Lisa Jensen was.

Going in, I had no doubt the Methodology would help me determine Lisa's identity. But I also understood it would be a much more difficult search than it was for most of my unknown-parentage cases. With an adoptee, you usually know *something* about them: when and where they were adopted, maybe when and where they were born, family stories that shed light on the adoption, and other anecdotal or documentary evidence. Even one tiny piece of personal information can point you to the part of the haystack where you will find your needle.

But with Lisa I had next to nothing. Imagine knowing so little about yourself and having no family records—no birth certificate, no adoption papers, no date of birth, no knowledge of where you are from, not even a name you can be sure is your own. Imagine how it must feel to be so rootless in the world, with no known connection to anywhere or anyone—except for the man who had abandoned you. This was the position Lisa found herself in. All I had to work with was her DNA.

I did have one tiny scrap of additional insight: I knew that Gordon Jensen/Curtis Kimball had lived in Quebec, in central Canada, around the time it was estimated that Lisa was born. But he had also traveled all over the United States in roughly the same time frame, so I did not really know if Lisa was from the United States or Canada. Like I said, it was just a scrap.

On my first day working on Lisa's case, I ordered a 23andMe DNA kit for her, and I downloaded her raw DNA profile from AncestryDNA and uploaded it to both FamilyTreeDNA and GEDmatch. That way her DNA profile would be on all the major sites.

The overall number of users in the databases was still relatively small in 2015—for instance, there were only about one million people in AncestryDNA's database. And the direct-to-consumer sites did not share their data with one another (they still do not). If you are an adoptee or someone else seeking to identify biological relatives, you have to fish in all the ponds to make any real progress. Lisa gave me permission to control all her online accounts and to reach out to any possible matches of interest on her behalf.

I put together a small group of volunteers to help me with Lisa's case. I knew most of them from the Monterey County Genealogy

Society (MoCoGenSo), the home base for many talented researchers in my area. The people I recruited were not law enforcement professionals; they were people like me who were working on their family histories. Some were fairly new to genealogy, while others had been in the field for years. But they were all smart, and they had backgrounds and research skills that I thought would prove helpful.

I also set up a DNA Special Interest Group (SIG) that met once a month at our local Family History Center. The purpose of the group was to help teach the members—including the folks in my group of volunteers—about the best ways to use DNA in family history research.

It would take several weeks to get Lisa's match data from the kit Lisa sent to 23andMe, and several days for her matches to appear after the uploads to FamilyTreeDNA and GEDmatch. But I had Lisa's genetic matches from AncestryDNA, and that was enough for me to get started.

I began with the closest match from Ancestry: Jean DuPont, an eighty-one-year-old man of French Canadian ancestry who, given his and Lisa's ages, was a possible first cousin twice removed to Lisa. Jean had a huge family tree on Ancestry (it featured more than six thousand people), which I used as the starting point of the speculative family tree that would lead me to the identity of one of Lisa's parents.

When the results from the other DNA test sites came in, I found that Lisa had three close matches on 23andMe as well.

The closest match, unfortunately, was listed as anonymous. This meant I knew nothing about this match other than that he was male. My only way to get in touch with Mr. Anonymous to find out more was to contact him through 23andMe's internal messaging system. I did just that, but the match did not respond to my messages.

The next closest match was a forty-year-old man named Adam. With any luck, Adam would happily cooperate and produce a tree full of biological relatives who would bring us closer to Lisa's identity.

But—no such luck. Adam's profile listed him as having been adopted. This was *not* something I was hoping for in a match. Ideally, I would find someone whose family tree included names in common with Jean's tree, but with Adam, I had no names at all. As for the remaining high match, he responded that he had no interest in helping me. That left only Adam.

But before Adam could ever be of help in Lisa's case, I would have to find out who he was, too.

I sent Adam a note through the 23andMe site, explaining who I was and what I was doing. My goal was to persuade him to upload his DNA profile to GEDmatch so I could compare his DNA to that of the match from Ancestry, whom I believed he was likely related to. Adam ignored my first note, so I tried again. However long it took, I would have to keep trying. I needed this guy's help because I needed to know who his ancestors were in order to solve Lisa's case.

Adam eventually responded, but he was deeply skeptical about my motives, and even about Lisa's kidnapping, which I had described to him in my note. "It was like something you'd see on a Thursday night TV crime show," Adam later explained. "I thought, 'This type of stuff doesn't actually happen to real people.'"

Like so many others I have reached out to in unknown-parentage cases over the years, Adam was afraid of being scammed or badgered for money. I gave him Deputy Headley's phone number and asked that he call him to verify that this was a legitimate case. Adam did call Deputy Headley, but even after being reassured Adam remained skeptical and needed more persuading.

So I bartered with him: I told him I would help him identify his biological parents if he helped me with Lisa's case.

Finally, Adam agreed to help. He shared the login information for his 23andMe account and gave me permission to upload his DNA profile to GEDmatch.

So now I had Adam, Lisa's 23andMe match, on board.

Next, I needed Lisa's Ancestry match—Jean, her eighty-one-year-old first cousin twice removed—to agree to help me, too.

Luckily, Jean was happy to join the search. He gave me permission to upload his DNA profile to GEDmatch, and that led to the discovery that Jean had a considerable X chromosome match with Lisa. Since Jean's X chromosome came from his mother, that meant Lisa was related to Jean through one of his maternal lines. Knowing that would prove helpful.

But then there was an even bigger break.

A new match for Lisa suddenly appeared on AncestryDNA. His name was Mason, and he was about the same-size DNA match to Lisa as was Jean. Mason had a private tree on AncestryDNA, which he agreed to share with me.

Mason's tree was instrumental in identifying a most recent common ancestor. His great-great-grandparents, I learned, were a French Canadian couple named Louis-Adolphe Doyon and Marie Leontine Jolin.

Louis-Adolphe and Marie also appeared in Jean's family tree; they were Jean's maternal grandparents.

There they were—the people I had been hunting for. The people who connected two of Lisa's matches, Mason and Jean. Now I had our precious MRCA—the most recent common ancestor.

I had Mason upload his DNA profile to GEDmatch, and on that site I could see that he matched not only with Lisa but also with both Adam and Jean on the same segment of DNA.

Since both Lisa and Adam matched with Jean and Mason, and they all matched with one another on the same segment of DNA, Lisa and Adam *had* to be descendants of Louis-Adolphe Doyon and Marie Leontine Jolin.

Next, I had to identify all the descendants of Louis-Adolphe Doyon and Marie Leontine Jolin down to the time period when I believed one of Lisa's parents, and Adam's father, would have been born. In theory that would lead me straight to the true identities of Adam and Lisa.

Based on their ages (Adam was born in 1975, and it had been estimated that Lisa was born around 1981), I surmised that Adam's father would have been born in 1955 or earlier. Lisa's parents would have been born in 1961 or earlier. Any descendants of Louis-Adolphe and Marie born around those years could be the descendants I was looking for. I hoped Louis-Adolphe and Marie had only one or maybe two children, so I would not have to build down the descendant lines of a whole slew of children.

In fact, Louis-Adolphe and Marie had *fourteen* children.

No one ever said determining Lisa's identity would be easy.

4

I gave Deputy Headley and Lisa access to the speculative tree that I was building based on Jean DuPont's family tree to keep them both updated on my progress. Lisa could see that, despite the complexity of her case, steady progress was being made in identifying her biological relatives.

Since it would give me a third data point if I knew who Adam's biological parents were, I tried first to directly identify Adam's biological parents rather than using genetic genealogy.

While Lisa knew next to nothing about herself, Adam did have a few facts at hand. He knew where he was born (San Diego) and he knew that he had been adopted there when he was four months old. He also had a birth certificate with the names of his adoptive parents, including his adoptive mother's maiden name.

It was possible to take that maiden name and perform what is called a reverse lookup, and for help with that I contacted a talented search angel named Diana Iwanski, who had access to a reverse-lookup microfiche for births in California that included the time period when Adam was born.

Diana, working with Adam's adoptive mother's maiden name and the date and county of Adam's birth, was able to locate the maiden name of Adam's birth mother, and even Adam's birth name.

As for Adam's father, there was no listing for him on Adam's birth certificate.

However, Adam had a copy of his "Non-ID"—nonidentifying information issued by his birth county. The Non-ID had no names in it, but it did list information on several of Adam's relatives, and it indicated that Adam had half siblings. Adam has a computer background, and the three of us—Adam, Diana, and myself—used Adam's mother's unusual maiden name and the Non-ID information to build a tree for Adam's maternal line. Things seemed to be moving along.

Then—another setback.

On GEDmatch, Adam was a DNA match not only with Lisa, but also with Jean and Mason, both of whom were of French Canadian ancestry. So I looked for any of Adam's maternal ancestors with the same roots.

His biological mother's admixture (ethnic background or bio-ancestry), was Dutch and Mexican. This meant the connection between Adam and Lisa likely was *not* on his maternal side.

It was on his father's side—and I did not know who his father was.

Somehow, I had to get information from a person who *did* know who Adam's father was—specifically, Adam's biological mother, who was still alive.

But before Deputy Headley could contact her, he had to confirm the information I had obtained from the reverse lookup that identified her as Adam's mother. To do that, he petitioned the court in San Diego to open Adam's sealed adoption records on the basis that the information would potentially help solve a criminal case. That process took several weeks, but Deputy Headley eventually received the file, which confirmed the information that we had. Deputy Headley was now able to contact Adam's mother in the hopes of learning who Adam's father was.

When he finally reached Adam's mother, he broke the news to her about her son and asked her to take a DNA test. She agreed, and the test confirmed that she was Adam's birth mother.

However, as I suspected (based on the mother's admixture), she did *not* match with Lisa.

Helpfully, Adam's mother gave us the name of a man she said was Adam's father. When we located and tested him, though, he did *not* match with Adam. Adam was of course bitterly disappointed, but he did have the thrill of meeting his birth mother and other relatives, with whom he felt an instant connection, discovering so many traits and talents in common with them that he had never had with his adoptive family.

Had Adam's mother been wrong about the man that she believed was his father? Or had she given me the wrong name as a way of protecting someone? Either way, I still did not have a name for Adam's father, and I would have to identify him through Adam's DNA alone.

To do that I focused on Jean and Mason, Lisa's big AncestryDNA matches.

What relationship were they to Adam? Jean was likely a first cousin twice removed, the same as Lisa, which meant Adam's father would be a first cousin *once* removed—as would be one of Lisa's parents. Plus he would have been born in 1955 or earlier and would likely have a connection to Southern California, and possibly San Diego, in the time period during which Adam was conceived.

That meant finding *all* the descendants of Louis-Adolphe and Marie's children who were born in 1955 or earlier—many of whom, I was disheartened to learn, had eight or ten children of their own.

It was an enormous amount of precise, painstaking work to build down so many lines, but with the help of the volunteers on the Lisa Project, I got all the way to the generation I believed corresponded to one of Lisa's parents and Adam's father.

I was now about three months into the Lisa Project. The amount of effort involved in doing the reverse tree build-down was staggering. I found the work to be nearly all-consuming, and I would often be at my laptop for twelve hours straight without even realizing it. The work was so engrossing that I began to set alarms for myself so I would not miss important calls and appointments. This was the beginning of my understanding that to be successful at this kind of work I had to be, at some level, obsessed with the case. I had to allow myself to be swept up by it. Building trees requires intense focus and persistence, and it is not something you can do halfheartedly, a half hour here and an hour there. When things start to fall into place it can be thrilling, but when they do not it can be crushing.

To succeed, you have to be fully committed to finding your answer, no matter how many trees you have to build, or how many hours it takes to build them.

I felt like I was working just as hard as I had before I retired.

Once the build-down to the right generation of Louis-Adolphe and Marie's descendants was complete, I created what is known as a Kinship Report, which shows how people in a family tree are related to one specific person—in this case, Jean DuPont. The report listed all of Jean's first cousins once removed—our pool of folks that should include both a potential parent for Lisa (I still did not know which parent) and a biological father for Adam.

There were *ninety-four* first cousins once removed to Jean in the Kinship Report.

Ninety-four. When I printed out the list in descendant format, it covered twelve sheets of paper in landscape format. When I taped all the sheets together, the final product stretched the length of a room. Somewhere among all these first cousins once removed was Adam's father and one of Lisa's parents.

The narrowing down of this pool of ninety-four people went quickly in terms of identifying Adam's father. The crucial question: Did any of the ninety-four first cousins once removed live in Southern California, where Adam was born? The answer was yes—I found one family in San Clemente. That family included four brothers.

Based on the ages of those four brothers, I concluded that one of them almost certainly had to be Adam's father.

But one brother was deceased, and the other three were criminals who were, as Deputy Headley put it, "in the wind" and nowhere to be found.

Luckily, Deputy Headley found a sister who was alive, and he approached her to take a DNA test. But she flatly refused, believing

Deputy Headley's real intention was to find and arrest one of her fugitive brothers.

I kept going. Although Deputy Headley and I worked separately and in different arenas, we were essentially a team, following up on each other's leads and assembling the puzzle together, him in the field, me at my computer. I felt a mutual respect building between us as we both realized, more or less at the same time, how profoundly influential this new technique could be to the future of law enforcement.

"It was like the moon and the stars were aligning perfectly," Headley says. "Barbara was working as an unpaid consultant, totally pro bono, as were her team members. She was identifying people to test to give her additional data points and I was cold-calling people who might be related and sending out DNA kits to those who were willing to help. And Barbara and her team were slowly putting this tree together that would help solve Lisa's identity. Barbara and I both wound up spending a lot of our own money on these DNA kits. But I was getting good at persuading people to test, and she was jumping in with the new data points to add to the tree. I could tell we were getting closer."

Now Deputy Headley had to track down one of the three missing San Clemente brothers *and* persuade that brother to submit to a DNA test. Incredibly, he succeeded. The brother he located had only one condition: he wanted me to maintain his anonymity, and he did not want Deputy Headley to ask him any questions about where his brothers were hiding.

The brother submitted a DNA test kit to FamilyTreeDNA, and the results contained good news.

His test revealed that he was Adam's uncle.

Which meant that I had been right: one of the other three brothers *had* to be Adam's biological father.

Adam, of course, desperately wanted to know which brother was his father (sadly, the brothers' family flatly refused to have anything to do with Adam and asked that he not contact them). But in terms of identifying a parent for Lisa Jensen, which was my original goal, just knowing the line from Adam to the most recent common ancestor was all I needed in order to proceed. I built out Adam's paternal family tree up through his grandparents, then to his great-grandparents, and finally to his great-great-grandparents: Louis-Adolphe Doyon and Marie Leontine Jolin.

There were two more surprises.

Adam was related to Lisa's Ancestry match Mason on his paternal side through two different families, *and* he was also doubly related to Lisa's other Ancestry match, Jean DuPont, through two families, including one on Jean's paternal side.

These kinds of double matches imply endogamy, or marriage within a family or clan or tribe. Normally, biologically unrelated parents have relatives who connect on only one side of the family or the other. But if you have endogamy, you can end up with matches who are related on both the maternal and the paternal sides of the family tree. Historically, endogamy was common among certain ethnic, religious, and geographic groups, and it can be a problem for genetic genealogists because, at first glance, people appear more closely related than they actually are, since you are not getting the customary 50 percent dilution of DNA from generation to generation. And that can throw you off.

But two-way matches can also limit the options of who the person you are searching for might be, and that can be a step forward.

From the X chromosome match between Jean and Lisa, I knew that Lisa was related to Jean on his maternal side. What we did not know was whether Jean was related to Lisa on her paternal or maternal side. Based on the chromosome makeup of the DNA match, I hypothesized that Lisa was most likely descended from a *son* of Marie Leontine Jolin.

This male descendant became the new subject of our search.

I knew Marie had twelve children who survived to adulthood. And I knew I was looking for a specific father-daughter relationship. So I looked at Marie's more recent family lines and found only two sons who had lived into adulthood.

If either of these men had a daughter or daughters, one of those women was Lisa Jensen's grandmother.

But *neither man had a daughter*.

Now what?

My hypothesis had been incorrect. Lisa was *not* descended from one of Marie's sons.

She was descended from one of her *daughters*.

Jean, Mason, and Adam were each descended from a different daughter of Marie Jolin. Lisa therefore had to be a descendant of one of Marie's remaining seven daughters' lines. I asked Deputy Headley to approach the oldest living person in each line.

One of the people he contacted was a man named Armand Beaudin, the son of Marie Leontine Jolin's daughter, Marie Cora Alice Beaudin née Doyon. Armand, who lived in New Hampshire, was an elderly man and, not surprisingly, skeptical about my intentions. He even traveled to his local police department to verify that Deputy Headley was who he said he was. Armand was assured that this was a legitimate and open case, yet he still refused any further contact.

Had he cooperated, I probably would have solved the case within the week.

But because he did not, I had to keep digging—for *another eight months*.

In those months, the Lisa Jensen Project team and I spent thousands of hours filling in Marie's seven remaining daughters' descendant lines. We pulled hundreds of records—marriage licenses, birth and death certificates, census data—both in the United States and Canada. When we found new relatives, Deputy Headley made dozens and dozens of phone calls, nearly begging people to cooperate with the search. A great many people he contacted refused to help.

Coming up on a full year of working on the project, we still did not know who Lisa was. And yet there was never any doubt that we *would* know. Deputy Headley was like a dog with a bone. Eventually I learned he felt the same way about me.

"With Barbara, I could tell she was tenacious," he says. "If she was an investigator, she would be one of those investigators who never gives up and sweats every detail. I could also tell that she was convinced of the rightness of what we were doing and that she was certain that she would identify who Lisa is."

Yet no matter how tenacious you are, sometimes you need to catch a break. And sometimes, just when you need it most, you catch it.

My lucky break came in the form of another new match for Lisa that miraculously popped up one day on AncestryDNA: an older man named Raymond Gelinas. And the size of the match indicated that he was a close relative.

Having a big new match suddenly appear is wonderfully lucky. But it was even luckier that Raymond was a retired intelligence agent who enjoyed games and puzzles and mysteries. Learning he could be part of our search for Lisa's identity was thrilling for him, and he cooperated fully. He liked telling me stories about his old days in a spy agency, and I liked listening to them, and some nights we spent hours on the phone unraveling his far-flung adventures. Talking with Raymond was a pleasant diversion as well as a helpful boost of energy. His enthusiasm for spycraft and intrigue strengthened my resolve to finally crack the case.

Although he was also of French Canadian ancestry, Raymond, it turned out, was not a match to Lisa's other matches of French Canadian ancestry, Jean, Mason, and Adam—which told me that Raymond was related to Lisa through different lines. Raymond convinced two of his cousins to test for me, one from each side of his family tree, the maternal and the paternal.

The results of testing these two cousins were a surprise.

Both cousins were strong matches with Lisa.

After encountering so many relatives who declined to test, and processing so many tests that provided no matches, suddenly I had another of those odd *double* matches—a confusing abundance of shared DNA. I went back through Raymond's family lines and focused on his most recent ancestors, on the theory that, in a closed or tribal family line, relatives often marry, blurring the distinction between lines.

I did not find any intermarriage among Raymond's immediate ancestors, but I did discover that two sisters on Raymond's line, his maternal grandmother and his great-aunt, had married two brothers, his grandfather and his great-uncle—causing the anomalous double-sided match further down the line.

What did this tell me?

- One of these two brothers was likely the father of Lisa Jensen's biological grandmother.
- This biological grandmother was married to Armand, the elderly man who refused to cooperate with us months earlier, even after verifying this was a legitimate case.

If I could somehow confirm beyond a doubt that Armand was Lisa's grandfather, I would be on the verge of cracking the case.

Why? Armand inherited an X chromosome from our most recent common ancestor, Marie Jolin, and I knew that the preservation of the X chromosome implied a mother-to-son-to-daughter sequence. If Armand was indeed Lisa's grandfather, his only daughter *had* to be the daughter in the mother-to-son-to-daughter sequence.

And this daughter would then have to be Lisa Jensen's mother.

Indeed, when we found and tested two of Armand's daughters' first cousins—one of whom was Armand's nephew—*both cousins matched with Lisa.*

Armand, therefore, was Lisa's grandfather. And Armand's daughter was Lisa's mother.

Now it was time to confirm this theory with actual documents. Armand had a son, Randall, who had died a number of years earlier. Randall's obituary mentioned a sister, Denise, as a surviving family member. Likewise, a 2008 obituary for Armand's wife, Georgette Beaudin, née Gelinas, noted that Georgette had been survived by a daughter, Denise.

Unfortunately, I could not find any records of a Denise Beaudin, other than the two obituaries that had been tracked down by Junel Davidsen, a member of the Lisa Project team.

Around this time, I got another unexpected—and decisive—good break.

Armand's nephew finally convinced a reluctant Armand to take a DNA test and help in our search. The results confirmed that Armand was Lisa's biological grandfather.

And that finally confirmed that *Armand's daughter Denise Beaudin was Lisa's mother*.

I had found her.

I contacted Deputy Headley and told him I knew the identity of Lisa's birth mother. A couple of hours after he opened my email, he called me. His response was *not* what I expected.

"Denise Beaudin," Deputy Headley said, "doesn't exist."

I had not worked for more than three thousand hours to find Denise Beaudin only to be told that she did not exist, so my response to Deputy Headley was pretty direct: "Yes she does."

Denise was mentioned in obituaries for two family members, her brother and her mother, so she most certainly *did* exist. But, beyond the obituaries, Deputy Headley could not find a single trace of her anywhere.

It was as if she had been completely erased from public records.

Which led me to believe I had found the right person. Given what had happened to Lisa, I did not think Lisa's mother was still alive. And a lack of documents and records from the last few decades supported this belief. Law enforcement databases are built from voting records, driver's licenses, death certificates, and other public records. The fewer such documents someone possesses, the harder they are for law enforcement to trace. In the case of Denise Beaudin, there was a *complete* lack of any such records, meaning Denise had fallen off the grid, either assuming a new identity or, in the worst-case scenario, dying young. Something dramatic had happened to her, and that alone was enough to make her whereabouts something Deputy Headley had reason to investigate further.

Denise Beaudin's father, Armand, told police he had last seen his daughter on Thanksgiving Day 1981, when Denise, her baby daughter, and her boyfriend abruptly left Armand's home in Manchester, New Hampshire, after a family argument.

The boyfriend's name, Armand recalled, was Bob Evans.

According to Armand, Bob Evans later told him that he and Denise were leaving Manchester, but he gave no compelling reason. Armand heard from others that they were fleeing some kind of debt. Whatever the reason, Armand never heard from Denise or Bob Evans again. Neither he nor any of her relatives reported Denise or her daughter missing.

But they never forgot her, either. Every year on her birthday, Denise's brother cried and prayed for the sister who had vanished so mysteriously from his life.

Deputy Headley now had a name to work with. He investigated Bob Evans, hoping to find a criminal record, and indeed he did: Evans had been arrested in Manchester for writing bad checks and for stealing electricity from a neighbor. Headley requested Evans's mug shots from those arrests, and when they arrived, the face in the pictures was very familiar.

Bob Evans, it turned out, was Gordon Jensen.

Headley learned more about Bob Evans from a Beaudin cousin. "He told everyone they owed money to some really bad people, drug dealers, so they had to leave town," Headley says. "Apparently Bob Evans was really good at telling these stories." Headley shared that he had noticed a disturbing pattern to Evans's behavior.

"Bob Evans had a method," Headley told me. "He would find single women with young children and take up with them, groom them. Then he would kill the mother and steal the child and go somewhere else where he would pose as a single father, which is how he would lure his next victim. He would bring along the child of his previous victim and tell women his sad single-father stories and start the process all over again."

It was a horrifying chain of abduction and murder and child molestation, and Lisa Jensen only escaped it thanks to Kathy Decker's daughter, who called the police on Gordon Jensen in San Bernardino.

Deputy Headley learned other biographical details about Lisa. She was born in 1981 to Denise and a man who at the time was Denise's husband. That marriage ended just four months later, and Lisa's father dropped out of the picture. Denise then began dating Bob Evans in Manchester, New Hampshire. At some point after she was last seen by her family in Manchester—no one knows exactly when—

Denise disappeared. In 1986 Bob Evans—now calling himself Gordon Jensen—appeared with Lisa in Southern California. For decades afterward, Lisa had no idea who her mother was, or who she herself was.

That was about to change.

In an interview with a family member, Deputy Headley learned Lisa's given name. On July 3, 2016, a little over a year after I started the search for Lisa's identity, Headley called Lisa.

"Would you like to know your birth name?" he asked.

"Yes," Lisa answered.

"It's Dawn. Dawn Beaudin."

Finally, Lisa Jensen had something her mother had given her that no one could ever take away: her name.

Lisa was eventually able to meet her grandfather Armand, and other relatives, at a gathering in New Hampshire. When Lisa and I spoke on the phone, she told me all about the gathering and how special it was for her. After believing for so long that her only relative was the man who turned out to be her abductor, Lisa now had hundreds of relatives—a real family that included a grandfather and many close cousins. Deputy Headley obtained a copy of Lisa/Dawn's original birth certificate, so now she had an authentic birthday, too. Slowly, she was piecing together an identity that had been taken from her and shattered into shards.

Because of the Methodology and the secrets unearthed using her DNA, I was able to help Lisa fit those pieces back together.

There were a few loose ends. Denise Beaudin's whereabouts were unexplained, and her body had never been found, though eventually she was declared legally deceased.

As for Bob Evans, he never faced the full measure of justice due to him—he died in prison in 2010, several years before I uncovered either his or Lisa's identity.

Still, I had accomplished the goal of the Lisa Project—to restore to a crime victim at least one of the things that was stolen from her:

her identity. In the end, the number of ancestors on the tree I built with the help of the team reached to nearly eighteen thousand names. The paternal line added another four thousand names. With the help of Deputy Headley and my team, I located and connected with hundreds of relatives, and DNA-tested dozens of them. I estimated that my small team of genealogists, on its own, put in some twenty thousand hours of work, while Headley and his investigators worked many thousands more.

For me, the Lisa Project was a hugely meaningful success. To be able to help Lisa reach some kind of closure in such a tragic case was rewarding, and I was thrilled to hear her say that she could now move on with her life in a way that she had not been able to before.

The case also confirmed for me that, in a DNA search, the answer is *always* out there. It may be extremely well hidden or seem all but inaccessible. It may take twenty thousand hours to find, or even a hundred thousand hours. I may run out of time searching for it. But it is there, somewhere, in the data, waiting to be discovered. And with enough time and skill, I began to believe, *any* case with available DNA evidence could be solved.

After concluding the Lisa Project, it did not take very long for me to wind up in a situation where I would put that theory to the test. In fact, it was the evidence I unlocked in the course of the Lisa Project that led Deputy Headley and me into another criminal case, this one even darker and more terrifying. It was a case known as the Allenstown Four.

Or, in some tellings, the Bear Brook Park quadruple-murder case.

PART TWO

THE BEAR BROOK MURDERS

JANUARY 2017

5

The Lisa Project was the first case I ever worked on with law enforcement. But even while I searched for Lisa's identity—a good part of 2015 and 2016—I continued helping adoptees identify birth relatives through DNAAdoption. After that case was closed, however, and as word spread within the law enforcement community that I had solved the mystery of Lisa's identity, the balance of my genealogy work changed. I received numerous requests by phone and email from detectives all over the country seeking assistance in solving their most haunting and impenetrable cold cases—the ones they simply could not walk away from. I felt compelled to assist in solving these long-cold cases, and I took on as many of them as I could. Suddenly I was working on several criminal cases alongside all of my adoptee cases.

Genetic genealogy is, as I have mentioned, time-consuming work. When I started working with Karin Corbeil, she estimated that the average adoptee/unknown-ancestor search took a minimum of a thousand hours to solve—which meant that if you worked on the case for twenty hours per week, a single case could take a year to solve. This proved true on the Lisa Jensen case, which took me over a year to solve. With the increase in the size of the databases like AncestryDNA and 23andMe, that is no longer true, and I can generally solve an unknown-parentage case within a day or two.

There is something else that I learned about DNA early on: every answer you discover leads to another question. A question you might feel driven to answer.

Such was the case with the Lisa Project.

Not long after my team and I discovered Lisa Jensen's true identity, one of my team members, Junel Davidsen, made a startling connection.

Once we knew that Lisa's mother was Denise Beaudin, we learned that Denise—before vanishing in 1981 with her then-boyfriend Bob Evans—had lived in Goffstown, a pleasant little town just a few minutes from the city of Manchester, in southern New Hampshire. Maps are an important component of traditional family history research, in that they help in visualizing migration routes: rivers, trains, passages through mountainous areas. Junel, as she usually did when working on a family history project, had put together maps of the area where Lisa was from. Junel studied a map of New Hampshire and, in a flash of revelation, noticed that the town of Manchester was only a few miles south of Allenstown, a tiny community of fewer than five thousand people best known for its sprawling ten-thousand-acre wooded preserve, Bear Brook State Park.

Bear Brook, Junel recalled, was the scene of a truly haunting crime that had gone unsolved for more than forty years—a quadruple murder. She wondered: Did the proximity of Manchester and Allenstown suggest a connection between the cases?

Independently, but at the same time, two other people who had worked long and hard on the Lisa Jensen case—Ashley Rodriguez, a forensic case manager at the National Center for Missing and Exploited Children (NCMEC) in Washington, D.C., and her supervisor, Carol Schweitzer—also noticed how close the two towns were to each other, and they asked the same question: Were the Lisa Jensen case and the Bear Brook murders connected? They contacted law enforcement with their hunch.

"I got a call from Ashley Rodriguez and she said, 'We've got this case down the road, the Bear Brook murders,'" recalls Deputy Peter Headley. "There are similarities."

After that call, Deputy Headley contacted me again.

All my life, mysteries have called out to me to be solved.

My earliest attempts to explain the unexplained took place on the North Island of New Zealand, in the quiet city suburb of Remuera in Auckland, where I grew up with my parents and my two younger brothers. When I learned how to read, I devoured everything I could get my hands on, which, when I was a teenager, even included my father's rather lurid collection of science fiction novels with their salacious covers (my mother was a bit alarmed by that). My favorite reading material, however, was encyclopedias. I still recall the cherished set my mother bought just for me, with their elegant maroon leather binding and gold trim and lettering on the spines. I would simply pull out a volume and sit on the floor and read it cover to cover, endlessly fascinated by all the new information. To this day I am someone who will read anything, even a milk carton, if that's all I have nearby.

Back then my mother told me I had a grasshopper mind. What she meant was that my thought process wasn't exactly linear, or at least not like her own. I tended to ask questions that at first seemed strange and off topic to her. But as I kept asking questions, my mother could see that I was, in fact, circling the topic, coming at it from odd angles, and finally landing on some insight or other. This was just the way my mind worked—I have learned that I look at things a little differently from most people.

As a girl, I collected insects that struck me as beautiful and fascinating but nearly everyone else as truly vile. These insects both intrigued and confounded me. Why did they look the way they did? How did they function? What made them special? I started with little caterpillars I found inching around the plants in our garden, and I kept them in tiny matchboxes I scooped up after my father tossed them away. I had questions about caterpillars, so I ran gentle experiments: Would they thrive on eating some plants and not others? Would their excrement change color if I fed them different-colored flowers?

For some reason, I needed to know these things.

Then I stepped up to wetas, large cricketlike insects common to New Zealand. Often when my family went to the beach, where the insects had no predators, I'd delight in spotting rodent-size wetas and giant huhu beetles that utterly horrified others. My paternal grandmother had a friend, Bruff, a squat-shouldered fire watcher who manned an isolated tower in the dense Waitakere Ranges to the west of Auckland for six weeks at a stretch. Bruff asked me if I would like him to try and collect even bigger, more exotic insects for my collection. Emphatically, I said yes.

Bruff came back with a hand-size green centipede and other strange creatures he had collected impaled in a large cigar box. The sight of them made my mother shriek.

Looking back, I can see that this was not just idle childhood curiosity. If there was something I didn't know, it became something I *needed* to know. Any gap in my knowledge was an opportunity to learn—a chance I felt compelled to seize. I never wanted to understand just a little about a subject; I wanted to know as much about it as I could. At the age of ten, for instance, I memorized the periodic table of elements. Why? Because the elements fascinated me, and I needed to know more.

I did not fully realize I was this way until one day many years later when, in a conversation with my grown son, Christopher, I watched him pick up his phone to instantly research a topic that came up in our talk. He did not know anything about the topic, and he needed to. *I do that*, I thought. *I do just that. I need to know what I don't know.* It took me recognizing the trait in someone else to understand what it was that was driving me.

There was something else about the way my brain worked that would eventually serve me well as a genetic genealogist. When I was young I realized I could remember things and events visually, often better than adults. I learned this when I lived with my paternal grandmother, whom we called Mumma, for several months when I was in high school.

After my grandfather, a former jockey and horse trainer, died relatively young from a massive heart attack, Mumma took what she knew about horses and horse races and became a bookie. My straitlaced mother (whom we kids had nicknamed Queen Victoria) was scandalized by Mumma's new vocation and forbade my father from taking us to visit her on any day the horses were racing. My father, of course, ignored the directive, and when we visited I would find Mumma sitting in her phone nook, cigarette dangling from her lips, glass of gin in hand, taking bets on the phone.

Mumma also hosted a regular card game where she and her friends gambled away somewhat more than pocket change. When I was fifteen and went to live with her, Mumma let me sit in on her games. She would stake me to a few dollars and sit me right at the big table with her usual players, including Bruff the fire watcher. The game was poker, or Ride the Bus, or some other gambling game. I did not expect to win; I was thrilled just being invited to play.

It turned out I was pretty good at cards. In one particular game, in which cards were turned faceup, then facedown, I could visualize the cards being turned over and remember which facedown card was which. I won a lot of consecutive hands thanks to this power of visual recall. I am sure Bruff and the others were not as delighted with my newfound prowess as I was, and I know for a fact my two brothers were not—when I corralled them into card games at home they soon tired of losing and refused to play with me anymore. (To this day they *still* refuse.)

Over the years I have come to rely on this ability to visualize past events in my head, almost like watching a movie. If I misplaced my car keys, I could simply unspool the movie of my actions over the last couple of hours and "see" exactly where I had left them. During tests, I could visualize my class notes as I had written them in my notebooks. I suspect Ian Fleming, author of the James Bond books, may have had a similar type of memory; there is a scene in one of his books in which he describes Bond doing the same mental unspooling to recall an event.

Later on, when I dove into genetic genealogy, this ability came in quite handy, as I found I could remember connections among people simply by visualizing where they sat on a particular family tree, even if it was a tree that I had not looked at in days.

This skill would one day help me sort through the staggering number of names, dates, and facts that emerged in the quest to solve the gruesome Bear Brook murders.

6

Some children playing hide-and-seek in the forest found it first—a rusted, greenish fifty-five-gallon metal drum knocked sideways on a pile of dead leaves near a skinny birch tree. The children ran around the old drum and kicked its sealed lid, just for fun, until the lid came loose and a black trash bag spilled out. That spooked the children, and they scurried away.

A few days later, on November 10, 1985, a hunter roamed the same woods in New Hampshire's Bear Brook State Park, a heavily forested preserve teeming with deer, moose, turkey, and, predictably, black bears, and strewn with campgrounds, cabins, stone cookeries, hiking trails, and vast lonely stretches along pine-covered valleys and ridges. The hunter came across the rusted, kicked-over metal drum and its spilled contents. He looked at the black trash bag and saw something so disturbing it would take him ten years before he was able to hunt in those same woods again.

Sticking out of a tear in the trash bag was a human foot.

The hunter alerted police, and the gruesome discovery was retrieved. Medical examiners in New Hampshire determined what was in the trash bag: the dismembered and badly decomposing remains of not just one but two humans, a woman and a young girl. They had been dismembered, wrapped in plastic, and tied with electrical tape.

The best guess was that the two females had been murdered several years earlier.

Unfortunately, the bodies were so badly degraded that identifying the victims seemed all but impossible. After months of investigation, the remains were released for burial and interred in a steel casket to better preserve them should they ever need to be exhumed. The casket was buried beneath a donated gravestone that read:

> Here lies the mortal remains known only to God of a woman age 23–33 and a girl child age 8–10. Their slain bodies were found on November 10, 1985 in Bear Brook State Park. May their souls find peace in God's loving care.

Fifteen years passed, and the double murders remained unsolved.

Then, in 2000, New Hampshire State Police sergeant John Cody, assigned to the long-cold case, decided to recanvass the crime scene in the endless woods of Bear Brook Park.

There he made another shocking discovery.

Just a hundred or so yards from where the hunter had found the first metal drum in 1985, Sergeant Cody found a second rusted drum.

When investigators opened this one, they found the decomposed remains of two more victims—both young girls—wrapped in plastic and tied with electrical tape.

Now there were four unidentified murder victims, three of them children, and the long-cold case assumed a new urgency. A double homicide was now a quadruple murder, and a feeling of unease settled over Allenstown, a small, scenic hamlet of some forty-seven hundred people and twenty square acres, half of which were consumed by the deep bogs and dense forests of Bear Brook Park.

Autosomal DNA extracted from the bones and tissue from each of the four victims was irreparably contaminated by bacterial DNA and could not produce a sample that would allow for identification of the bodies. But investigators were able to obtain mitochondrial DNA (mtDNA), which allowed them to conclude that the woman and two of the children were maternally related. The third child was not maternally related and remained a complete mystery.

Despite this startling new development, the case went cold again.

Another fifteen years would pass before Junel Davidsen, as well as Ashley Rodriguez and Carol Schweitzer at NCMEC, made the connection between Allenstown and Manchester. Their curiosity reenergized the investigation into the murders.

By then, investigators knew a little more about Bob Evans/Gordon Jensen, the man who was Denise Beaudin's live-in boyfriend in 1981—and who had abducted Denise's daughter, Lisa Jensen, after Denise disappeared.

Born in Colorado in 1943 one day before Christmas Eve, Evans dropped out of high school in Arizona to join the U.S. Navy, where he trained as an electrician. He was married in 1969 and had a son and three daughters, but his wife took the children and left him shortly after giving birth to their fourth child. She claimed that she came home from the hospital after the birth to discover cigarette burns on her son's buttocks—the same atrocity Bob Evans later inflicted on Lisa Jensen. Many years later, when police eventually questioned Bob Evans's son, he remembered his father burning him with cigarettes and described Evans as having "dead man's" eyes.

Following his divorce in 1978, Evans relocated across the country to Manchester, New Hampshire. There he was arrested in 1980 for writing bad checks and stealing electricity by diverting an electrical current. Just one year later, in 1981, Evans disappeared from Manchester, along with his new girlfriend, Denise Beaudin, and Denise's daughter, Lisa.

After that Bob Evans assumed the alias Curtis Kimball and was arrested for drunk driving—and endangering young Lisa, who was in the car with him—in Cypress, California, in 1985. Evans/Kimball skipped town before he could be indicted and assumed yet another identity: Gordon Jensen. It was as Gordon Jensen that he abandoned Lisa after their stay at the Santa Cruz Ranch RV Resort in 1986, but once again he eluded capture, disappeared, and changed his name. Finally, as Gerry Mockerman, he was arrested in 1988 on suspicion of stealing a car, and police unraveled his many false identities. It was the crime of abandoning Lisa in 1986 that finally landed him in prison—but not for long,

Evans/Kimball/Jensen/Mockerman served only two years in prison for abandoning Lisa, and when he was released he began a new life in Richmond, California. For years, whatever fresh criminal exploits he perpetrated remained under the radar. In 2001, he married Eunsoon Jun, a chemist in her early forties, in a ceremony in the backyard of her home, where they both lived. It was not an official marriage.

By then, Bob Evans had a new alias—he was now Larry Vanner. And, as Vanner, he had a new mysterious tragedy to explain: the disappearance of his wife just a few months after the informal wedding ceremony.

Vanner told a friend of Eunsoon Jun's that she had left town on her own, but the friend was suspicious. She told police that Eunsoon would never leave without first saying goodbye. That simply was not her way. The friend kept pushing police until they sent officers to Eunsoon's Richmond home to look around. In a basement area they found something strange:

Two hundred and fifty pounds of loose kitty litter in a big pile.

Police dug through the mounds of litter, pulling away dusty handfuls at a time, until they came upon the horror: a mummified and dismembered body wrapped in plastic and electrical tape.

These were the remains of Eunsoon Jun, killed, apparently, with a sledgehammer.

Police brought Vanner in for questioning. He volunteered to be fingerprinted, believing, perhaps, that it would take time for his prints to be processed—time he could use to get himself released from custody and disappear yet again. But since his last brush with the law years earlier, fingerprinting technology had vastly improved, and Vanner's prints, processed in real time, immediately connected him to crimes that he had committed under two aliases: Bob Evans and Gordon Jensen.

That was enough for police to arrest Vanner and, after further investigation, charge him with second-degree murder for the killing of Eunsoon Jun. Vanner pleaded not guilty, but at a pretrial hearing he surprised prosecutors by suddenly changing his plea to no contest. Captain Roxane Gruenheid of the Contra Costa County Sheriff's Office, the officer who started the investigation into Lisa Jensen's identity, believed Vanner changed his plea because he overheard her in court mentioning his possible connection to Lisa's case.

"I think . . . he believed if he pled guilty," Gruenheid explained to a reporter, "I would stop investigating that aspect of his past."

Authorities sentenced Vanner to fifteen years to life in prison. He served seven of those years at the High Desert Prison in Susanville, California, and in 2010 he died there, of natural causes.

A long and heinous criminal record, it seemed, had finally logged its last crime.

But had it?

7

Bob Evans/Larry Vanner (let's call him Vanner for now) emerged suddenly as a suspect in the Bear Brook murders for several reasons. We knew Vanner had lived in Manchester, New Hampshire, just fourteen miles south of Bear Brook Park. We knew he was capable of murder—he was imprisoned for brutally slaying his wife Eunsoon Jun. And we knew there were similarities between the killing of Jun and the murders in Bear Brook Park (the victims were dismembered, wrapped in plastic, and tied with electrical tape). All of this led investigators like Deputy Headley to begin looking much more closely at Vanner as a suspect.

Headley reached out to Michael Kokoski, the New Hampshire State Police detective working on cold cases at the time, and "together," says Headley, "we began connecting the dots."

It was about this time that Headley called me and filled me in on the case. He wanted to know if the methodology we used to identify Lisa could now help us identify not only the four Bear Brook murder victims, but also who Bob Evans really was.

This was exciting. I was working on other criminal cases at the time, but none were like this one. For one thing, the Bear Brook case had now been cold for forty years, making it seem all but unsolvable and presenting quite a challenge. For another, it was looking more and more likely that Detective Headley had a serial killer on his hands. I simply could not pass up the chance to help him solve the case and find the murderer. "Yes, I believe it is possible to identify the Bear Brook victims," I told Deputy Headley in our first call about the case, "but I'm going to need autosomal DNA from each of the four victims, and from Vanner in order to identify him."

There was, however, one big problem: at the time no such DNA was available, either from the four victims or from Vanner.

A DNA sample had been taken from Vanner while he was under arrest for drunk driving as Curtis Kimball, but not enough DNA extract from that sample remained to be of any use. Unfortunately, when he died in prison in 2010, no relatives had emerged to claim his remains, and he was cremated. Vanner's ashes were tossed into the sea, eliminating any chance of retrieving usable DNA from his body.

This initially seemed like an insurmountable hurdle—without his DNA, we had nothing.

But then I remembered something I had once read, a stray fact that for some reason stuck with me and now pushed its way forward. I remembered that when California prisoners die, they are automatically autopsied, and some of their blood is drawn and put on specialized absorbent filters. Once the blood is dry, the sample can be safely stored away. It is called a blood card.

Was it possible Larry Vanner had been autopsied and a source of his DNA remained? Deputy Headley said he would look into it.

Sure enough, he discovered that Vanner *had* been autopsied, and a hair sample and a blood card had been generated.

But there was no guarantee the California penal system still had the hair sample and the blood card in storage. Deputy Headley had to fill out form after form just to get someone to look for the autopsy items. Eventually, he learned that the California blood card and Vanner's hair sample were stored in a facility in Nevada. More forms and signatures were required in order to obtain them.

Finally, Headley learned that after a certain number of years the blood cards are routinely destroyed. When a staffer dug through the card files, he found that Vanner's card was officially slated for destruction.

But it had not been destroyed yet.

Headley succeeded in getting the card, and with that lucky break we were able to have Vanner's DNA extracted and tested. Before long I went to work building out a speculative family tree from his matches that we could use to identify him. As with the Lisa Jensen case, all I had to work with was his DNA. I had no idea where he was from or how old he was—all his aliases came with different ages and birth dates. One possible clue: he spoke several languages (including French), and he had possible connections to Quebec. I enlisted Junel Davidsen to help me unearth his true identity.

We did both Y-DNA and autosomal DNA testing. Vanner had hardly any Y-DNA matches, and his autosomal DNA matches were not particularly close, suggesting that his ancestors were probably fairly recent immigrants. It took us a long time to find a most recent common ancestor (MRCA) for a set of Vanner's autosomal DNA matches. Eventually, we did find an MRCA, allowing us to build down all of the MRCA's descendant lines and identify ten of the MRCA's male descendants who roughly fit Vanner's age criteria.

One of them, in theory, was Larry Vanner.

Junel and I, each at our own laptops, scoured public records for information about these ten men, looking for photos or anything else that might help us narrow down the list and possibly hit on the person who Vanner really was.

We assumed that someone who had for years been using aliases would have a sketchy or even nonexistent trail of records, as was the case with Denise Beaudin, who was presumably deceased. In other words, he would at some point early in his life have stopped generating contemporary records, such as a driver's license, marriage records, divorce records, and birth records of his children. We also knew that he was an electrician by training and had continued to work in that field. While researching the ten men, we found that one of them—a man named Terry Rasmussen—had a document trail that went cold in 1978 after he was divorced in San Mateo County, California. Junel obtained a copy of his divorce papers, which listed Terry Rasmussen's occupation.

He was an electrician, just like Larry Vanner.

We needed more. We needed some kind of confirmation. Then we found it: an old high school photo of Terry Rasmussen. The man in the photo looked familiar—extremely familiar. In fact he looked a whole lot like Bob Evans/Larry Vanner.

Had we finally discovered this man's true identity?

More research into the man in the photo revealed his full name: Terry Peder Rasmussen. The divorce papers indicated Rasmussen had a son, and as final proof that we had identified the correct person Y-DNA testing was done on the son. The son's Y-DNA matched with the Y-DNA that had been extracted from Vanner's blood card.

Bob Evans, Gordon Jensen, Larry Vanner, Curtis Kimball, Gerry Mockerman—they were *all* Terry Peder Rasmussen.

With that name in hand, Deputy Headley found employment records and other data that allowed him to piece together some of Rasmussen's past. He had many aliases Headley had not known about, including Jerry Gorman, Don Vannerson, Ulos Jensen. He had so many aliases and identities that the press eventually nicknamed him the Chameleon Killer. Rasmussen was, apparently, unusually intelligent, capable of retaining the swaths of information that helped him appropriate other people's identities.

"All the aliases he used came from real people he met," says Deputy Headley. "In 1988 he got arrested with a stolen car and came up with the name Gerry Mockerman. He knew this man's date of birth and Social Security numbers. I later spoke with the real Gerry Mockerman and he said his ID papers were stolen out of his truck eighteen months before Rasmussen's 1988 arrest. Rasmussen was a smart guy with an incredible memory."

For Rasmussen, outsmarting investigators was a game he seemed to enjoy.

"I've always tried to live by the motto that there's no defense against the truth," he told one prison interrogator. "But sometimes it's hard to find what the truth is."

Rasmussen's DNA, however, did not lie.

Employment records showed that Rasmussen, as Bob Evans, worked briefly as a handyman for a New Hampshire company called Carol Cable.

Carol Cable, it turned out, *was located very near the Bear Brook Park murders crime scene.*

But that was not all. It also turned out that Denise Beaudin had worked briefly at Carol Cable Company at the same time Rasmussen worked there.

This was simply one too many connections to be a coincidence, and, sure enough, the evidence kept piling up. Further research revealed that the electrical cables used to tie up the four Bear Brook Park victims were manufactured by the Carol Cable Company. Then, analysis of Rasmussen's DNA matched traces of DNA found in one of the rusted metal drums, further implicating him.

The Chameleon Killer, it seemed, was the Bear Brook Park killer, too.

Deputy Headley sent all our findings to the New Hampshire State Police cold-case detective, and Rasmussen was officially identified as the suspected killer behind the Allenstown murders.

What remained unknown were the identities of the victims. Was the adult woman Lisa Jensen's mother, Denise Beaudin? And who were the three children? Denise Beaudin was ruled out as the adult female but, shockingly, a DNA comparison of the four Bear Brook Park victims and Terry Rasmussen revealed that he *was the biological father of one of the child victims. Furthermore, it determined that the child was not* maternally *related to the other three victims.* This raised the question as to whether the mother of this child was another of Rasmussen's victims.

Unfortunately, the contaminated DNA subsequently isolated from the victims was not useful for the kinds of tests we needed to perform to determine their identities. Technically, the human DNA in the contaminated samples could be amplified, but the process would have been prohibitively expensive and time-consuming. Sadly, it appeared we had reached a dead end.

"At this point in time, we are almost at our full—if not, we are at the final line—of what science can do to help us based upon their remains to identify where they came from and who they were," New Hampshire's senior assistant attorney general Benjamin Agati announced decisively at a 2015 press conference.

As far as I knew, he was right.

But I also knew that, in the exploding field of genetic genealogy, what is true one minute might not be true the next.

8

In March 2017 I was surfing around the internet on my iPad, hopping from site to site and catching up on some reading, when I came across an extraordinary article.

It was about a paleogeneticist at the University of California, Santa Cruz. His name was Richard "Ed" Green. Professor Green was best known among fellow scientists for his research into the Neanderthal genome. He was, in fact, part of a team that developed the genetic-sequencing technology that made it possible to read DNA extracted from fossilized bones. Professor Green had helped sequence the entire Neanderthal genome, a game changer for scientists studying human evolution. "We went from zero reliable ancient genomes," Green later explained, "to thousands and thousands."

The article I read, however, did not have to do with his work with Neanderthals or another of his specialties, dinosaur bones. It was about the identification of the remains in a small coffin found buried beneath a concrete slab in a San Francisco home that was being renovated. An excavator felt his shovel clank against something solid, which proved to be a thirty-seven-inch-long ornate cast-iron casket with small panes of glass on top. Tucked tightly inside the airless coffin were the well-preserved remains of a little girl, two or three years old, in a white embroidered dress, with a cross of lavender on her chest and rose petals and eucalyptus leaves strewn around her. The small child was clutching a single rose, and there was no headstone anywhere.

The mystery of the girl's identity captured the imaginations of local residents and, once the national media picked up the story, people around the country. Why was the girl buried there all alone? Why was her coffin so ornate? Who was she?

Research revealed that her distinctive coffin—which was 145 years old—had been left behind at the site when some twenty-nine thousand other remains were exhumed from the Odd Fellows Cemetery in San Francisco in 1902 and reburied in Colma, south of San Francisco, so that new homes could be built over the old cemetery grounds.

Over a century later the excavator discovered the casket, and it was disinterred so the girl could be reburied in a larger casket. But before she was, an archaeologist, Jelmer Eerkens, cut a few three- or four-inch strands of hair from the child's head. He hoped chemical analysis of the hair might help pinpoint the year of her death and the area where she lived. The goal was to figure out who she was—and to give her a name.

Eerkens knew, however, that DNA from hair without the root attached could not be used to identify the child. At the time, it was possible to extract mitochondrial DNA from strands of rootless hair, perhaps revealing maternal connections to other people. But to conclusively identify a person, autosomal DNA was required, and back then, it was believed that there was no autosomal DNA in a rootless hair. As hair grows, the cells go through apoptosis, or a programmed cell death, during which it was believed nuclear or autosomal DNA would be hopelessly degraded.

Elissa Davey, project director of the Garden of Innocence, a not-for-profit charity group that provides dignified burials for unidentified children—and that was overseeing the coffin girl's reburial—placed a call to Professor Green and asked if he could help with identifying her remains. Professor Green, a true-crime aficionado, agreed to try.

Born in the small town of Conyers, Georgia, Green dropped out of the University of Georgia after his sophomore year because he found his studies as a business major "mind-numbingly boring," he says. It was not until he reenrolled at the university and took an introductory genetics class (at the urging of his advisor) that a spark was lit and Green's life changed. "Genetics was real stuff that really mattered and that was a revelation to me—that it can be your job to figure out things that no one else has figured out," he says. "I loved it and I really ate it up."

Green was an associate professor of biomolecular engineering at the Baskin School of Engineering at UC Santa Cruz when he got the call from Elissa Davey about the girl in the casket. Working out of UC Santa Cruz's Paleogenomics Lab, he attempted to adapt the technique he had used to retrieve DNA from old dinosaur fossils to extract DNA from a strand of rootless hair that was at least a century old. He took some strands of the hair from the remains in the small coffin and produced a usable genetic profile. By then, researchers guided by Elissa Davey had pored over scale plans of the Odd Fellows Cemetery that had once existed at the site where the house undergoing renovation had been built, as well as hundreds of years of birth, death, marriage, and property records, all to identify two possible families the girl might have been part of (a process, Davey says, that took several researchers around three thousand total hours). A volunteer genealogist assembled one of the families' trees back to the 1600s and located a living relative who agreed to submit a saliva DNA sample.

"That was the *real* legwork," says Professor Green.

Next, the casket girl's DNA profile was compared to the profile of the living relative.

Would there be a match?

In fact, the girl and the relative were a 12.5 percent match.

They had found her. The casket girl was the living relative's great-aunt, and her name was Edith Howard Cook. Death records showed that she had died in 1876 at the age of two years, ten months, and fifteen days due to marasmus, a term for severe undernourishment likely caused by disease or infection. Edith was reburied on a sloping hill in Greenlawn Cemetery, just south of San Francisco, in a ceremony attended by the living Cook relative, Edith's great-great-nephew, Peter Cook, then eighty-two—as well as Professor Green, the man who found a way to reclaim her identity. "A name is a dignity every human being deserves," Elissa Davey said in her remarks that day. "To be called *something*."

When I read about Professor Green and his work with rootless hair on the Edith Cook case, I could hardly believe my good luck. I had only recently learned that the available DNA in the Bear Brook case was too contaminated to be of any use, and that setback had left me feeling deflated. But I also knew that hair strands from all four of the Bear Brook victims were available, and here, suddenly, was a technique that could be used to extract autosomal DNA from hair without the root. This was a remarkable breakthrough, and it happened precisely when I had reached a dead end in the Bear Brook case. The serendipity of these events syncing up was simply thrilling.

I called Deputy Headley and asked him to contact Professor Green to see if he might be interested in working with me on identifying the victims in the Bear Brook case. Luckily, the professor indicated that he was up for the challenge. I arranged to meet him for lunch at the Whole Enchilada restaurant in Moss Landing, a sort of halfway point between our locations on opposite sides of Monterey Bay. I asked for my usual order, chile verde, while Professor Green had the enchiladas. Our conversation roamed over several topics: my work as a patent attorney, his love of biotechnology, the early days of genomics, his developments in extracting DNA from hair. I also briefed him on the stalled Bear Brook murder case.

There was a kinship between us, in part because of the similarity of our situations: somehow, despite neither of us having any law enforcement experience, we had both suddenly found ourselves in the business of solving crimes.

"I thought that after the casket girl that was the end of my work on these types of cases, and then Barbara showed up," Professor Green says. "It didn't take much arm-twisting to get me on board; in fact, I was hooked from the very beginning."

As the professor later explained to Deputy Headley when he officially joined our team, "This sounds more interesting than dinosaur DNA."

It was Professor Ed Green who discovered that, in fact, small fragments of the autosomal DNA remain, and those fragments *can* be analyzed. Professor Green went straight to work developing a protocol to extract autosomal DNA from strands of hair from each of the four victims—hair that had sat in barrels exposed to the elements for five years (first barrel) and twenty years (second barrel). Green had discovered that the cuticle of the hair shaft protects the cortex, where the DNA is located, from damage. Retrieving the DNA was a two-step process. The DNA in the hair shaft was in tiny pieces, so the first step was to put the DNA back together using a process called whole-genome sequencing, or WGS. From there he used an algorithm to create a DNA profile (specifically a SNP profile) that I could upload to GEDmatch and FamilyTreeDNA.

The human genome—the sum of *all* the genetic data in our DNA—contains a staggering amount of genetic information, and it is by analyzing mutations that occur in our DNA that we are able to determine which humans are closely related to which other humans. These mutations, or variants, are formally known as single nucleotide polymorphisms, or SNPs (SNP is pronounced "snip"), if they occur in at least 1 percent of the population. A SNP profile generally contains information on around 700,000 to 800,000 SNPs.

Analyzing such degraded DNA "is a little like chopping a stack of newspapers into confetti, tossing the bits of paper into the air on a windy day, and then trying to reassemble them into something you can read," one article about Professor Green explained. Or as Green himself puts it: "It is real grunt lab work and a process of trial and error." That process was painstaking, and the white board that Green used to map out calculations was filled and erased many, many dozens of times.

"The solutions are not easy to come up with," he says. "It's the difference between being told how to hit a baseball and then being able to hit a home run."

It took him about a year before he had something that he believed could help identify the Bear Brook victims.

To test his new technique, he created a genotype file from a strand of his own hair. Using an algorithm, he extracted data from that file on the SNPs that are used by the DTC (direct-to-consumer) companies and uploaded this algorithm-derived SNP profile to GEDmatch. He wanted to know if this file would work the same way as a typical SNP array file (created from autosomal DNA isolated from saliva). Would the hair-derived SNP file Green uploaded to GEDmatch even match with anyone at all?

To his delight, Green matched with the very same relatives through both the hair- and saliva-derived profiles. "It was my eureka moment," he says.

Professor Green had to continually tweak and refine the algorithm in order to provide reliable results. As he finished a set of refinements, he would send me the resulting file, which I would upload to GEDmatch to gauge the quality of the SNP profile produced.

The Bear Brook samples were perfect for evaluating the efficacy of Green's algorithm. I had one definite set of parent and child (Rasmussen and his daughter, the maternally unrelated child found in the second barrel) and a possible second set: the female victim found in the first barrel and the two maternally related children. This information served as my control. The first couple of times I uploaded the files that Green sent me, I did not find a match at the proper parent-child matching level (I saw only about half of the expected amount of matching DNA). Green kept refining his algorithm, and after a few more iterations, I finally did get a result with the level of matching expected for a parent and child, both for Rasmussen and his daughter and for the unidentified woman and the two maternally related girls. Additionally, the two girls matched each other at the level expected for half siblings, not full siblings.

The year it had taken to develop and validate the hair protocol was time well spent, because without Professor Green's work, there would have been no other way to identify the Bear Brook victims.

I was now ready to begin using the Methodology. Because I now had good matches for the adult female, things went fairly quickly. I built a speculative tree from her matches and identified an MRCA. Building down from this MRCA, I was able to determine the likely name of the adult female Bear Brook victim within just a couple of days.

She was, I learned, Marlyse Honeychurch.

Knowing her identity meant we would also be able to find the names of the two child victims who, the initial match information showed, were her daughters.

I emailed Deputy Headley with Marlyse's name—a name that was long thought impossible to know. This was another of those thrilling moments of discovery—the brief interval of time during which I may have been the only person in the world who knew that a long-held secret was, at last, no longer a secret. That moment made all the months of digging and building trees worthwhile.

I wish I could say this singular thrill lasted for days or even weeks, but for me it was fleeting. For one thing, everything about the Bear Brook murder case was dark and sad and tragic. Solving the case called not for celebration, but rather for contemplation. It was the best conclusion to an irredeemably evil series of events, a small measure of grace following endless suffering. It was something to be thankful for, and perhaps even a harbinger of future successes that might *prevent* some nefarious crime. But the emotions of the search for, and the discovery of, the victims' identities could not be separated from the punishing reality of the murders.

This feeling was new to me. Finding an adoptee's birth relatives is almost always a moment of triumph, of promise and possibility, perhaps even of salvation. It was easy to celebrate such victories, as I did when I attended ninety-eight-year-old Ellen Law's joyous family reunion in San Bernardino. Even the Lisa Jensen case had ended on a note that was positive and life-affirming, with the discovery that Lisa's maternal grandfather was still living. But the long-cold Bear Brook murder case was different. Far too much had been lost to allow for anything other than a modest rush of satisfaction when, finally, it was solved.

In a sidenote, a woman named Rebekah Heath—a research librarian from Connecticut and a nearly lifelong murder-mystery fan who favored Agatha Christie's Miss Marple series—had taken a special interest in the Bear Brook case and spent ten years working on her own to determine the identities of the four victims. The case became a crusade for the amateur sleuth. Eventually, she found messages on a genealogy forum about two missing women: a twenty-four-year-old mother and her young daughter Sarah McWaters. Both roughly matched the estimated ages of two of the Bear Brook victims. Rebekah dug around and found a relative who told her more about the mother: she was born in Fairfield, Connecticut, and had two daughters, one with each of two ex-husbands. In 1978 she introduced her latest boyfriend to her mother, who told her she thought the man was far too old for her.

The argument that followed was bad enough for the woman to march out of the house in La Puente, California, and disappear from her mother's life. That was around Thanksgiving 1978, the last time family members ever saw or heard from the mother or her children again.

The woman's name was Marlyse Honeychurch. And the name of this missing woman's boyfriend? Terry Rasmussen. Because Junel Davidsen's and my research showing Bob Evans's real name was Terry Rasmussen had been published in newspaper articles, Rebekah was able to connect the dots in her own research.

I was never in contact with Rebekah Heath and only later learned about her work. It was easy for me to recognize, and admire, the tenacity she had shown in searching for answers. I could also guess at the frustration she must have felt at not having any way to confirm her discovery. Rebekah Heath represents the enormous strides a dedicated researcher can make toward solving long-cold cases, as well as the limits of what can be achieved without DNA.

Fortunately, thanks in large part to Professor Green's expertise, I was able to confirm beyond any scientific doubt that the adult female victim was Marlyse Honeychurch. The New Hampshire police collected DNA samples from Marlyse's two living sisters and a half brother, as well as a sample from one of her ex-husbands, the man believed to be the father of one of Honeychurch's daughters, Marie Elizabeth Vaughn. When I uploaded these reference samples to GEDmatch, I was able to confirm conclusively the identities of three of the four Bear Brook murder victims: Marlyse Honeychurch and her daughters, Marie Vaughn and Sarah McWaters.

The information I uncovered about the victims told a sad and fractured story. Marlyse Elizabeth Honeychurch, born in Connecticut in 1954, was a high school sophomore in Stamford when she and her mother moved to Southern California. In 1970 Marlyse enrolled in Artesia High School in Lakewood, California, and began seeing a boyfriend. Just one year later the young couple were married in Las Vegas, while Marlyse was still a teenager. That December Marlyse gave birth to a girl she named Marie.

Mother and daughter bounced around after that—back to Stamford, then to Fall River in Massachusetts, then back to Lakewood. Marie's father and Marlyse divorced in 1974, and that same year Marlyse married her second husband, with whom she had a daughter, Sarah, born in 1977, before they separated. Marlyse's family last saw her in November 1978, just after she introduced them to her new boyfriend on Thanksgiving.

It appears that Marlyse and Rasmussen moved to Manchester, New Hampshire, where Marlyse may have assumed a new identity, Elizabeth Evans—the name found on a document linked to Rasmussen's Manchester address.

In 1985, seven years after her family last saw Marlyse, the remains of a woman and three children were found in two metal barrels in Bear Brook Park—victims who, more than thirty years later, I identified as Marlyse Honeychurch and her daughters.

A haunting mystery that spanned decades had for the most part been solved in just a few days after DNA profiles for the victims were uploaded to GEDmatch. This marked the first time in the history of U.S. law enforcement that autosomal DNA from rootless hair samples helped solve a crime—*and* the first time genetic genealogy had been used to obtain the true identity of a criminal.

The fourth victim remains unidentified, beyond the fact that she was the biological daughter of Terry Rasmussen. Unfortunately, the current genetic matches that I have for the child are quite distant. But I have not given up on finding her, and I have been making progress. This child deserves a name, too, and I continue to work on restoring that to her.

In the meantime, the remains of the other three now-identified Bear Brook victims were reinterred. At a memorial service held in the Saint John the Baptist Cemetery in Allenstown, New Hampshire, on a chilly day in November 2019, several relatives gathered to honor Marlyse Honeychurch and her daughter Marie, who was about six years old when she was murdered. Their remains, held in two small urns, were laid to rest side by side in a small grave. Marlyse's other daughter, Sarah McWaters, who was only one when she died, was buried separately closer to other relatives.

In Allenstown, some who attended the ceremony brought flowers for Marlyse and little stuffed bears for Marie. A new gravestone was placed next to the old one that spoke of "mortal remains known only to God." This new stone included names and dates of birth and death, evidence that Marlyse and her daughters had lived and mattered. Marlyse's siblings David Salamon, Michelle Chagaris, Paula Hodges, and Roxanne Barrow, who had not seen or heard from their sister in thirty-four years, came to Allenstown from California, Oregon, and Oklahoma. They wore winter coats against the afternoon chill and sat on chairs covered in green velvet and wept as the heavy new stone was wedged into the earth above the two buried urns.

"Through the years we never stopped searching," David Salamon, the youngest sibling (who was only six when his sister disappeared), said on the day of the service. "We searched and we searched and we never gave up." About 150 other mourners gathered at the gravesite and formed a protective circle around Marlyse's family.

"Love conquers all things," Deacon William R. Lavallee said solemnly in his graveside sermon. "It can conquer hate. It can conquer death."

Deacon Lavallee also spoke of the significance of what had been accomplished on behalf of Marlyse and her daughters.

"A name is a very powerful thing," the deacon said. "Having a name makes a huge difference. They are no longer just the Allenstown Four. They have names."

I was not at the memorial service, but when I later read Deacon Lavallee's sermon, I found it moving. In a case that had provoked so many emotions—anger, sadness, despair, hope—it was difficult to reach any kind of coherent conclusion as to what it had all meant. But Deacon Lavallee's words were clarifying.

The world now knew who at least three of the long-unidentified Bear Brook victims were, and the world also knew who had killed them.

This mattered. It mattered quite a bit. It made, as the deacon preached, a real and meaningful difference.

Of this, at least, I was sure.

PART THREE

THE GOLDEN STATE KILLER

MARCH 2017

9

Deputy Headley and I had now worked together on two high-profile, long-cold cases in two years, and we had solved them both. It was a good partnership. We had met only one time, but we had an easy, productive relationship based, I believe, on mutual trust and respect. Deputy Headley was soft-spoken and tended to use even, measured tones. He was never rushed or excitable, but rather steady and confident, always ready to help, whether by cold-calling people and persuading them to provide DNA samples or identifying relatives of matches using law enforcement databases.

Deputy Headley began his law enforcement career helping hikers stranded on perilous mountains before spending ten years in the emotionally taxing field of crimes against children. It seemed to me that he had developed the hard shell necessary for that kind of work without sacrificing any of his humanity or innate goodness. His steely demeanor, along with his graying hair and sturdy mustache, put me in mind of a rugged, badge-wearing cowboy.

The two cases we had worked on together were, for me, an auspicious introduction to a new method of crime fighting that would become known as investigative genetic genealogy (IGG). In many ways, Deputy Headley and I were defining this new discipline as we worked our cases. There were no rules, no precedents, no set protocols—

other than the basics of the Methodology—for how to use DNA to identify suspects in violent crimes such as rape and murder. Deputy Headley and I were, as a member of my group quipped, "building the airplane as we flew it."

Deputy Headley was so excited about what we had accomplished that he shared the story of the Lisa Project with what seemed like *all* his colleagues.

"I told everyone about what we did," he says. "I was just so happy that we were able to identify Lisa after the case had been cold for such a long time."

Deputy Headley was on a conference call about another case in early 2017 when he mentioned our success with Lisa to Steve Kramer, a Wisconsin-raised, Los Angeles–based now former FBI attorney. Kramer had worked with FBI special agents on so many cases that most people believed he was a special agent himself. Kramer asked Deputy Headley questions about the Lisa case and was briefed on the DNA technology we used.

"I told him how it works—all the steps, the blood cards, the DNA, everything," Headley says, "and I said, 'You *have* to talk to Barbara Rae-Venter.'"

Not much later, Steve Kramer shared the success story of the Lisa Project with another law enforcement officer named Paul Holes, a cold-case investigator for the Contra Costa County (CA) Sheriff's Office.

At the time, Steve Kramer headed up the investigative team that was trying to capture an elusive California-area serial killer known as the Golden State Killer (he took over the case from Paul Holes). This was a high-profile case in which the suspect was completely unknown to law enforcement—and, despite the number of victims involved, a case lacking a single recent clue about who or where the suspect might be. What's more, the Golden State Killer's last known crime had been committed more than thirty years earlier. Paul Holes had spent twenty-two years working on this case, and as he neared his retirement from the sheriff's office, this was the one case he most wanted to solve before leaving the job. After speaking with Kramer, Holes wondered if the same technology we used to identify Lisa Jensen could be used to identify a suspect.

In March 2017, Paul Holes called me and posed this very question: Did I think investigative genetic genealogy could help identify an unknown assailant with only his decades-old crime-scene DNA to work with?

I told Paul Holes I believed it could.

In that first phone call, Paul declined to tell me anything about the criminal we would be trying to identify, other than to say the case was very high profile and would be a real feather in my cap if I could somehow solve it. I asked him to send me whatever he could about the case, which, because I was not officially part of law enforcement, turned out to be nothing at all. Still, I assumed I would learn more about our suspect in my next phone call with Paul.

But that call did not happen for several more months. Paul Holes did reach out to me again, several times. But I did not respond to any of his calls or emails.

"I just didn't hear from you again," Paul told me when we reconnected. "I figured you didn't want to work with law enforcement investigators."

But that was not the case at all.

The reason I did not call Paul back was because I could not.

I was in a hospital, coping with an illness that very nearly cost me my life.

In the eighteen months before Paul Holes called me in March 2017, I had gone to a hospital emergency room five separate times.

Each time was for a different alarming reason. The first trip was for what was diagnosed as supraventricular tachycardia—a rapid heartbeat that can cause heart palpitations. It had developed while I was playing tennis. Luckily, when it happened, one of my opponents on the court was an emergency room nurse who took my pulse and called 911, all the while telling me everything was fine.

After that, I wound up in the ER again for shortness of breath. Another time it was badly swollen legs. I also went in for a searing but inexplicable upper-left back pain. With each visit, doctors prescribed medication to deal with the presenting symptoms. There seemed to be no overriding disease or condition that connected all the symptoms.

In late 2016, a few months before Paul Holes's call, a friend and I went on a family-history research trip to Inverness in Scotland. Our idea was to research family records while we were there but also enjoy the beautiful Scottish countryside. My friend and I were wandering cheerfully along on a city street one Monday morning when I suddenly felt like I was having trouble talking and breathing at the same time. I tried to speak but could not utter a single word. It was a new and very strange sensation, and I was frightened and baffled: What could possibly be wrong with me that would not allow me to breathe and talk?

My friend took me to the nearest hospital. In the emergency room I gathered myself and was able to speak again, though my chest and lungs still felt strange and uncomfortable. And though I had been in Scotland for about ten days by then, my legs and feet were still quite swollen from the long flight from California. The ER doctor speculated I might have some kind of cardiac issue. It was hardly a specific diagnosis, and all she could do was prescribe medication that would temporarily make it a little easier for me to breathe.

"See a cardiologist when you get home," she advised.

Back in California, I tried to follow her advice, but when I called my doctor's office to make an appointment I learned that my doctor's practice had split in two and I was now considered a new patient of the cardiology practice. That meant I would have to wait several months before anyone could see me.

On Christmas Day 2016, I hosted a dinner party at my home for several friends, and I spent most of the day cooking in the kitchen. Late in the afternoon, I felt a sudden horrible, excruciating pain in my upper-left back. The pain was so bad that I slumped down on the kitchen floor and cried. My brain was telling me to go to the emergency room, but I had a turkey and a lamb in the oven, so I went ahead with the party and did my best to mask my extreme discomfort.

It did not work. The pain was simply unbearable.

"Excuse me," I finally said to my guests during dinner, "but can one of you please drive me to the hospital?"

In the emergency room a doctor diagnosed the source of the pain as a muscle spasm, pumped me full of Valium, and sent me home with a prescription for a muscle relaxant. Once again, only a single symptom had been addressed.

Over the next few weeks, the pain returned on and off. Then, right after my first phone call with Paul, in early 2017, I went to see my doctor to get a refill for the muscle relaxant prescription. This time, I talked to the doctor about my experience of not being able to breathe and talk at the same time.

"Asthma?" the doctor said, more asking than telling.

I told her I did not think so, but she called in a prescription for an asthma medication inhaler anyway.

And then, right there in her office, I had an attack.

I could not talk. I also could not *breathe*. The doctor immediately hooked me to an EKG machine, scanning the results for an explanation.

"Things don't look right," she finally said. "You need to immediately get an echocardiogram stress test."

She referred me to a cardiologist in her practice and I took the test. The diagnosis, based on the echocardiogram, was mitral valve prolapse, a kind of leak in the valve between the heart's two left chambers. Blood was regurgitating into the left atrium of my heart.

The doctor said I needed a valve repair. I called my daughter-in-law, a psychiatrist in San Francisco who works with a heart transplant team, and I asked if she could recommend a good cardiothoracic surgeon. She connected me to one of the best surgeons in the state. I checked into the California Pacific Medical Center in San Francisco a day ahead of schedule so additional tests could be carried out. The surgeon ordered an angiogram, and a small tube was inserted into a large vessel in my arm, followed by a contrast dye that would make it easier for doctors to see the flow of blood through my arteries and to my heart.

The angiogram revealed a blockage.

Not a minor blockage, but a *90 percent* blockage in a bifurcated artery. I would require double bypass surgery as well as the mitral valve repair.

I was a heart attack waiting to happen.

I was extremely lucky to receive my diagnosis when I did. My surgery lasted for several hours and was successful. When I regained consciousness, I could breathe normally again. I spent eight days recovering in the hospital and the next several months going through a fairly extensive cardiac rehab program, with strenuous exercise three times a week while hooked up to a cardiac and other monitors. It was hard work, but the monitoring equipment made me feel safe while exercising, and I finished the program feeling healthy and strong, a blessing I am enormously thankful for.

Only later did it occur to me that the initial confusion about my diagnosis was similar to the early stages of a DNA-based investigation.

No one had been able to tie all my different symptoms together until it was almost too late. It was the last-minute angiogram that finally revealed the connection between them all. The supraventricular tachycardia was caused by an enlarged heart, the regurgitation from the leaky mitral valve caused my breathing problems, my back pain was likely angina, and so forth.

It was all there, waiting to be connected, and yet it had not been for years.

Why not? One reason no doctor correctly diagnosed me early on could be that, unlike men, women tend not to exhibit the traditional overt signs of an impending heart attack: chest pain, intense sweating, a feeling of extreme indigestion. But the truth was, I had a bad family history of cardiac disease, and the genetics likely were not good. My father had his first heart attack at fifty-seven—ten years younger than I was in 2017. And my paternal grandfather (late husband of Mumma the bookie) died of a heart attack at the age of sixty-seven. Yet, even with my family history, no one connected the dots, as each of my symptoms on its own did not make sense or suggest a proper diagnosis.

Similarly, the early matches that come up in a DNA search often seem to lead nowhere, and even subsequent research can leave you with a tangle of apparently unrelated names as clues. There are times when the connections you are hoping to find simply do not appear and nothing seems to make any sense at all. Maybe someone you think is a biological relative was adopted, or a parent or other ancestor changed their name, or had a secret affair, and that blocks you from getting the results you *know* you should be getting.

The mystery remains stubbornly unsolvable, an infuriating collection of facts that simply will not tie together.

But, of course, they do. What is missing is the single insight—the suddenly clear, undiluted view—that transforms the names in the trees from random puzzle pieces into a coherent image. This is what we do in the field of investigative genetic genealogy: we spend hours and hours chasing that one single insight that will pull together all the clues and produce, at long last, the elusive identity of a person of interest.

When my life finally resumed a kind of normalcy, it was October 2017—six months after Paul Holes first reached out to me. I am normally good about returning phone calls and following up on obligations, so I was surprised to realize, when I went through weeks and weeks of unopened emails, that I had not at least let Paul know why I had not returned his calls.

Finally, in October, I did call him back, and I explained what had happened to me.

"Do you still need help with that case?" I asked.

"Absolutely I do," Paul replied.

This time, Paul told me the subject of our search.

"It's the Golden State Killer," he said.

10

Paul Holes likely expected a big reaction when he mentioned the Golden State Killer, but the moniker meant nothing to me. Back in the 1970s I lived in Buffalo, New York, and I returned to Northern California long after the Golden State Killer had faded from the headlines. I had not heard of this serial killer and knew nothing about him. So I turned to Google to learn about the case, unaware of the darkness I was about to engage with.

The articles about the Golden State Killer's individual crimes were jarring enough, but the fact that there were so many, and so much violence and death, gave the case an added gravity that was overwhelming. At least thirteen brutal murders. More than fifty rapes. One hundred burglaries, and maybe many more. Any number of unknown or unreported atrocities. All in the span of just twelve years. He was far more active than either of California's other infamous terrorizing serial killers: the Night Stalker and the Zodiac Killer. This was, I discovered, a reign of terror and mayhem unlike anything I had ever heard of—an exhibition of truly depraved, sadistic behavior; lives ended or utterly ruined with neither remorse nor hesitation; the civilization of friendly neighborhoods mocked by one man's zeal to violate and destroy.

What made it even more horrific was his success at remaining unknown and unknowable. He left clues, but nothing that was truly revealing of who he was. He had many signatures, many discernible patterns—but nothing defined him more than his elusiveness. Each cruel assault was aggravated by the taunting reality that he was almost certain to get away with it—and the sickening expectation that he would soon strike again.

No one knew what he looked like. Survivors offered descriptions, but they were all partial, since most of the time the intruder wore a mask. The picture of the suspect that emerged from these descriptions was unsettlingly average: a white male, approximately five foot ten, with a lean build, possibly blond hair, possibly light brown. The sketches varied—some featured him with short, neatly kept hair swept to the side, others with shaggy, nearly collar-length locks parted in the center. His facial features were nondescript, though one sketch depicted him sneering slightly, as if with contempt. His voice—left on answering machines in dozens of chilling, menacing phone calls to victims—was deep, hoarse, and demonic, but likely exaggerated for effect (his victims reported his voice during their ordeals as being whispery). He appeared to be familiar with firearms, and there was speculation he may have served or had an interest in the military or law enforcement. Sketches of the suspect showed a man in his mid-twenties or so. When I started working on the case, it was estimated he would now be between sixty and seventy-five years old.

And that was it. No distinctive limp or physical features that would make him stand out in a crowd. In a way he was not only nameless but faceless as well. He was a cipher, a blank slate people could project their very worst fears onto. He did not even seem human. Devoid of features, compassion, and restraint, he might as well have been a terror machine.

It is likely the mysterious Golden State Killer got his start committing lesser crimes in the town of Visalia, in central California's San Joaquin Valley, as early as 1973, perhaps with break-ins, vandalism, or petty theft of unusual items like photographs and piggy banks. A series of such crimes led to his first nickname: the Visalia Ransacker. On February 5, 1975, a journalism professor named Claude Snelling heard noises in his San Joaquin Valley home around 2:00 A.M. and confronted a man in a ski mask in his carport. The intruder was wrestling with Snelling's sixteen-year-old daughter, who had been dragged outside from her bedroom. Without warning, the intruder pulled a gun and fired twice at Snelling, sending him staggering back into his house. The man in the ski mask fled. Snelling, tragically, died in the ambulance on the way to the hospital.

This was the intruder's first murder—the cowardly, cold-blooded killing of a father in front of his daughter in the dark of night.

His assaults continued, confined always to sleepy, residential central California towns, and mostly to ranch-style homes with neatly paved driveways and trimmed shrubbery and serene elm, cedar, and cypress trees that provided just enough isolation for the killer to belie the illusion of security.

One year after shooting Claude Snelling, the killer turned up in areas just east of Sacramento, 211 miles north of Visalia. There, in June 1976, he broke into a woman's Rancho Cordova home and raped her repeatedly. More attacks followed, all against women who were home alone. By November, police believed the same man had committed eight rapes, including four in a month.

"Fear Grips Serene Neighborhoods," *The Sacramento Bee* declared, describing small towns "in the clutches of fear caused by a faceless man who wears hooded masks."

By then, there was a new nickname: the East Area Rapist.

The attacks intensified. Carmichael, Citrus Heights, Orangevale—all quiet towns, all changed forever. On January 19, 1977, a pregnant housewife who was home alone was awakened at 4:00 A.M. by a stranger in her bedroom. She was tied up and raped several times. Five days later a twenty-five-year-old woman separated from her husband and living alone was asleep when a man broke in, bound her hands with rope, threatened to kill her with an ice pick, and raped her several times. That March, a sixteen-year-old girl whose parents were away for the weekend came home from work at 10:45 P.M. and found a man holding an ax in the living room. The intruder assaulted and raped her repeatedly.

At one meeting to discuss the East Area Rapist, an investigator voiced the opinion that the attacker was a "wuss" because he only went after women who were alone. That soon changed.

In October 1977, a man in a ski mask, armed with a knife and a gun, broke into a Sacramento home through the garage. Both the husband and wife were home, and the assailant tied up the husband and raped the wife—while their two children slept nearby. A headline in the *Los Angeles Times* read, "Rapist Claims 25th Victim."

The offender was usually stealthy but sometimes brazen and leisurely. His victims often heard him prowling around a backyard before breaking into their homes. He was nearly caught on two occasions but both times eluded police by jumping over fences and racing away into the woods, which indicated a confidence in his athleticism. Sometimes he would slip into an empty home the day before an attack to leave windows and sliding glass doors open, or to stash rope beneath sofas to use later to bind his victims. On several occasions he phoned a victim the following day to taunt her, or to threaten to return and kill her. On one occasion he phoned a victim just to say, "Merry Christmas, it's me again!" He often spent hours in people's homes, and he liked raiding their kitchens for turkey or apple pie in between assaults. One survivor recalled hearing him cry in another room while she lay bound and blindfolded; another heard him sob and say "Mummy" over and over. Another time he mentioned the name Bonnie. He frequently rummaged through homes to find odd personal objects he could take with him, small trophies to mark his heinous deeds.

He relished his power over his captives—relished terrifying them. His game was subjugation. He usually blinded women with a flashlight as soon as the creak of a floorboard or the yawn of an opening door awakened them. Often he forced women to tie up their husbands, after which he placed a stack of dishes on the men's backs. If the dishes rattled, he warned the husbands, he would kill their wives and then kill them. He would then force the wife to another room, where he would rape her repeatedly. Victims were left haunted by different lingering memories of their unthinkable imprisonment: the gentle tinkle of disturbed chimes, the strong smell of aftershave, the intruder's strange, whispery voice.

Between 1976 and 1979, he raped at least fifty women, and probably more. Two of his victims were only thirteen.

He was a nightmare come to life. Anyone could be next, so everyone lived in fear. He invaded homes but also invaded the consciousness of towns and cities across Northern California, causing people to change the way they lived. They began keeping their porch lights on all night. They installed new locks at a record pace. In some homes families slept in shifts. One boy with a sliding door in his bedroom took his BB gun to bed every night. The monster destroyed all that was good and decent and normal.

And, of course, he ended lives in cruel and godless ways.

Keith and Patti Harrington were newlyweds when they encountered him in their Laguna Niguel home late on August 21, 1975. He used a blunt object to kill them both—his first known double murder.

Brian and Katie Maggiore were out for a walk with their dog not far from their Rancho Cordova home at 9:00 P.M. on February 2, 1978, when he confronted them on the street. They ran for their lives and he shot them both from behind, killing them.

He stalked Robert Offerman and his wife, Debra, both doctors, before, on December 30, 1979, breaking into their Avenida Pequena condominium in Goleta. He raped Debra and killed them both.

He used a fireplace log to bludgeon two married doctors in Ventura, and he murdered a young couple housesitting for a friend in Goleta. On May 5, 1986, he raped and killed eighteen-year-old Janelle Lisa Cruz in her Irvine home while her parents were away on vacation.

As it turned out, Janelle was his final known victim. After 1986, he was not linked to any other crime. All told, he directly victimized more than seventy people, and many tens of thousands more who were lucky enough not to encounter him but unlucky enough to live within his zone of savagery. To burrow into the details of his crimes, as I did, is to have your understanding of human nature challenged and, ultimately, changed. It is to bear witness to what can only be described as profound, rampant evil.

The more I read about his crimes, the more determined I became to identify him. Very quickly, the case became personal for me. I could see why so many others had become obsessed with catching him over the years—sheriffs, detectives, police officers, journalists, true-crime enthusiasts. The thought of this monster still free on the streets was maddening and intolerable.

In 2001 the unsolved rapes were finally connected to the murders through a DNA match, creating a larger, more sprawling case—one that proved no less difficult to solve. The writer Michelle McNamara, a true-crime blogger and one of the obsessed, coined the moniker that stuck in 2013: the Golden State Killer. There have been many serial killers who were never caught—including the Zodiac killer, the Freeway Phantom, and the Long Island serial killer—but none, it seemed, who had left behind so many tantalizing clues and signatures and such a sheer volume of casework, and yet who remained so far out of reach.

From the early days of his crime spree, when six police investigators and three FBI agents were assigned full-time to find him, to the day Paul Holes called me decades later, the Golden State Killer had been one of the most earnestly hunted human beings in all of history. Careers came and went; the killer remained unknown.

Few people were as devoted to catching the killer as Paul Holes.

Paul grew up in many places—Salt Lake City; Washington, D.C.; San Antonio—before his family settled, more or less, in central California, right in the middle of the Golden State Killer's sprawling crime field. His father was in the air force, and Paul was a military brat. Inspired by his favorite TV show, *Quincy, M.E.,* about a Los Angeles County medical examiner, Paul planned to go to medical school and become a forensic pathologist. But his grades were not quite good enough for that track, so he instead earned a bachelor of science in biochemistry.

After seeing a booth at a job fair that featured a model of a crime scene—"a guy laying on a kitchen floor with a pool of blood around his head"—Paul switched his interest to criminalistics and, in 1994, took a job as an investigator for the Contra Costa County Sheriff's Office in Martinez, California. The final impetus had been a book his parents gifted him on his twenty-first birthday: *Sexual Homicide,* by the eminent FBI manhunter John Douglas. "I was passionate about the investigative and forensic parts of the job, but when I read that book I also embraced the behavioral aspects of crime fighting," says Paul, who further refined his focus to serial predators and cold cases.

One day in 1994, out of curiosity, he wandered into the new library built for the sheriff's department by a team at UC Berkeley. "I was a young kid starting out and I was constantly in that library, going through files," he says. On one visit, he noticed a file cabinet stuck away in a corner, off on its own. He opened the bottom drawer first. "It was chock-full of these old manila folders, and on their tabs, written in red marker, it said 'EAR.' "

The acronym, he learned, stood for East Area Rapist.

Paul could hardly believe it. A serial rapist in the Bay Area, right where he grew up? And he still had not been caught or even identified? Paul checked out the case files and pored over them whenever he had time. The statute of limitations for the sex crimes had long since run, so working on them, Paul says, "was more of an academic exercise, not work on an actual open case."

Still, he found the mountain of evidence fascinating, and through a new forensic DNA program in the department's crime lab he was able to make a small but significant advance in the case: Paul proved conclusively that three of the rapes, the only ones for which he had DNA, had been committed by the same man.

What Paul could not assemble—what *no one,* it seemed, could assemble—was a list of suspects. Paul called up one high-ranking lieutenant and asked a basic question: Do you have or did you ever have one or two good primary suspects?

The lieutenant's reply was stark.

"We don't have anybody," he said. "The people we thought might be good were eliminated. Now we have no one."

Paul had little choice but to try long-odds searches. He put together a list of all the male inmates in the California Department of

Corrections, which ran to forty thousand names. Another list was even more imposing: everyone who lived in the crime-scene zip codes at the time of the crimes. That list contained many tens of thousands of names.

"There was no way to realistically sort through all those names," Paul says. "Coroners' reports, public records, prison rolls—it was just a massive amount of people to try and narrow down."

Over the years the case would be revisited, thanks to one or another technical advancement, but, stubbornly, it remained a stone-cold case. Paul even returned the original manila folders to the bottom drawer of the file cabinet, their lonely home for the foreseeable future, and perhaps forever.

Paul, however, was not done with the case.

He was eventually promoted to division commander in the sheriff's office, a position he found too administrative. Once more, on his own, he went back to the file cabinet in the library and, after more than ten years away from the case, retrieved the familiar old folders. In his final months at the sheriff's office, Paul wanted to take one last vigorous shot at catching the man who had consumed so many of his thinking hours.

I was now part of that last shot.

11

Once I signed on to work with Paul Holes in late 2017, I was anxious to start putting together a profile of the man I was looking for. This is one of the first things that I do when I agree to work on a case. I knew there had been a Snapshot composite profile of the Golden State Killer produced by a DNA lab that had previously worked on the case, and I asked Paul if I could see it. (Snapshot is a forensic DNA-analysis tool that attempts to create a likeness of unidentified persons by pinpointing phenotypic characteristics such as hair and eye color.)

Paul explained that because I was a civilian and not a law enforcement officer, he was not permitted to provide me with any official documents. All he sent me was one page of the lab report describing the killer's bioancestry information, which, I later discovered, was not even completely accurate. Paul did not send me any phenotypic data—for instance, hair color, eye color, freckled or unfreckled skin, or other information that might have been useful.

Up until then, I had been reporting to both Paul and FBI attorney Steve Kramer, but because Paul was in the process of wrapping up his cases ahead of his retirement, Steve Kramer became my sole point person on the investigation. Steve was assigned to the FBI's Los Angeles field office, and I called him there to ask for a copy of the Snapshot profile. Steve was friendly, but he did not waste time. He, too, said he could not send me anything. I simply was not authorized to see any official material regarding the case.

"You are asking me to identify this guy and you won't give me any information at all?" I asked, probably sounding more impatient than I intended.

"It's not up to me," Steve said. "It's Orange County. They're not letting any of it go."

Orange County was just one of several California counties in which the Golden State Killer had struck. As Paul Holes also explained it to me, there were a lot of internal politics at play between counties, and a few grudges that long predated my entry into the case. Whatever the reason, it meant I would not have access to any official paperwork.

This was frustrating, but I had experienced such interdepartmental-type squabbling before. When I was a first-year graduate student at UC San Diego, I was caught up in a rivalry between two laboratories supervised by two professors, and I was even falsely accused of contaminating one of the labs with radioactive iodine by an unscrupulous postdoctoral fellow. I understood how competition between departments could get in the way of productivity.

I also knew that it was possible to begin a case having next to nothing to work with and *still* solve the case—as I had with the Lisa Jensen Project. In fact, I only really needed one thing to identify the Golden State Killer: his DNA.

But that, too, was a problem.

Apparently, we did not *have* his DNA.

In the course of his twelve-year crime spree, the Golden State Killer left behind a wealth of DNA evidence, primarily hair, skin cells, and semen found at his many crime scenes. Over the decades that followed, however, each new advance in DNA technology led to some of that evidence being used to conduct whatever the new tests were, in hopes of generating fresh leads.

For instance, in the late 1980s the FBI began developing a national DNA database that would come to be known as the Combined DNA Index System, or CODIS for short. Essentially, CODIS was a vast store of DNA profiles drawn from criminals and crime-scene DNA. Law enforcement can compare DNA from their crime scene against the CODIS database. As soon as CODIS was operative, officials working on what was then called the East Area Rapist case submitted DNA samples they had preserved from earlier crime scenes.

Unfortunately, those samples did not match any existing DNA profiles in CODIS. The new database was powerful but limited—if a perpetrator had no criminal record, the crime-scene DNA was not of much use.

Early DNA tests also required a relatively large amount of high-quality DNA material. This caused the supply of the Golden State Killer's DNA to shrink quickly. Investigators had to balance the desire to keep up with new DNA technology against the risk of eventually running out of DNA material to test. (It is only in recent years that testing methods have progressed to where much less DNA is needed for an accurate test, which means that crime-scene DNA will last longer—but still not forever.)

That was the reality of the Golden State Killer case. In a way, it was a desperate race between rapidly improving technology and a rapidly dwindling supply of the killer's DNA. What would happen first—the key breakthrough in DNA analysis that would lead to the identification of the killer, or the very last DNA sample being wasted on another dead end? Who would win the race—the good guys or the murderer?

By the time Paul Holes called me in March 2017, he had run out of all the Golden State Killer's crime-scene DNA to which he had been given access. He was going to have to find another county that still had DNA and was willing to share it with him. The obvious starting place was Orange County, the third-most populous county in the state, and also the scene of four of the Golden State Killer's murders.

In the fall of 2017, around the time I was able to work on the case in earnest, Paul reached out to the Orange County Sheriff's Office for help.

They turned him down.

Once again, I was astonished. How could officials from nearby counties not find a way to work together to solve such a high-profile case? With resignation in his voice, Paul again cited a network of internecine spats and grudges that seemed to govern intercounty cooperation in California.

"That's Orange County," he explained. "That's just the way they are."

But, as it turned out, the race was not quite over—and failing to get a sample from Orange County proved a blessing in disguise.

While Paul Holes went down the list of California counties in search of a DNA sample, I went to work building an initial profile of the serial killer with what little information I had, and with whatever I could deduce from newspaper accounts and public records.

What did I know about the suspect? *Well,* I thought, *let's start with his age.* I knew he had begun his rape spree in the mid-1970s, and I surmised that when he had escalated from burglary to rape in 1976, he had to be at least twenty years old. Why did I think that? Because he did not rape just one time, he raped multiple times. If we were looking for someone who had committed only one assault, I would have to allow for the possibility that the perpetrator could have been as young as, say, fifteen, and that the attack had been an isolated impulse offense. But given that he had struck so often—and that he had been able to elude police by scaling tall fences and outrunning them in the woods—I guessed that he had to be at least twenty when he started. He had to be capable of a certain level of physicality. This was not a boy committing these heinous, often strenuous acts.

These were a man's crimes.

So if he were twenty or older in 1976, he had to have been born in 1956 or earlier. He likely lived in California—possibly Northern California—and had either a military or a law enforcement background. Forty years previously he had been described as athletic, about five foot ten and having blond or light brown hair. Beyond this, there was not much material that I could use to build a profile, although I would be able to get some additional information, such as eye color, from his DNA.

Paul Holes had not only built his own extensive physical and psychological profile of the killer, he had also described his profile in detail in a four-part TV series. The series aired right around the time I started work on the case, and I watched all four segments and took notes.

One of Paul's theories was that, since many of the rapes had taken place in new housing developments, the Golden State Killer likely worked in an occupation that had something to do with real estate, such as a Realtor or developer. Possibly, Paul guessed, he might have worked in the construction business.

Paul's profile was based primarily on supposition, whereas my profile included only factual information or educated biographical estimates—a possible year of birth, likely residential locations, or observed physical characteristics. To these, I would add verifiable data that would, hopefully, be revealed by the killer's DNA.

For two months—October and November 2017—Paul came up empty in his quest for DNA for our project. Many other county investigators had run out of DNA material, too, or did not have enough to share, or had samples that were too mixed with a victim's DNA to be of much use. To achieve the results we wanted, we needed a preferably single-source, uncontaminated sample of the Golden State Killer's crime-scene DNA. It was beginning to look as if one might no longer exist outside of Orange County.

I did not know it at the time (although I have certainly learned it since), but solving really challenging DNA cases or crimes often seems to require a random twist of fate—a moment when something unexpected happens that defies probability and ends up being just the thing you need to keep going. When that happens, it feels as if the universe is nudging the case along. A document that was believed destroyed is found; a person who refused to do a DNA test has a change of heart; information that once appeared completely inaccessible no longer is. I have referred to these lucky happenings as my guardian angel.

In this case, it was one of the serial killer's tragic victims—one of the two he slaughtered most violently—who reached out from the past, through decades of silence, and gave us precisely the thing we needed most.

Everything seemed off.

A side door that was normally unlocked to let in the landscapers was locked. The front door was open, although it usually was not. Three days' worth of newspapers were stacked up on the front porch. Inside the home, the living room looked a mess, with sofa cushions out of place, although the house was always kept tidy. A wake-up alarm rang from behind the bedroom door, even though it was nearly noon.

Gary Smith, then twelve years old, had bicycled to his father's home in Ventura County to mow the lawn—his weekly chore—and he had no idea why things seemed so strange that day, March 16, 1980. He walked into his father's bedroom and saw the bedcovers pulled up over two people and, inexplicably, a thick fireplace log placed between them on the bed. Slowly, Gary pulled back the bedcover on one side, and saw his father, Lyman Smith, lying there.

The back of his father's head was caved in.

Gary called the police and waited in a daze on the front porch for them to arrive. The house filled with investigators. Both Gary's father and Gary's stepmother, Charlene Smith, were dead, bludgeoned by a blunt object, presumably the bloodied log, which the intruder had apparently taken from a pile outside the house. Lyman Smith was found naked and facedown, his hands and ankles bound with a length of cord from the drapes. Charlene had on a T-shirt and was faceup, her wrists also tied. Both were bound, and the cord was tied using a distinctive knot called a sailor's knife lanyard knot, or diamond knot. In the days after the brutal double murder, newspapers referred to the unknown assailant as the Diamond Knot Killer.

Shortly after the bodies were found, the Ventura County assistant medical examiner at the time, Dr. Peter Speth, arrived at the house. Not all medical examiners attended crime scenes to collect samples;

most preferred to take their samples when the bodies arrived at the crime lab. But Dr. Speth almost always made it to the scene of a rape. He believed that moving and transporting bodies caused seminal fluids in a body cavity to shift and mix, compromising the purity of a sample later taken in a lab.

In the Smiths' bedroom, Dr. Speth went to work.

Because DNA testing was not yet possible in 1980, Dr. Speth concentrated on tests for blood groups and enzymes, which could be used to identify possible suspects, provided the samples were as close to pristine as possible. Employing a standard sexual assault kit that had been created just a few years earlier, Dr. Speth used a swab to take a vaginal sample from Charlene and put the swab, cotton-end up, in a rack of vials. He air-dried the vial, sealed it with a capsular desiccant, and put it on dry ice he had brought to the scene with him. Once he was back in the Ventura County forensics lab, the sealed vial went into a freezer.

The process went smoothly and without incident, and Dr. Speth had the pristine sample he needed. His work at the crime scene, in theory, should have been finished. But it was not.

In the bedroom of the Smiths' tragically violated home, Dr. Speth did something that was not part of any rule book, not required of any medical examiner, and not a common practice among any medical examiners anywhere—not in 1980, and not today.

If Peter Speth was not, as he believes, the only medical examiner in the world to routinely do what he did next, he was certainly among an infinitesimally small number of forensic practitioners who have done it.

Over the years, Paul Holes had been judicious with the DNA material from the three Golden State Killer crimes that had occurred in Contra Costa County. Still, he had no choice but to dip back into the samples every time there was a breakthrough in DNA technology. Advances in DNA analysis using Y-STRs, or short tandem repeats on the Y, or male, chromosome, looked promising enough that Paul spent six years—and the last of his DNA material—working the new technology to try to get a surname for the suspect. Unfortunately, he came up empty again. There were just no useful matches, suggesting that the men in the suspect's paternal line may have been recent immigrants.

When I joined the case, Paul was running out of counties to ask for DNA samples. Finally, he and Steve Kramer briefed Steve Rhodes, a Ventura County prosecutor and a member of that county's cold-case task force, on the new technology that I had used to identify Lisa Jensen. Ventura County was the scene of two of the GSK's (Golden State Killer's) murders: Charlene and Lyman Smith. Paul asked Rhodes if he had any GSK crime-scene DNA available to share.

"Let me dig around," Rhodes said.

At least it was not a no.

Rhodes called the Ventura County Medical Examiner's Office and asked a technician there to look through the sexual assault kits stored in the lab's freezer.

It turned out that the county's chief medical examiner, Dr. Ann Bucholtz, recently had begun the process of cleaning out the lab's cluttered and disorganized freezer, which was packed with samples and other evidence that no one seemed to need. Many of the samples had already been transferred from an older freezer, and if that transfer had been handled improperly, it was likely that the samples had thawed out and been ruined. Dr. Bucholtz assigned a technician the task of cleaning up the freezer and told her, "You can probably discard everything."

The technician, Janelle Payne, methodically went through the samples. At the very bottom of the freezer she found a tub, and in the tub was an old but still sealed rape kit and other sealed evidence bags. She was surprised to find an unopened rape kit, since rape kits were almost always opened and the samples analyzed early in an investigation. Yet here was a completely pristine kit. That was uncommon enough for Payne to bring the kit to Dr. Bucholtz's attention.

"Why do we have this unopened old kit?" she asked Dr. Bucholtz.

"I don't know. Let me call the prosecutor's office."

The prosecutor Dr. Bucholtz talked to had no idea as to whom the kit belonged, either. Eventually, though, the existence of the kit was made known to Ventura County investigator Steve Rhodes—the man Paul Holes and Steve Kramer had asked for Golden State Killer DNA.

Rhodes asked for the name and date on the rape kit.

The name was Charlene Smith, and the date was in 1980.

Peter Speth had long wanted to be a pathologist—the medical professional who conducts lab tests, studies body tissues, and helps reach diagnoses. "A pathologist is the doctor's doctor," says Dr. Speth. "You have to know every disease in every part of the body, and you have to be able to recognize it by how it feels, and also simply by eyeballing it. Why did this person bleed from the bowel? What kind of brain tumor is this? You need many years of training to become a pathologist."

Dr. Speth underwent that training and earned a fellowship under Dr. Boyd Stephens, San Francisco's first-ever chief medical examiner and a world-renowned expert in forensic pathology. "He was a unique guy, in that he went to every crime scene and established himself as the boss there," says Dr. Speth. "Nowhere else was the medical examiner in charge of investigators and the other criminalists at the scene of a crime."

Dr. Speth, who drove everywhere in a small red Renault (his CB handle was "Red Rascal"), tagged along with Dr. Stephens to every crime scene and learned how to be aggressive and persistent in retrieving and processing good samples. But he developed his most distinctive practice all on his own. "It occurred to me that we, as doctors, should somehow be able to preserve evidence so that it will be available for future research using new technology," he says. "It just seemed logical to me to save evidence from every single case I worked."

Dr. Speth saved evidence by taking not just one sample at a crime scene, but *two* samples—something no other medical examiner did.

One of the samples was for the investigating officers working the case. The second one was safely stored away, its seal unbroken, should there ever be a need to reexamine the evidence.

At the home of Charlene and Lyman Smith, Dr. Speth took four vaginal swabs and placed two of them in one red-topped vial, and two in a different vial. He eventually sealed both vials and labeled them precisely to begin and preserve an impeccable chain of custody. Whoever it was that broke the seals would be photographed doing it and become part of the custody chain.

The first vial went to the investigators assigned to the Smith double murder. The second vial was stored away in a freezer.

That second vial, miraculously, survived unopened and forgotten for the next *thirty-seven years*—until technician Janelle Payne found it in a tub at the bottom of a crime lab freezer that was deemed so disastrously disorganized its contents hardly seemed worth saving.

Dr. Speth, for one, had no idea the second kit had survived, nor did anyone tell him when it was found. "The Charlene and Lyman murder scene had haunted me since 1980," he says. "I lived year after year waiting and hoping that the true monster who carried out those murders would be caught before he died, and before I died."

So it was that Ventura County prosecutor Steve Rhodes called Paul Holes and Steve Kramer and delivered the most remarkable news: he was in possession of a *pristine* unopened rape kit from the scene of the Smith double murder. The odds of such a thing happening were incalculably small. And yet it had happened—the second kit existed. Because of Dr. Speth's unique practice of assembling two kits, Paul Holes now had the precious DNA sample he had hoped beyond hope to find. He now had, he told people, "a gold mine of Golden State Killer DNA."

What lay ahead was unprecedented and historic, and would, in time, introduce to the world the use of investigative genetic genealogy to identify a suspect in cases involving violent crimes.

12

Paul Holes called me with the news about the discovery of the pristine second rape kit in late November 2017. I was amazed that such a kit had survived and thrilled by the possibility that I might soon have a DNA profile that I could use for IGG. My guardian angel had come through again.

The first step in the process was to extract DNA from the semen in the rape kit and create something called a SNP profile.

In 2017, the only laboratories that were capable of creating a SNP array profile were the handful of commercial, direct-to-consumer DNA-testing companies that existed then. The big question was: Could we convince one of them to create a SNP profile for us from the DNA in the semen sample in our rape kit?

Steve Kramer reached out to all the direct-to-consumer companies, but only Bennett Greenspan, the founder, president, and CEO of FamilyTreeDNA and a true pioneer in the field of genetic genealogy, was willing to entertain the idea of working with law enforcement. I knew Bennett Greenspan from speaking with him at FamilyTree-DNA's annual meetings for its project leaders, and he had granted me permission to have FamilyTreeDNA create SNP files and upload them to its database in two previous criminal cases on which I had worked, one of which was the identification of Terry Rasmussen.

Growing up in Omaha, Nebraska, Bennett Greenspan showed an interest in genealogy from an early age and enjoyed interviewing relatives at funerals. He built his first family tree at age eleven. "I was the only one in the family who was interested in it," he told one reporter. "My parents didn't understand, but it was great because it gave me an excuse to talk to my grandparents and great-aunts, and of course they loved that." As an adult, he hit a dead end trying to prove his grandfather was related to a man in Argentina. The only thing that could help him was a DNA test, but no company offered such tests to the public for genealogical purposes. Bennett teamed up with a university genetics professor and in 1999 created FamilyTreeDNA, the first American company to offer DNA testing to the public. Its motto: "History Unearthed Daily." By 2017, when Steve Kramer reached out to Bennett, FamilyTreeDNA had a database of more than 1.5 million test takers.

Kramer discussed two specific crimes with Bennett, including one of the rapes in the Golden State Killer case. If Kramer expected Bennett to politely defer reaching a decision and take time to gather other opinions, that did not happen.

Instead, Bennett gave Kramer his permission right then and there.

"I have made decisions on my own for a long time," Bennett later explained to *The Wall Street Journal*. "In this case, it was easy. We were talking about horrendous crimes. So I made my decision."

The one thing Bennett requested was that the involvement of FamilyTreeDNA in the Golden State Killer case be kept confidential and not made public.

Bennett Greenspan's quick decision did not surprise me. At the time of Kramer's contact with him, I personally did not feel that there were any pressing ethical issues stemming from the use of commercial DNA sites in criminal cases, and I agreed with Bennett that solving horrendous crimes was more than enough of a reason for him to grant us permission. It simply did not strike me as a complicated ethical issue—and I was someone who had more than a passing interest in ethical dilemmas. In fact, I had very nearly made studying them a career.

In high school in New Zealand, I tended to do well in the subjects that interested me, such as science, and not so well in those I found boring. I did not know why that was the case until many years later, when a psychologist diagnosed my son, Christopher, with attention deficit disorder. She then tested me and found that I had the same disorder, which is not surprising since it tends to be genetic.

At seventeen I stopped my schooling—after a dispute with a teacher cost me the chance to enter university in New Zealand—and took a job as a lab technician for a company named Lever Brothers (now Unilever) in Wellington. The company was delighted to be able to hire a high schooler with an aptitude in science for a university-graduate-level job (and pay her significantly less). The lab made soap out of lard, and one of my tasks was keeping track of the glycerin, a valuable byproduct of the process, that was produced.

Eventually, I did go back to school, this time in the United States. I graduated from the University of California, San Diego, with a BA in psychology and biochemistry and a PhD in biology, and after a postdoctoral fellowship at Roswell Park Memorial Institute in Buffalo, New York, I accepted a position as an assistant professor at the University of Texas Medical Branch (UTMB) in Galveston, Texas. There, as a member of the Medical School Admissions Committee, I interviewed many prospective students, nearly all of them high academic achievers with perfect GPAs. What I noticed, however, was that only a few of them were well-rounded students. They often did not have a broad range of experiences or interests.

I began to ask the candidates questions about controversial medical issues: abortion, surrogate parenting, frozen embryos, end-of-life practices. I wanted to see if they understood, or had even considered, the ethical dilemmas that might be created by the work they would do. Most of them had not given these issues a thought, and some were not even aware of them.

In the process I discovered I was especially drawn to medical ethics. I found the issues involved so compelling that I changed my plans and applied for admission to an accelerated program at the University of Texas at Austin School of Law. My new plan was to pursue a career in medical ethics, and after accepting a coveted place at the law school, I resigned from my position at UTMB.

Two years later I changed my plans again. When I interviewed at law firms and attended job fairs, a number of people noticed all the science on my résumé and suggested that I consider becoming a patent attorney. The field was expanding and patent attorneys tended to be well paid. After graduation I took a job as an associate attorney with a Dallas law firm that specialized in patent law, but I soon switched firms to work with the fabled patent attorney Bertram Rowland. Dr. Rowland was known and heralded for obtaining the first-ever patent in biotechnology. The patent was jointly owned by Stanford University and the University of California. Known as the Cohen-Boyer patent, it was the genetic-engineering patent that essentially launched the biotech industry in the 1970s. Professors Stanley Cohen and Herbert Boyer, the inventors, had created the first organism containing recombinant DNA—a gene containing DNA spliced into it from a foreign source.

Cohen and Boyer's work was so groundbreaking that scientists called for a halt to any further work so that the ethical implications of the new technology could be discussed and its future uses considered. For example, recombinant DNA could theoretically be used for human germ-line intervention to replace a defective gene, or for genetic enhancement to an embryo to increase intelligence, or to alter eye or skin color, or even to clone humans—all sci-fi-sounding technologies that had vast moral and ethical implications and deserved vigorous debate.

In other words, should humans be messing around with DNA?

As the debate continued, the technology surged ever forward. The emergence of the internet and the dot-com boom of the late 1990s spurred the biotech industry even further, and patent attorneys were suddenly a hot commodity. Over the years I worked for several different firms and developed a stable of loyal clients who followed me from firm to firm. In 1995 I finally launched my own company, the Rae-Venter Law Group.

Along the way I developed a unique way of working with biotech inventors. Quite often, their view of their invention and its applications was fairly narrow. They had worked on their inventions with such hyperfocus for so long that they often did not see past their original goal. My job was to persuade them to consider other possible uses for their inventions, in addition to the way they had intended. This was where my grasshopper mind came into play.

It was my job to thoroughly understand an invention so that the legal claims I drafted would encompass the invention, its uses, and how it was made as broadly as possible. I had to persuade inventors to consider alternate embodiments of their inventions, something that I needed to do very carefully. Patent attorneys generally do not want to play a critical role in the development of an invention, because to do so would make them inventors as well. It is preferable to ask questions that tease out alternate embodiments, along the lines of "Could X be used for Z?" or "Is there another way to produce Y?"

Sometimes, when I asked my questions, an inventor would look at me with a puzzled expression, disappear in thought for a moment, and then say, "You know, if I tweaked this and that, then, yeah, I guess it *could* be used for Z."

My questioning mindset—*Is there some connection here that we're not seeing?*—turned out to be an asset not only in patent law, but, eventually, in genetic genealogy as well.

One of my earliest clients as a patent attorney working with Dr. Rowland was Calgene, a small biotech company in Davis, California. They introduced a new product called the FLAVR SAVR tomato— the first-ever genetically engineered fruit to be cleared for human consumption by the FDA. The Flavr Savr was a genetically modified tomato, altered so that it could be picked off the vine perfectly ripe. Its existence, however, sparked a powerful anti–GMO (genetically modified organism) movement, a collection of skeptics and ethicists who derisively dubbed such genetically engineered creations "Frankenfood."

I was unprepared for this backlash. There were arguments that genetically modified organisms could damage the environment, or make farmers dependent on commercial seeds, or prove harmful to humans. A group of Catholic bishops called GMOs "morally irresponsible," while the environmental lobby Greenpeace also came out against GMOs.

The most powerful arguments on the other side include the potential for GMOs to alleviate world hunger and possibly to prevent blindness due to a vitamin A deficiency in the millions of children whose diet consists primarily of rice. This has been accomplished in the form of "Golden Rice"—rice in which a gene that adds beta-carotene, a precursor of vitamin A, has been inserted. There is also the potential to create genetically modified plants that can thrive in a warming world or with less water, or even in salt water. So far, these potential positive uses have not been enough to lessen the stridence of the technology's critics.

Certainly any new technology deserves debate, but I knew from the extensive research done by Calgene that their GMOs were safe. I also understood that consumers tend to balk at change, and at anything they don't quite understand. When something is new and innovative, it can also be, to some, a bit scary. Certain groups sounded the alarm about horrible foreign substances being inserted into their food, and conspiracy theories arose about evil corporations bent on controlling humanity. Over the years, the Frankenfood contingent succeeded in shaping a negative public perception of GMOs.

As for the Flavr Savr, our firm helped it obtain a groundbreaking patent that cleared the way for the tomato to be sold commercially, and it was, in 1994.

Little did I realize that my battle with the Frankenfood folks would prepare me for the even more intense ethical dogfight that resulted from my work on the Golden State Killer case.

When I agreed to help Deputy Headley and the New Hampshire State Police on the Lisa Jensen Project and the Bear Brook murders case, and then Paul Holes on the Golden State Killer case, I had no apprehensions about doing so. Identifying victims and criminals felt like a good and noble endeavor, and I did not see it as a two-sided issue: If the technology existed, why should we not use it in pursuit of violent criminals and in identifying their victims? There were no ethical discussions of which I was aware about adoptees using all of the direct-to-consumer databases and GEDmatch to find their birth families, or about other people of unknown parentage, such as those conceived via egg or sperm donation (even though egg and sperm donors were guaranteed anonymity). Thus it was a surprise to me that the use of the DTC databases and GEDmatch for investigative genetic genealogy would suddenly become an ethical issue.

But it has.

When FamilyTreeDNA founder Bennett Greenspan agreed to create a SNP profile for the Golden State Killer and upload that file to FamilyTreeDNA's database of 1.5 million users, the controversy about direct-to-consumer DNA sites and law enforcement had yet to erupt—mostly because nobody knew about the collaboration. Soon enough, though, Bennett's decision not to tell his customers about helping law enforcement would be heavily criticized. Although I did not realize it at the time, by agreeing to work on the Golden State Killer case I was thrusting myself into a fierce ethical debate. It was, at least for some in the genetic genealogy community, a fraught gray area they preferred not to enter.

"I saw how vitriolic people in the community became when investigative genetic genealogy first began," says Richard Weiss, a prominent genealogist and an adoptee who, like me, was one of the students in the original autosomal DNA class offered by DNAAdoption (he is the group's former director). These days, Richard declines to work on criminal cases. "IGG completely fractured the community, and I did not want to bring that into DNAAdoption," he says. "There are people who believe that helping law enforcement is a violation of privacy and just flat wrong. They argue that people's data is being used in ways that they never agreed to."

But Richard also notes a key distinction that often gets overlooked in the debate: the meaning of privacy versus anonymity.

"No one has a legal right to anonymity," he says. "Who you are, where you live, your birthday, that is all publicly accessible information. You do, however, have every legal right to *privacy*, especially from the government. But that doesn't mean you can hide who you are. No one is entitled to have a relationship with you, but everyone has a legal right to contact you."

Some people believe direct-to-consumer DNA testing in general should be more regulated, so that users are better informed about the potential risks involved in unearthing family history.

"The biggest danger is that folks don't seriously consider that their very sense of who they are can be totally upended by these tests," says Judy Russell, a former federal prosecutor, defense attorney, and professor who has a popular blog called The Legal Genealogist. Judy is a prominent critic of unregulated investigative genetic genealogy. "People don't believe [genetic genealogy] will tell them anything new and are utterly shocked when it does. That includes everything from learning about the increased risk of certain diseases to unanticipated relatives to discovering that those they believed to be biologically related are not. They don't understand how an unexpected result can reverberate through the entire family."

Russell is dead set against law enforcement accessing a genealogy site without the consent of its users. "I would support a ban on allowing *any* third party—law enforcement, pharmaceutical companies, insurance companies, and more—to use genealogy databases without users' consent," Russell says. "Just because there's new technology doesn't mean we toss out essential guarantees."

I believe, however, that the emergence of new technology can sometimes lead people to focus on issues that are not especially relevant to the technology's use and purpose. Fingerprints, for example, were considered an invasion of privacy when they were first used in the United States around the turn of the century to identify and help convict criminal suspects. My thinking, however, at least early on, was far more straightforward: the more I learned about the Golden State Killer and his heinous crimes, the more convinced I became of one simple fact: *This man needs to come off the streets.* Thankfully, Bennett Greenspan felt the same way.

"If we can help prevent violent crimes and save lives and bring closure to families," he later explained about his thought process, "then we're going to do that."

And so it was that, with Bennett's help, we were finally able to get down to the business of solving who the Golden State Killer was.

FamilyTreeDNA developed a SNP profile from our crime-scene DNA and uploaded it to their database. In February 2018, Steve Kramer and Paul Holes emailed me a text file that represented the Golden State Killer's DNA profile. I uploaded the file to GEDmatch on February 18, 2018, under a fake profile.

It would take several days for each site's matching algorithm to compare the SNP profile that we had uploaded against other profiles in its database. Any people identified as having matching DNA with our DNA profile, over a threshold amount, would be considered to be genetic cousins of the Golden State Killer. The amount of matching DNA between our profile and the genetic cousin would be used to estimate how closely related the genetic cousins were to the Golden State Killer. With that information, we could begin to build family trees for the closest matches.

While we waited for this process to complete, I ran some of GEDmatch's utilities on the DNA profile that we had uploaded.

At the time, the technology behind DNA analysis was growing exponentially, and new tools were becoming available seemingly every day. For instance, a site called OhMyGene could identify a single gene that might lead to Crohn's disease. Another site, Athletigen, was tailored to athletes and analyzed DNA with an eye toward health, nutrition, and performance. Infinome promised analysis that could help people lose weight and "fit better into our genes!"

I started with a tool offered by GEDmatch: an eye-color estimator. The tool used information from the many SNPs related to eye color to predict a person's specific coloring. A typical line of data produced by the tool might be: *GG at rs7174027—blocks some melanin; often gives light-colored eyes,* or *TT at rs1129038—penetrance modifier; blue eyes.* It was by no means a foolproof test, and it tended to work better for people with European ancestry. What it could do, however, was provide me with another piece of data that could potentially narrow down our list of potential suspects.

I ran the eye-color estimator on GEDmatch on the Golden State

Killer's DNA profile, and the results were clear—the killer's eyes, the tool predicted, were blue.

Next, I turned to a site called Promethease (the name is a take on the Greek god Prometheus, who sculpted mortals out of clay and bestowed fire on humanity). The site scans your raw DNA data to determine gene variations and match them to existing scientific reports about the variations and the diseases they could cause. It was another predictive tool that had its limitations but that could yield a potentially crucial bit of data.

The analysis confirmed the GEDmatch estimation that the killer's eyes were blue.

It also indicated our killer would likely be prematurely bald.

As I would learn after we had solved the case, I was not the first person to use the Golden State Killer's DNA to predict his likely eye color. A Snapshot report had been obtained years before I had begun working on the case. That report predicted that the eye color of the Golden State Killer was green or hazel. That lab also declared that its test results specifically *ruled out* the possibility that the Golden State Killer's eyes were blue. Although I did not have access to this report, the other folks on the team all did.

That is why they all believed they we were chasing a green-eyed monster, while I was looking for one with blue eyes.

These tiny bits of biographical data about the killer were the modest beginnings of what we hoped would be a complete unmasking of his identity.

In other words, the hunt for the Golden State Killer was on.

13

Paul Holes had assembled a small team to work with him on the DNA side of the Golden State Killer case. He christened the group Team Justice. Along with me, he brought in two law enforcement officers from Sacramento, where the killer had struck five times: Lieutenant Kirk Campbell of the Sacramento County District Attorney's Office and investigative assistant Monica Czajkowski. The FBI's Steve Kramer and intelligence analyst Melissa Parisot rounded out the team. One of the things I would be doing, in addition to building speculative trees for DNA matches with the killer, was training this small group of crime fighters in IGG.

The challenge of building out speculative trees for matches in a forensic case begins with identifying which matches are the best ones to build trees for. Ideally you want to find people who match as close cousins, which increases the chance you will find common ancestors. Once the best matches for tree building have been determined, the next important step is properly identifying that very first person in the tree—the match themselves.

Once you have that name, you can start building a tree for that person using whatever records you are able to find. One thing that you should *not* do, if it happens that the match already has a family tree posted somewhere online, is to copy that match's tree and simply add the names to your speculative tree. For one thing, if you do not know how a particular name came to be added to someone else's tree, you risk including a false connection that can contaminate your entire search. Many trees on AncestryDNA, for instance, are not sourced in any way. Every name we added to our Golden State Killer speculative family tree had to be based on what was considered a primary source—i.e., birth and death certificates, marriage licenses, gravesite records, and census records. If you found something relevant on Facebook, for instance, or in a published obituary, you had to independently verify it. Facebook is an incredibly valuable source: a seemingly innocuous photo (someone wearing a sweatshirt with the name of a college; someone standing near a street sign; a photo caption listing family members) can provide the lead that breaks a case open. But a Facebook find is only a lead and needs to be confirmed by poring over other sources to verify the information.

IGG is about going the extra step to make absolutely certain that your tree is correct, because one errant name can set a search back countless days or even months—or possibly lead to identifying the wrong person. The discipline of IGG is about not taking shortcuts but making sure that your tree is *perfect*.

In law enforcement, some detectives tend to trust their guts and follow hunches, but in the field of IGG, hunches can be disruptive. With IGG, you have to focus only on what matters and can be proven: verified matches, relevant leads, estimated date of birth, estimated relationship to a match, geography, and bioancestry and phenotypic characteristics gleaned from the DNA.

You must always ask: *What is the DNA telling me?*

We now had the Golden State Killer's DNA profile uploaded to both FamilyTreeDNA and GEDmatch. GEDmatch is a useful site because people can upload DNA profiles there from the various direct-to-consumer sites. GEDmatch was designed to help family historians search for relatives who had DNA-tested at sites other than the ones they used. At the time I uploaded the Golden State Killer's DNA profile to the site, its terms of service stated that the site could be used for purposes beyond family history research. In other words, GEDmatch was open to anyone for any use at all.

A few days after we uploaded the Golden State Killer's DNA profile to the site, the matching process was completed and a list of hundreds of matches was posted to our pages on both FamilyTreeDNA and GEDmatch (nearly every DNA profile upload generates that many matches). The results, at least to me, were a bit disappointing. Our closest match on FamilyTreeDNA was at 52 centimorgans, or cM. Since we share about 3,700 cM with each parent, but only between 20 and 85 cM with a fourth cousin, our 52 cM match suggested a fairly distant relative. The closest GEDmatch result was only slightly better at 62 cM. Because both matches were to such distant relatives, we knew right away that we would likely need to build a lot of family trees to identify our suspect. If we had found a second cousin, for instance, we likely would have had to build far fewer trees and been able to solve the case fairly quickly, possibly within a day or two.

Still, these two distant matches were a start.

Now we had to identify family connections among the matches. We could do that using the technique at the heart of DNAAdoption's Methodology: DNA segment triangulation. Basically, segment triangulation involves three people (Persons A, B, and C) who all match one another on the same chromosomal segment of DNA. The goal is to find the most recent common ancestor (MRCA) to Persons B and C. Since Person A must also be a descendant of this common ancestor, finding the MRCA is a major step toward identifying Person A.

And in the case of the Golden State Killer, Person A was the killer himself.

∞

At this early point in the case, not only did we not know the identity of the crucial most recent common ancestor, we did not even know if our closest genetic matches—Persons B and C— matched the Golden State Killer on his paternal or maternal side.

Not surprisingly, these early parts of the search were a bit chaotic.

All six members of Team Justice eagerly jumped into the tree-building process. But besides myself, the others simply did not have the necessary experience to be able to identify matches who were good candidates to build trees for (for instance, people whose matches overlapped with other matches). Instead, they were more or less randomly picking matches to build speculative trees for.

Early on, we found that many genetic matches traced back to Italy. That made things more difficult. Many Italian ancestral records had been scanned and were available online, but most of them had not been digitized. That meant we would have to manually review each record. Reviewing records manually is hard enough to do in English, but it is even harder when the types of records are unfamiliar to you and are also in a foreign language. Rather than get too bogged down in that endeavor, we chose to focus on non-Italian relatives.

And so we built our speculative trees. We used AncestryDNA's software, which suggests documents pertinent to the people who are being added to a tree. We used those documents—birth certificates, census reports, marriage licenses—to verify any new relative, and only when we were 100 percent sure of a name could we move on to the next generation. Sometimes we used other sources in other databases, such as FamilySearch or MyHeritage, to find the verifying data that we needed. As a group we dug up literally hundreds of documents, moving methodically from generation to generation—all in search of the elusive most recent common ancestor.

It was slow going. Weeks passed. A month into the search, we found that we were stuck.

And then, suddenly, we weren't.

The big break came when I uploaded the Golden State Killer's SNP profile to MyHeritage, which at the time was a relatively new direct-to-consumer company that was growing its database fairly quickly. I had an existing account at MyHeritage, which I used for my own family history research and an occasional unknown-parentage case. I knew that MyHeritage accepted uploads of SNP profiles produced by other sites, so I suggested to Steve Kramer that we upload the GSK's profile to this newer site, too, and he gave me the go-ahead.

A few days later, there it was:

A beautiful new match.

This time, it was a mother and daughter who matched the Golden State Killer's DNA. I could see that the family tree they had posted would connect to the tree for another of our existing matches. The mother, it turned out, matched the GSK at the *second-cousin level*.

This was huge. Before, we had had only a possible third- or fourth-cousin match at 62 cM. Now we had a solid second-cousin match at *240* cM, and this person connected to both the Golden State Killer *and* to the third- or fourth-cousin match. We now had the three people we needed to employ DNA segment triangulation—the key to the Methodology. Fourth cousins share a set of great-great-great-grandparents, but second cousins share a set of *great*-grandparents.

Once we knew which set of great-grandparents was the most recent common ancestor, we could build a reverse tree all the way to the time period during which the Golden State Killer was born—knowing that he had to be a descendant of that couple.

As I have said, this is not quite as simple as it sounds. We had narrowed down our search to just one set of great-grandparents, but if they happened to have an especially large family, that would still mean a *lot* of building down of descendant lines.

Even so, seeing that second-cousin match in the list of matches on the MyHeritage site was the moment when I first thought: *We've got him.*

14

Anyone who has spent time building family trees knows how absorbing the process can be. You sit down at the computer and before you know it five hours have passed, or ten, or more. Temporal matters fade away as you dig deeper and deeper into records— appointments are missed; cats go unfed and plants unwatered. It is so easy to lose yourself in the work, with the jumble of names and dates rattling in your brain and pushing out everything else. For me, few activities have ever been quite as compelling, maybe even as addictive.

With the Golden State Killer case, I also felt something else: a pressing urgency based on the nature of the crimes. The killer's atrocities were never too far from my mind, and the absolute horror of his actions was just too overwhelming to ignore. When I first steeped myself in the details of the case, my eyes were opened to a side of human nature I had never had to consider before. Not just bad or ugly, but monstrous, unthinkable, absent of remorse or humanity.

"He punched me in the face and broke my nose," remembered Patricia Murphy, who was raped in her parents' Sacramento home in 1976, the fourth known victim of the assailant then known as the East Area Rapist. "I had a concussion from falling backward and hitting my head on the pavement. I did what I had to do to survive. He truly is an evil monster with no soul."

"He broke into my home, blindfolded me, tied me up, threatened my life with a knife, and raped me," Phyllis Henneman said of her assault in 1976, when she was just twenty-two. "Life as I knew it irrevocably changed that day. He is the devil incarnate." The rapist phoned Henneman two years after the attack just to taunt her, and after that, the mere ringing of a telephone terrified her.

These brutal details are impossible to forget, and I did not want to forget them. I did not want to lose the urgency I felt to finally attach a name and face to this nameless and faceless creature. That urgency is what drove me to work as hard as I did—sometimes twelve or fourteen hours a day, sometimes more. I truly felt I was on a mission, and that the work I was doing was meaningful and worthwhile. And it would not end until we had our man.

What I did not realize was that working on the Golden State Killer case was changing me, in both subtle and fundamental ways.

Every time you undertake an absorbing, immersive new task—going to university or starting a new job, for instance—your life begins to change around you. And you change, too. You spend more time with colleagues and less with other friends; you let go of some time-consuming pursuits; you begin to see the world differently, through the prism of the new environment that you are entering. This is what was happening to me, although I did not realize it—not until a friend who is a detective invited me to dinner.

After the dinner my friend's husband, a retired assistant chief of police, asked if I would like to attend a workshop he was going to be presenting to two hundred California game wardens. (California has more than four hundred game wardens, I learned, who are all sworn peace officers.) I joined my friend's husband at the workshop and listened intently as he lectured about the emotional impact of working in law enforcement.

"When you are dealing with the dregs of society and untold horrors on a day-to-day basis, things that are not particularly important begin to irritate you," he explained. "You will hear someone go on about something trivial, and you will think in your head, 'This is bullshit.'"

I thought: *Yes. That is happening to me.*

I remembered having dinner with a group of friends a few weeks earlier and listening to one woman complain endlessly about a matter that struck me as fairly unimportant. And I remembered just how irritated I was by what seemed to me to be petty and privileged whining. Ordinarily I would have ordered another glass of wine and simply let her go on, but on this night, the more she complained, the more my patience wore thin. After several more minutes I simply could not stand it any longer, and I excused myself and left.

I don't want to waste my time being around this woman, I thought. *I would rather be home, working on my cases.*

During the Golden State Killer case I got to the point where I valued my time so highly that I could not bear to waste it. Working on a case, finding answers for people, spending time with people I cared about—these things were good and worthwhile. These were the things I wanted to do. So I chose not to be around certain types of people, and I focused on my work.

Being exposed to the evils of humanity, the extremes of depraved behavior, can change you. And the Golden State Killer case was changing me.

Finding a second-cousin match to the Golden State Killer was a breakthrough moment. There was still a lot of work to be done, but it seemed not only doable, but also something we could do fairly quickly. Having people common to both trees meant that we could combine two of the twenty-five separate trees we were working on into one speculative tree. And in this combined tree we were able to identify our first most recent common ancestor, a set of great-grandparents of the second-cousin match. Now that we had identified a most recent common ancestor in our speculative tree, we could start building down the descendant lines from the MRCA to the time that I had estimated the Golden State Killer was born. We would continue that build-down until we were sure that we had *all* the descendants of the MRCA in the tree who had been born in the relevant time period.

Once that build-down was complete, we could look for men who matched the little bits of information that we had about the Golden

State Killer: his likely date of birth, places he had lived, and bioancestry and phenotypic characteristics based on victim statements and his DNA.

What we were doing, in essence, was putting together a list of potential suspects.

To do this, the only tool available to me at the time was a Kinship Report, which I had used in the Lisa Jensen case to identify Adam Keim's father's family, and which shows how people in a particular family tree are related to any one specific person. There are more sophisticated tools available today for narrowing down candidates, such as DNA Painter's What Are The Odds? (WATO), but Kinship Reports were all that I had available to me at the time.

From the amount of matching DNA and the relative ages involved, I knew that the GSK was most likely a second cousin to the new match who had appeared on MyHeritage. So I ran two Kinship Reports: one for all the people in the speculative tree who were second cousins to the new match (Person C), and another for all the people who were third cousins to the original match from FamilyTreeDNA (Person B).

It took just a few minutes to run the reports, which produced quite a few names common to both lists. Now I took two of the earliest deductions I had made about the killer—that he was likely born in 1956 or earlier, and that he had at some point lived in California, the scene of all of the crimes—and I applied these two basic criteria to all the men who appeared on both Person B's and Person C's Kinship Reports. Applying the age and geographical criteria to these men produced my first list of suspects.

This list contained just *nine* names.

This was a breathtaking moment. We now had something that had never before existed in the forty-year search for the Golden State Killer.

An honest-to-goodness suspect list.

One of these nine men, I was certain, was the monster who dwelt in darkness. Now all we had to do was identify him and drag him into the light.

15

Before California authorities turned to IGG—back when they relied only on traditional investigative methods—the Golden State Killer suspect list never shrank to fewer than several hundred names. There was no way to link the crime-scene DNA to any of the tens of thousands of men who had lived within or near the massive crime-spree field, which spanned nine California counties. Investigators would have needed an extremely lucky break, or a serious misstep by the killer, to narrow the suspect list.

And because the Golden State Killer apparently stopped his assaults in 1986, there had not been a break in some seventeen years, since the cases of the East Area Rapist and the Original Night Stalker—another name coined for the GSK—were connected in 2001.

But now, in just a few weeks, we were down to a suspect list of *nine names*.

It was a heady time for Paul Holes, but also a tricky one. There is something that happens when an IGG search gets closer and closer to the subject of the search—what I call the temptation to chase bad rabbits.

When you begin adding living people to a speculative family tree that you are building, you often have to turn to sources such as Been-Verified or TruthFinder for information about the person's relatives and where they have lived. In my experience that information is generally reliable, although sometimes we have found conflated files (files for two people with similar names combined). So you have to remain alert and be thorough.

On occasion, the information from sources like BeenVerified includes references to criminal records. If you are working on identifying a suspect in a rape case and you see that the person in your tree has arrests for sexual assault, it can be tempting to focus on that individual. That temptation, I have seen, can be *extremely* strong. This phenomenon is sometimes called confirmation bias—trying to make the facts fit a preconceived conclusion. The temptation is to focus in on that one person without making sure that they fit *all* the criteria in the profile that you have developed for your suspect—criteria such as their estimated ethnic background from their DNA, their relationship to the suspect, their estimated age, and any known physical characteristics either from witnesses or from the DNA. When you succumb to confirmation bias, you also potentially are ignoring solid leads.

Or perhaps someone who is a potential suspect checks some of the boxes in the profile you created for your suspect but not all of them. That, too, can lead you to play a hunch.

But that is *not* what you are supposed to be doing in an IGG case. In such a search, there is no room for hunches, only identification of potential suspects based on the DNA.

Paul Holes followed a hunch when he seized on one of the names on our nine-man list as a potential suspect. Research showed that the man Holes focused on had owned property in Citrus Heights—the scene of many of the rapes. This man had also worked in the real estate business. He had a connection to Los Angeles, the scene of one of the Golden State Killer's crimes, and he fit the age range we had established for our killer. All of that squared with the theory Paul had developed—that because so many of the Golden State Killer's crimes occurred near new housing developments, the killer might have been connected to the housing or real estate industries. Paul focused on this man and became convinced he was the killer.

But there was a problem. While Paul's preferred suspect did fit the profile he had assembled, he did *not* fit with what the DNA was telling us.

Our crime-scene DNA showed that the Golden State Killer's bio-ancestry included 44.4 percent southern European heritage, which explained why we were seeing so many matches who were of Italian ancestry. When I researched Paul's preferred suspect, however, I learned that his ancestors all traced back to the United Kingdom. His ancestry was purely English. In fact, he did not seem to have a single ancestor who had ever set foot in continental Europe.

Based on the DNA, Paul's choice for a suspect could *not* be the killer.

I told Paul about this finding, but he responded that the admixture could be wrong, and he refused to allow the admixture report alone to rule out his man as a suspect. After all, he argued, his suspect checked so many other boxes in his profile of the Golden State Killer.

Paul had worked on the Golden State Killer case for a long, long time, and being this close to finding him, and especially so close to his own retirement, had to feel to him as if his man was right there, within his grasp, and all he had to do was reach out and grab him. No matter what I told him, I was not able to shake Paul off his hunch.

Even before Paul had focused on his chosen suspect, though, what turned out to be a potentially crucial piece of information had emerged.

This information was in an old newspaper article discovered by Sacramento County investigative assistant Monica Czajkowski, the member of Team Justice who was digging up documents relating to the nine men on our list. The short article she found appeared in California's *Auburn Journal* on, appropriately enough, Wednesday, October 31, 1979—Halloween.

GUILTY OF SHOPLIFTING

Joseph DeAngelo, former Auburn policeman, was found guilty of misdemeanor shoplifting charges by a Sacramento County jury Friday.

He was given a $100 fine and six months probation by Sacramento Municipal Court Judge Thomas Daugherty.

DeAngelo was fired from the police force shortly after his arrest last July 2, at the Pay N' Save store off Greenback Lane.

His Chico attorney, Maureen Whelan, Tuesday was unavailable for comment on the status of the appeal, but it will be heard Nov. 9 before the Auburn Personnel Board.

During the three-day trial, a store employee testified he saw DeAngelo take a can of dog repellant from the waistband of his trousers. Another employee told jurors that he pulled a hammer from DeAngelo's trousers.

DeAngelo took the stand Thursday afternoon and denied he was trying to steal the items.

Joseph DeAngelo was one of the nine men I had identified as potential suspects. DeAngelo's brother was also on the list.

As soon as I read the article, I emailed Paul and Steve and asked them if Joseph DeAngelo had been ruled out as a suspect for any reason. When I was younger and living in the San Francisco Bay Area, I used to ski at Palisades Tahoe, and when I did I always took Interstate 80 north from Sacramento and stopped in Auburn for coffee. I knew exactly where Auburn was, and I knew it was a straight shot down I-80 from Auburn to Sacramento, maybe a thirty- or forty-minute drive from Auburn to the scene of so many of the Golden State Killer's crimes.

Paul and Steve told me that Joseph DeAngelo had not been ruled out.

Now I was excited. Here was a former police officer, well versed in crime scenes and evidence, whose surname indicated he likely had Italian ancestry, which fit the man we were looking for. He had also been convicted of a crime, which made him an especially tantalizing bad rabbit. And he had lived in a city where three of the rapes linked to the East Area Rapist had occurred. To me, there was no denying the arrows were pointing to Joseph DeAngelo.

Paul Holes, however, remained convinced that his Citrus Heights property owner was the best suspect. Paul managed to locate a woman who was closely related to his suspect (I am withholding the exact relationship to protect her identity). Paul's idea was to contact this close relative and ask her to take a DNA test. When I learned this, I quickly sent an email to Paul and Steve suggesting that if we were going to DNA-test anyone, we should surreptitiously test one of the DeAngelo brothers.

"John and Joseph [DeAngelo] are second cousins to [our MyHeritage match, whose name I have not included] and first cousins twice removed from our FamilyTreeDNA match," I wrote in my March 22, 2018, email. "They live in California and have an Italian grandparent (Samuel DeAngelo 1882–1942). Joseph was the former police officer arrested for shoplifting. Any chance [the East Area Rapist] would have used dog repellant and a hammer [the items DeAngelo stole]? Odd things for a police officer to be shoplifting."

Paul responded that he still planned to focus on his preferred suspect. Steve shared with me that Paul believed it was unlikely that someone who was a police officer could have committed the heinous crimes attributed to the GSK. So Paul went ahead with his plan. He contacted the close relative to his suspect, and she agreed to take a DNA test. If the test showed that she matched the crime-scene DNA at the level of her close relationship to Paul's preferred suspect (and if his suspect did not have a male sibling), there would only be one conclusion: Paul's preferred suspect *was* the Golden State Killer.

FamilyTreeDNA expedited processing of the woman's sample. Still, it took several days before we had match results. In that time I continued researching all nine suspects on my list. I did not believe Paul's suspect was the killer, but I was still eager to see the results of the relative's DNA test. All the members of Team Justice had access to the FamilyTreeDNA account where the results would appear, and I am sure I was not the only one of us who repeatedly checked and refreshed the site while waiting, hour after hour, for the match results to be posted. On one day, it felt like I was accessing the site every few seconds.

Finally, late on a Friday night, around 10:00 P.M., the relative's matches were posted.

I drew a deep breath before I checked them, and then I dove in.

The woman's DNA did *not* match the Golden State Killer's crime-scene DNA at the close level of her relationship to Paul's suspect.

Paul's hunch had been wrong.

But—

—the woman *did* match the crime-scene DNA at the level of a second cousin.

This was significant. It meant that, without a doubt, we were working on the correct family line—and that our list of nine suspects, whittled down to eight with the elimination of Paul's preferred suspect, was solid.

The Golden State Killer was one of these remaining eight men.

But there was more.

The relative also had an X chromosome match with the GSK.

The X chromosome match indicated that the Golden State Killer was related to the relative through one of his *maternal* lines (men have a single X chromosome that they inherit from their mother). With that information, I would be able to narrow the suspect list even further by eliminating those men who could not have inherited the X chromosome.

I had barely taken in the new information when my telephone rang. But I knew who was calling.

Steven Kramer had access to the same FamilyTreeDNA account that I did, and I guessed that, though it was late, he had seen the same results and understood we had a close match—which meant we were potentially on the verge of identifying the GSK. I knew that Kramer would probably not want to wait even one more day to begin the process of shrinking down our suspect list. And I anticipated Kramer was going to ask me to keep working into the night, rather than catch a few hours' sleep and start fresh in the morning. Not that I would have, anyway.

"Barbara," Steve said cheerily when I answered the call, "how about I send you an espresso from Starbucks right now?"

16

I worked at my computer for the next several hours, until around 3:00 A.M. That is when our suspect list changed. The X chromosome match with the relative allowed me to eliminate some names from the list.

It no longer ran to eight names.

Now it ran to only six.

Six potential suspects.

Six men, all of them white, all of them over sixty, and all of them one-time California dwellers. All of them were grouped together now by identifiers passed on through centuries and generations, invisible yet inevitable. Five of them were related to an infamous serial killer.

The sixth: the killer himself.

Among those six men: both DeAngelo brothers.

So—what did we now know about the Golden State Killer? Second cousins share a set of great-grandparents, which meant that the Golden State Killer and the relative who had tested for Paul were related through a set of the Golden State Killer's great-grandparents— a set of his *maternal* great-grandparents. What was more, I knew I had the tools at hand to narrow the list even further—potentially all the way down to one man—in a fairly short period of time.

I was as close to identifying the Golden State Killer as I had ever been. But it was not up to me, or Paul Holes, or Steve Kramer, to shrink the list to just one final name.

It was up to the DNA.

∞∞∞

As I explained, one of the first things I did once I had the Golden State Killer's DNA was determine his eye color. An eye-color estimator on GEDmatch told me that the Golden State Killer's eyes were blue. I sent the eye-color estimate to Paul Holes and Steve Kramer and asked them if we could reach out to the California Department of Motor Vehicles and pull up the driver's license eye-color data for all six of our potential suspects. The FBI retrieved those records but did not send me the actual license photos. What I received, however, was just as good: a collection of each person's personal details as listed on their license.

The data included the birth years, heights, and weights of our six men. A small box for each contained the eye color, and the boxes themselves were correspondingly colored: green, hazel, blue, and so on. That allowed me to quickly determine whether any of our six potential suspects had blue eyes.

Only one of the six boxes was blue.

That's him, I thought as I scanned and rescanned the document. *I've got him. This guy is the Golden State Killer.*

The only man with blue eyes was Joseph James DeAngelo.

It was an astonishing moment. I sat in my chair and stared at the little blue box for quite a while. In that moment, I might have been the only person in the world who knew the precise identity of the Golden State Killer (besides the killer himself, and any other accomplice or relative who might have known). Can you imagine that?

I turned to my keyboard and sent an email to Paul Holes and Steve Kramer.

"It's Joseph DeAngelo," I wrote.

Kramer was the first to call me.

"How sure are you?" he asked.

"As long as we correctly identified all the descendants of the MRCA," I said, "I'm sure."

Every bit of DNA evidence we had pointed to Joseph DeAngelo. Perhaps the most tantalizing news of all was that, despite theories suggesting that the killer's abrupt end to his crime spree likely meant that he had died, Joseph DeAngelo was very much alive and currently living in Citrus Heights, scene of three of the Golden State Killer's rapes. He was seventy-two years old, which would have made him twenty-nine when the crime spree began in 1976—a bit older than I had estimated, but squarely in the correct age range.

The only DNA-related step remaining was to obtain a DNA sample from DeAngelo and match it to the crime-scene sample in CODIS. A direct match would be conclusive proof.

We had done all we could with the DNA we had, and if I trusted what the DNA had told us so far, I had to believe Joseph DeAngelo was the Golden State Killer.

And so I told Steve Kramer, "I'm sure."

After that, I did not hear back from anyone on Team Justice for ten days.

When I emailed him about DeAngelo, Paul Holes was just about out of time.

He had been chasing the Golden State Killer for twenty-two years, but now, as the search neared its end, the date of Paul's retirement loomed. He had already begun the process of reassigning cases, moving files, and packing up his things. It was a bittersweet time, and for many retiring officers it would have been a quiet, contemplative time, but Paul was too busy to get emotional. He still had a few days left, and his nemesis had not yet been caught.

Shortly before my "blue eyes" email, Paul, as part of his regular investigative protocol, looked into the nine men on our original suspect list. He read the newspaper article about Joseph DeAngelo's arrest and made some calls. He reached out to Nick Willick, the Auburn police chief who decades earlier, in 1979, had fired Joseph DeAngelo after the shoplifting incident. Paul drove out and sat with Willick and asked him about DeAngelo.

According to Paul, Willick remembered DeAngelo as a bad cop who had a lot of stolen property in his house. Paul also says that Willick shared an eerie story about his daughter's possible interaction with DeAngelo. "My daughter comes to me one night and says, 'Dad, there is a man outside my bedroom window with a flashlight,'" Paul recalls Willick telling him. "I know that was DeAngelo." If that was true, it was yet another chilling piece of circumstantial evidence. A face in the window, a lurker in the dark—these were the hallmarks of the Golden State Killer.

Then another clue emerged. The voluminous case files contained a statement from the victim of a 1978 assault in Davis, California. The victim claimed her assailant repeatedly uttered a phrase the night of the attack, almost like a lament: "I hate you, Bonnie." The investigator interviewing her asked if she was sure the attacker said "Bonnie" and not "Mommy," something other victims had heard him say (as in "Mommy, please help me" and "I don't want to do this, Mommy").

"No, I assure you it was Bonnie," the victim insisted.

After I had produced our list of nine suspects, research had revealed that Joseph DeAngelo had once been engaged.

The woman he was engaged to, but did not marry, was named Bonnie.

Police rushed to interview this Bonnie, and she told them she had returned DeAngelo's ring and called off the engagement in 1971, after they'd spent a year together. She also said that two weeks after their breakup, DeAngelo began stalking her, and that he had once pointed a gun at her face through her bedroom window.

Five years later, the East Area rapes began.

It was another stunning piece of circumstantial evidence, and even spoke to a possible motive: retaliation.

Not long before his official retirement, and once he had wrapped up the last of his office business, Paul Holes climbed into an unmarked police car and drove to an address in the scenic central California city of Citrus Heights. He parked along a street called Canyon Oak Court, across from a one-story, three-bedroom, tan and brown home set on a lot with a side front yard and a small backyard. The house was modest and would later sell for $320,000, at the low end for the area. It was an unspectacular house in every way, except for one.

The house was owned by Joseph DeAngelo.

"I parked across from it where I couldn't be seen, and I just sat in the car, looking at the house, looking at the yard," Paul says. "I didn't tell anyone I was going to do it. I wasn't even logged in to the radio. I just needed to be there."

Paul was still not completely convinced we had the right man. But if DeAngelo was indeed the Golden State Killer—and at this point there was a very high probability that he was—then Paul's nemesis was now literally all but in his grasp.

"I was thinking, 'You know, we need to close out this guy, and I should just get out and knock on his door and tell him we want to eliminate him as a suspect, and go from there,'" Paul remembers. "There was just enough about him—the arrest, the Bonnie he was engaged to, all this stuff. But I knew I couldn't act prematurely. So I sat there for ten minutes, put the car in gear, and drove off. My wife blew up at me when she found out I did that."

Just a few days after that, on March 28, Paul turned in his badge. He was now officially retired.

Almost immediately after I emailed Steve Kramer and Paul Holes and told them I believed we had our man, they alerted Sacramento County sheriff Scott Jones, who promptly assembled a task force of investigators and began discreet surveillance of Joseph DeAngelo in his Citrus Heights neighborhood.

Over the course of the next several days, investigators observed what appeared to be an ordinary man living an ordinary suburban life. DeAngelo was meticulous about his front lawn and kept it tightly manicured. He owned a dirt bike and a small aluminum fishing boat, which he kept in his driveway. His large garage was stuffed with four vehicles: a 2014 Toyota Camry, a 2016 Suzuki motorcycle, a white Tacoma pickup truck, and a one-year-old trailer.

Since leaving the police force nearly three decades earlier, DeAngelo had worked as a truck-yard mechanic in the Save Mart warehouse in Roseville, four miles north of his home. But just a year earlier he had retired, and now he was home much more often. He was married but apparently separated from his wife. Neighbors knew him to be grumpy, and often heard him yelling or cursing in frustration. Some referred to him as "the freak" because of his furious grumblings. About the only thing that really stood out about DeAngelo, aside from the bad language and ill temperament, was that, at seventy-two, he was uncommonly spry. He poured concrete in front of his house. He lugged heavy objects in and out of his truck. He moved with a kind of springiness. During their surveillance, investigators followed DeAngelo onto a freeway and watched him race his Suzuki motorcycle at speeds up to one hundred miles per hour, weaving in and out of traffic as if trying to elude someone.

The investigators waited for just the right moment to get what they needed from DeAngelo: his DNA.

At last, the moment arrived. Officers followed DeAngelo in his car to the parking lot of the Hobby Lobby in Roseville, and when he was safely inside the store, police quickly swabbed his driver-side car door handle to retrieve a DNA sample. The swab was rushed to a crime lab for DNA extraction and testing. Around dinnertime that Friday night, an investigator called Sacramento County district attorney Anne Marie Schubert, who was at a high school fundraiser, to share the test results.

The DNA taken from Joseph DeAngelo's car door handle matched the DNA from a rape kit processed by Dr. Speth that was from the scene of the 1980 murders of Lyman and Charlene Smith. It matched at levels District Attorney Schubert later described as "overwhelming."

And yet—it was just one sample.

Investigators insisted upon a second DNA test. The stakes were too high to not be convinced beyond the slightest possible doubt. This time, police managed to retrieve a tissue they watched DeAngelo discard in his front trash bin. They extracted DNA from the tissue and sent it to a lab for an extremely expedited analysis.

The results were conclusive.

The DNA from the tissue *also* matched the crime-scene DNA. Beyond any shred of doubt, scientific or otherwise, Joseph James DeAngelo *was* the Golden State Killer.

One of the oldest and most puzzling criminal cold cases in the history of the United States had, at last, been solved.

The second DNA test lit a hot fuse under the investigation.

There was immediate concern for the safety of DeAngelo's neighbors and anyone else he might run into, should he figure out police were surveilling him. Though he appeared not to have been criminally active for decades, he still had to be considered a very dangerous man. Prosecutors scrambled to produce a hundred-page arrest warrant, and the very next day, Tuesday, April 24, 2018, police officers approached DeAngelo outside his home on Canyon Oak Court and served him the warrant. DeAngelo was shocked to see them.

He told the officers he had a roast in the oven.

The officers told him they would take care of it.

Joseph DeAngelo was whisked away. Officers wrapped yellow crime-scene tape around the perimeter of the house. Investigators kept the details of the arrest tightly under wraps until making a formal announcement the following day, April 25, 2018.

"Authorities announced Wednesday the arrest of a suspect in the case of the Golden State Killer, also known as the East Area Rapist, connected to at least twelve murders and forty-five rapes in the 1970s and 1980s, more than half of which occurred in the Sacramento region," a California radio station reported that day. DeAngelo was initially charged with two 1978 murders: the slaughter of Brian and Katie Maggiore, the young Rancho Cordova couple he confronted as they were walking their dog and shot to death as they tried to flee.

News of DeAngelo's arrest soon traveled around the world, creating a massive media frenzy few arrests have ever caused.

Paul Holes was not in California when the first DNA test matched DeAngelo to the Smith crime scene. He and his wife were in Colorado Springs, hunting for a new home. They were having dinner together at a P.F. Chang's, celebrating an offer they'd just put in on a house they really liked, when Paul's cellphone sounded. A member of Team Justice, Lieutenant Kirk Campbell, was calling. Paul excused himself and took the call outside the restaurant on the snow-covered front sidewalk.

"You can't tell anybody this," Paul heard Campbell say.

"That's when I knew," Paul recalls. "Kirk told me the lab was superexcited; there were twenty-one matching markers. I understood what that meant, and I said, 'Kirk, that's him.' Then I went back into the restaurant, and I didn't know if I should tell my wife, and she said, 'Did the DNA come back?' and I nodded my head. And she knew."

Paul did not react to the news in any celebratory way. "At that moment, I just felt numb," he says. "I'm not somebody that jumps up and down and hoots and hollers, and I understood we still had a ton of work left. Now we had to close it out. I jumped on the phone with Steve Kramer and we started strategizing about the next step."

It was only much later, when Paul was sitting in front of his computer late one night, a glass of bourbon neat in his hand, that he came across a photo of Joseph DeAngelo in an orange jumpsuit, sitting forlornly in a police station, and felt the enormity of what had happened.

"I looked at the photo," Paul remembers, "and I said to myself, in the dark, *We got you.* That was the moment."

Across the country, in Wenonah, New Jersey, a quiet, woodsy borough of some twenty-three hundred people along the Pennsylvania border, Dr. Peter Speth heard the announcement about the arrest of Joseph DeAngelo in the long-dormant Golden State Killer case.

"My first thought was 'That's my rape kit,'" Speth says. "That wasn't announced right away, but I just knew they had to have used the second rape kit from the Lyman murders." Not much later, Speth got a phone call from Jennifer Carole, the daughter of Lyman Smith, with whom Speth had remained in frequent contact over the years.

"She was the one who told me they had indeed used the rape kit from her parents' murder scene to get the Golden State Killer," he says.

During the call, Speth found himself in tears.

"Oh, I cried," he remembers. "I cried because out of the thousands of cases I've worked on, this was the one that haunted me. It haunted me because it had never been solved. And now, finally, it was."

Ten days after I emailed Paul Holes the words *It's Joseph DeAngelo,* he and Steve Kramer set up a conference call with me. They got right to the point.

"We arrested the guy," Paul said.

This was before the official announcement; in fact, Paul was on his way to the press conference where Sacramento DA Anne Marie Schubert would announce the arrest. This was also the first I was hearing about the DNA samples from the car door handle and the tissue connecting Joseph DeAngelo to the Lyman murders. In those ten days of waiting I had assumed investigators were doing whatever they had to do to bring in DeAngelo. But I did not know if they had found him, or if somehow he had eluded them. I had no doubt that DeAngelo was the Golden State Killer, but I was eager to see him captured and brought to justice. I wanted to see our collective hundreds of hours of work pay off.

When I finally learned DeAngelo was under arrest, I did not hoot and holler, either, but I did feel an instant and intense sense of relief and satisfaction—even though, at that moment, I did not understand the vast implications of what we had accomplished. I also felt a profound sense of pride, not just in myself but also in science itself. I had devoted my life to the sciences, and to the life-affirming truths and bold insights that result from clear-eyed scientific study. Later on, I encountered a number of law enforcement officers who resisted the idea that DNA could play a major part in solving crimes. I pushed through that resistance, and I followed the DNA, and now here we were: we had solved one of the most notorious U.S. criminal cold cases, and dragged a truly heinous monster out of his hiding place and into the light.

We had made history.

Four long months had passed since I had first become involved in the Golden State Killer case, and in those four months I had processed literally thousands of bits of data. I had worked twelve- or fourteen-hour days, and there were times when I forgot to eat, or even to stand up and stretch. I had allowed myself to be utterly consumed by the case, to the exclusion of almost everything else in my life, and there were days when the only living creatures I interacted with were my cats, Bijou and Emrys. I did all this willingly and happily, because I believed that what I was doing mattered.

And in the end, it was DNA that identified Joseph DeAngelo— a name that had never previously appeared in any investigative file, phone log, crime report, or anything else related to the Golden State Killer case.

DeAngelo had never been known to *anyone* who worked either casually or obsessively on the case, from seasoned investigators like Paul Holes and Steve Kramer to amateur sleuths who ran websites and forums devoted to finding the killer, to dedicated journalists like Michelle McNamara, who spent years writing a book about the case before her untimely death in 2016. Joseph DeAngelo simply did not exist as a suspect until his DNA told us he was the killer— despite the fact that he had been arrested for shoplifting just a short thirty-minute drive from where he committed his first known crime in 1976.

"The traditional investigative path would *not* have caught this guy," says Paul. "None of us were going down the road that led to him."

So I felt a mixture of all these things—pride, relief, satisfaction, happiness—even though, had you been sitting next to me at the time, you might not have been able to tell.

But there was one other thing I can say for sure that Joseph DeAngelo's arrest made me feel.

Concern for my safety.

Paul Holes spent his adult working life in law enforcement. So did most of the people investigating the GSK. Perhaps they had built up a kind of second skin, a defense against the darkness they routinely confronted. But I was new to seeing this level of violence and depravity, and I was not inured to the horrific side of human nature. I might have trained myself to block out the gruesome details of the killer's crimes while I followed his DNA trail, and to see him as a kind of inanimate target, but now that he had been captured he was very much a real human being—and an expert remorseless predator. Of course, I knew he was safely locked away, at least for now. But what if he was released on some unforeseen technicality? Would he come after his captors? Or those who had played a role in putting him behind bars? Or would others who had left their DNA at crime scenes realize I might be able to identify them, too, and be proactive in making sure that I did not?

I asked Paul about this, and he was honest with me: he said he knew of situations where criminals were released or escaped and did in fact come after someone they blamed for their arrest. That was a frightening scenario. I felt concern for my safety but also for the safety of my son, Christopher. I was also a bit overwhelmed by the amount of global attention DeAngelo's arrest received right out of the gate. The resolution of the Golden State Killer case was clearly going to be one of the most compelling stories of the year, and everyone involved in it would receive a lot of attention. And I was not sure if I was prepared for that.

I had worked on two other criminal cases before the Golden State Killer case: the combined determination of Lisa Jensen's identity and the identity of the murderer of the Allenstown Four, and a case in Washington State that involved identifying a suspect in the rape /homicide of a young girl. In both cases, once they were solved, I had asked to remain anonymous to the public.

When I started working on the Golden State Killer case, I told Paul and Steve that I wished to remain anonymous and not have my role in solving the case publicized.

Before the press conference, Paul and Steve asked me if I still wished to be anonymous. I told them that I did.

So when the biggest true-crime story in decades broke worldwide, by my own choice my name was not mentioned anywhere, and the role I had played in finding Joseph DeAngelo remained publicly unacknowledged.

PART FOUR

THE CLEARFIELD RAPIST AND THE BOY UNDER THE BILLBOARD

NOVEMBER 2017

17

It is late afternoon, the sun slanting in dusty diagonals across the room where we sit, my mother and I, sipping weak tea from cups of bone china. My mother is only four foot eleven inches, shorter now that age has shrunk her frame and osteoporosis has curved her spine. The skin on her face is thin, translucent, and it moves in soft folds when she smiles, as she does now.

She holds a banjo-ukulele—a family heirloom that hung for many years in my parents' dining room. It is a treasured memento that once belonged to my mother's beloved brother Reginald Joseph. Now she offers the instrument to me.

"Are you sure you want to part with it?" I ask.

My mother nods. "Keep it for Christopher," she says, pausing for breath. "Maybe he can learn to play it."

I take the banjo-ukulele from her. I run my hands over the smooth wood. It is burled walnut, a warm, satiny gold flecked with darkish knots. A fingernail catches in a small chip in the veneer on its back. All but one of the strings are broken and dangle dejectedly from the graceful neck. I pick at the remaining string.

Plink, plink, plink.

In the quiet of some afternoons I can almost hear the sweet sounds these torn strings and gentle wood once made.

This, after all, was no ordinary banjo-ukulele. It was the instrument my uncle Reg purchased years earlier with his wages as an apprentice metal spinner; the instrument he played for his friends around a driftwood bonfire on the beach as a teenager; the instrument he played again for his weary troops as they crowded in transport vans to return to base after a long day of sorties during World War II.

"Reg and his magical banjo-uke were also a success at social gatherings in the mess," my father, who flew a Spitfire under Reg's command, told me many years later. "The songs we sang were bawdy and at times probably well over the line, but with Reg's personality, he received only applause."

This, too, was the instrument my mother received in a package from the Royal Air Force, along with a telegram from the War Department informing her that her brother Reg had been killed in combat. The magical banjo-uke and a few other belongings were all that remained of Reg.

And so he would live on only in memories, in photos and in stories, and in the sounds of a piece of burled walnut, a precious gift from family past.

So many of us who have researched our family histories encounter such moments of sweet remembrance, when relatives long gone suddenly come into clearer focus, explaining, perhaps, a trait we ourselves possess or a penchant we could never quite understand. Many of us also run into stubborn little pockets of mystery: an affair revealed only decades later, an unexplained decision to relocate, some unexpected twist or turn in the linear lines we imagine depict our ancestors' progress through time.

I had been involved in family and DNA research well before I was contacted by Deputy Peter Headley in 2015, and I had some idea of the unpredictable nature of building family trees. But once I began working as an investigative genetic genealogist attempting to solve long-cold criminal cases, I gained new insight into the incredible complexity of human connectivity, and thus into my own family history and myself.

Specifically, I was learning about the impulses, motivations, and events that can define a personal history: the need to lie about or change an identity; the societal pressures that tear some families apart; the desires and urges that determine the course of our lives; the unfortunate decisions that end up resonating through multiple generations; and the losses that must be endured, and overcome, in order for families to soldier on.

I was gaining a deeper and richer perspective of human nature, and I was able to apply what I was learning to my own research into my family history.

I will give you an example. Not long after I shared that wonderful late-afternoon tea with my mother, I was asleep in my home on November 14, 2006, when, at 1:00 A.M., the telephone rang. I recognized the voice of my sister-in-law Lesley, but I had trouble comprehending what she was saying. It was something about my parents.

Slowly, then quickly, I understood. There had been an accident. A car accident. My father was driving and the car hit a tree.

My father was in intensive care, badly hurt.

"What about Mother?" I asked.

Lesley responded, "She's dead."

I remember my brother Grant got on the phone and tried to soften Lesley's brutal words by telling me what the undertaker had shared with him:

"She died instantly. She hit her head on the dashboard when the car hit the tree."

These words were meant to soothe, but they did not. Tears slid down my cheeks as I immediately flashed back to my mother, Veronique, gently waving goodbye to me after handing me her brother's precious banjo-uke. She was still beautiful then. She was *always* beautiful. And now she was gone. Going by what my mother had told people outside the family, she died at the age of eighty-eight.

But that, I had learned, was not true.

I had begun to question the timeline of my mother's life when I was in high school. She always referred to her brothers Ian and Reg as her "older" brothers, but that did not make sense to me. My uncles' war records indicated they were born in New Zealand. And yet my mother, I knew, was born in Newcastle upon Tyne in England, where her family had lived *before* my grandparents immigrated to New Zealand in 1913.

If my mother was younger than her New Zealand–born brothers, she should have been born in New Zealand, too—and yet she had not.

Had my mother lied to us about her age? A mystery solver by nature, I decided to snoop around a bit. Not knowing the truth bugged me. When I was a teenager, I went through my mother's purse and took a look at her driver's license. The license declared that she had been born not in 1920, as she had led us to believe, but rather in 1907. My mother had shaved *twelve years* off her actual age and sworn any relatives who knew her real age to secrecy. (When my sister-in-law divulged Mother's actual age, my mother did not speak to her for two years.)

My father was one of the few who knew the truth: my mother was actually forty years old when she married him (he was twenty-eight), and forty-one when she had me. And when she died in that car accident, she was ninety-nine.

I was not shocked by my discovery, nor did I ever confront my mother about it. If anything, I felt satisfaction at having solved the puzzle, and that was all. Over the years, and without any conversations about it with my mother, her real age simply ceased to be a secret among our immediate family; we all just knew.

After the accident I returned to New Zealand to be with my father while he recovered, first in an intensive care unit for two months, and then in rehab for another month. At my father's home I went through some papers in his office and learned that beyond deceiving her closest friends about her age, my mother had also deceived her insurance company and other corporations. My mother, it seemed, had managed quite an impressive deception for decades.

Why had she done it? Why was it important to her to appear

younger than my father? I never asked her these questions, so I will never know her reasons.

But now, with the experience I have gained as an investigative genetic genealogist, I understand better that such deceptions are not at all uncommon—that people manipulate their identities quite often, in different ways and for different reasons.

What was not a mystery to me was how my mother got away with it. She had a youthful beauty that never deserted her. In their wedding photos, my father—twelve years her junior—looks the older of the two, mostly because his harrowing experiences in the war had taken much of his hair and added years to his face, but also because my mother was as beautiful at forty as she had been at twenty. When my mother turned eighty, my father took her to lunch to celebrate at a restaurant that gave discounts to anyone over sixty-five. When they got their check, they saw the waitress had automatically given my father a discount—but not my mother. In fact, she had to produce concrete proof to qualify for the discount.

My mother *loved* telling that story.

What made me sad, however, was realizing how much my mother would have been looking forward to turning one hundred and receiving a letter from the queen (the English authorities, of course, knew my mother's actual age). Just one week after that monumental birthday, she would have celebrated her sixtieth wedding anniversary and received yet another letter from the queen. How tragic that she passed away before those milestones arrived.

What did it mean, then, that my mother had gone to such lengths to create, in essence, a new identity for herself?

I was not sure then, and I still am not. Her fabrication resembled the many surprising and often shocking twists we often encounter when we start peeling away layers of family history. It also made me think about the concept of identity. In the course of my DNA work I would often come across moments when the data revealed a crucial turning point in someone's life: an affair, an estrangement, an illegitimate child. Sometimes I could plainly see how these events had changed the course of a person's life, steering them toward one fate instead of another. Why these people did what they did—that was something that I generally could not determine. Were they simply trying to define who they were and what their lives would be like? Escaping an identity they were not comfortable with? Blindly following instincts?

Which led to even bigger questions: Are our identities defined mostly by our DNA—by the jumble of molecules, acids, coils, and codes that carry our genetic instructions for growth and function and behavior? Or are we free to define our identities and shape our destinies by reinventing ourselves along the way, or perhaps by shaving a few years off the calendar?

◄◅◉▻►

Sometimes, I was learning, the desire to be part of a family can be the most powerful and defining force in a person's life. I learned this from both the adoptee and criminal cases I was working, and from a story from my own past.

Nearly a year after a German plane shot down my father's Spitfire and forced him to crash-land in a field in 1943, my father received a letter delivered to him at the Stalag Luft III prison camp. It was from the woman who was his fiancée, and she had important news.

My father was, she told him, the proud father of a newborn baby boy. The baby, she said, had been born in England almost nine months to the day after my father was shot down.

Eleven months later, when my father was repatriated, he tried to find his fiancée and the boy he believed was his son. But by then another family in the UK had adopted the child, and the adoption could not be reversed. As for the boy, who was named Robin, he was told his father was Jack Rae (my father), a war hero who perished in combat.

Many years later, when Robin turned twenty-one, he was finally entitled to see his adoption records. When he obtained them he learned that the man he had been told was his birth father—Jack Rae—was actually still alive and living in New Zealand.

Robin contacted my father, who by then was married to my mother and had his three children with her, including me.

My father, who frequently made it known that he wished his first-born child had been a son instead of me, was delighted by the apparent revelation that he *did* indeed have a firstborn who was male, and he was quite happy to hear from Robin and wanted to bring him over to New Zealand to live with us. My mother was dead set against the idea. I remember my parents fighting bitterly about someone named Robin, though I had no idea who this person was.

In the end, my mother persevered in keeping Robin out of our home.

But Robin did not give up. He believed he had a father who was a war hero, and he held on to that belief tightly, almost desperately, for the next thirty years.

At one point he brought his wife and two children to New Zealand to see my father, a visit that did not end well (the children were rude to my mother, who threw them all out of the house). In 1980, when I was living in Texas, Robin asked to meet me. My brother Grant had a home in California at the time, and he and his wife flew to Texas to join me, and we all hosted Robin at my home. Robin looked nothing like my father (for one thing, he was six foot three, while all the Rae men were short), and I became skeptical that he was related to us at all.

Around the year 2000, Robin asked my father to acknowledge his paternity. This acknowledgment would have allowed Robin to obtain New Zealand citizenship and move there with his family. He sent my father a petition that described, in detail, the circumstances of his conception, as proof that he was in fact my father's son. When my father asked me to review the petition, I crossed out all of Robin's anecdotal evidence and added instead that he had to submit to a DNA test at his own expense before my father would agree to help him in any way.

The DNA test revealed Robin was *not* biologically related to my father.

Robin took another one to be certain, and that one, too, was negative.

That should have ended the matter, but it did not.

My father, for one, blamed me for ruining his relationship with

Robin and depriving him of the firstborn son he had always longed for. As for Robin, he refused to surrender his fantasy that his father was a war hero, and he had my father sign his name to his paternity petition behind my back. Robin filed it in the local court, which approved it—opening the way for Robin to claim New Zealand citizenship.

How did he persuade my father they were related even after the DNA test was negative?

Robin explained to my father that his open-heart coronary bypass surgery had altered his DNA—an impossibility—thus accounting for the lack of a DNA match.

Robin even joined my father at a reunion of Spitfire pilots and the crew of the USS *Ohio* in Malta in 2005. I was there, too, and I watched as, everywhere he went, my father proudly introduced Robin to everyone as "my son" while forgetting to introduce me at all. Hearing my father utter this lie over and over was extremely hurtful. I could hardly believe that even after seeing the evidence, he, too, held on to his cherished fantasy that his firstborn was a son. It became obvious that both Robin and my father wanted to ignore the DNA test and continue their shared fantasy. Even my brothers told me to let the matter go.

"It makes Dad happy," they said. "What's the harm?"

But I would not have it.

To me, this was fraud, pure and simple. What is more, even then, years before I ever pursued genetic genealogy, I respected the sanctity of DNA. Either Robin was or was not my father's son, and the DNA showed that he was not. To pretend otherwise was an offense I could not let stand. I asked a friend of mine, a practicing attorney in New Zealand, to alert immigration officials that Robin had failed the DNA test, and that his paternity petition was fraudulent. I also provided them with a copy of the DNA test results. That was enough for the petition to be thrown out.

In the end, Robin never joined my father in New Zealand. Had he been my father's son, he would have been welcomed. But the simple truth was that he was not.

Some of you may think my actions were a bit harsh. Was there any harm in allowing my father and Robin to have their fantasy? I understand that it is human nature to want to experience the things we have missed out on, the things we see our friends enjoying—the happy Thanksgiving dinners, the fun family outings, the camaraderie of loving siblings, all of that. Believe me, I understand that impulse.

It is just that this can be an unrealistic and even harmful fantasy. And, for an adoptee, that can lead to a second painful rejection by those who denied the adoptee these things in the first place by giving him or her up. It can also endanger relationships with the family the adoptee has—the people who love and need him or her.

The lie that Robin's mother told Robin about his paternity damaged me and my family, but it also deprived Robin of learning the truth about who he really was.

In the end, perhaps, we must all decide for ourselves what it means to be a family. Genealogy is a powerful tool that can connect us to our most ancient roots and deepen our understanding of our families and ourselves. It can make us richer and more emotionally nuanced human beings. Over the past twenty years, I believe I have really benefitted from having a better understanding of my family and myself through the lens of my new insights into family structures and dynamics.

This passing on of identity through the generations can be a truly beautiful and wondrous thing. As a child I loved my collection of what others saw as ghastly and hideous insects from the wild. Then, many years later, when my young son, Christopher, came home one day with a large and hairy tarantula and declared it was his new pet, I did not wonder what in the world was going through his head. I knew what it was.

It was that gravitational pull that binds family members to one another.

18

One warm spring night in 1992, in the family-friendly Salt Lake City suburb of Riverdale near the banks of the Weber River, a man broke into an ordinary home.

The invader, tall and hulking, entered through a sliding glass door. He crept quietly in the dark until he found an eleven-year-old girl in her bedroom. He put a knife against the girl's neck and told her not to scream. He then wrapped duct tape around her eyes. While he held her in silence she could hear one of her parents enter the kitchen and flick on the light. She heard the cupboard open and someone pour liquid into a glass. Her strange thought was how smooth the knife felt against her neck. Then she sent out a silent plea to whoever it was in the kitchen:

Please come around the corner and check on me.

But also: *Please* don't *come around the corner.*

"I didn't know what would happen if they checked on me," she later recalled of that night.

The kitchen light flicked off. A bedroom door closed. Silence again. The man took the girl out of the house and into his Pontiac Firebird and drove her to a desolate parking lot.

There, he sexually assaulted her.

"I thought I was going to die," she said.

The girl, Nichole Eyre, survived the ordeal, but the terror of that night never left her. It was a terror known to many others, at the hands of the very same man. In 1991 he crawled through a young girl's bedroom window and raped her at gunpoint; in 1996 he attacked a woman in Laramie, Wyoming; in 2001 he broke into a home wearing a nylon stocking over his head, bound five family members, and raped the mother and her nineteen-year-old daughter. His methods were consistent: forcing open sliding glass doors, binding victims, using a knife or gun to force them to comply. The same assailant committed at least eleven sexual assaults and, after four attacks in the same city, earned a nickname.

The Clearfield Rapist.

He became one of the most hunted and wanted men in the country, yet he eluded detection throughout his ten-year crime spree.

Then he just stopped.

Police did not link him to any further crimes. Nor did they make any progress in identifying him. Detectives and investigators came and went, theories were developed and dropped, but the Clearfield Rapist case went cold, and the monster remained at large, a haunting unsolved mystery, for three long decades.

I first heard from Detective Kyle Jeffries of the Clearfield City Police Department on October 4, 2017. Detective Jeffries was familiar with my work on the Lisa Jensen case, and he had reached out to me a few months before the capture of the Golden State Killer.

Clearfield is the city in northern Utah where four of the Clearfield Rapist's crimes occurred. The city's police department first began an investigation in 2000 while the spree was ongoing. They even obtained a John Doe DNA warrant—issued for suspects known only by their genetic data—as a way of starting an official prosecution and stopping the running of the statute of limitations. Still, another decade passed without good leads, and the case went cold.

The Clearfield Police Department reopened the case in 2012 and arranged to feature it on the investigative true-crime TV show *Cold*

Justice, hoping that would generate new leads. It did not. In 2017, the department assigned a new officer to be lead investigator on the Clearfield case: Detective Kyle Jeffries.

"I was given your contact information by Angela Williamson [of the National Center for Missing and Exploited Children]," Detective Jeffries wrote to me in his 2017 email. "I have been working several cold case rapes over the last few years, and we have eleven known victims linked by DNA to one suspect."

Detective Jeffries wondered if I might be able to help him.

We eventually got on the phone and talked about the case. The good news was that Jeffries had the rapist's DNA, and a lot of it. The questions the detective and I discussed were numerous: Would the DNA from twenty-five-year-old crime scenes be good enough to use? Did too many hours pass between the time of the rape and the collection of the DNA sample? Was the sample handled properly, both at the time it was taken and over the next two decades?

But even before determining those answers, we had to turn the crime-scene DNA—in this case, contained in rape kits—into a SNP file that could be uploaded to GEDmatch.

For help, I suggested that we turn to Professor Ed Green.

Earlier, I described how Professor Green's remarkable work on DNA retrieval from rootless hair helped my team on the Lisa Project identify three of the victims in the Bear Brook murders case. Professor Green was still interested in working with forensic samples, and he agreed to help me on the Clearfield Rapist case as well.

I asked Detective Jeffries to send a sample of crime-scene DNA to Professor Green so that he could create a SNP profile from DNA extracted from the semen sample. As he did with the hair samples, he performed whole-genome sequencing, but there was a difference. The hair DNA was already in small fragments; for the semen DNA, he first had to shear the DNA into fragments. From there, the procedure was essentially the same. It took him several months, but Professor Green came through again and sent me a SNP profile, which, in July 2018, I uploaded to both GEDmatch and FamilyTreeDNA.

A few days later, a list of matches was posted on both sites. Most of the Clearfield Rapist's crimes had occurred in Utah, and many of our initial matches were from Utah, indicating that the rapist was probably from that state. One of them was a very good match with the rapist—a woman named Amelia who came in as an estimated first cousin with an 840.6 cM match. The best match that ever popped up in the Golden State Killer case, by comparison, was a second cousin, so having a first cousin among our initial matches was indeed a good break.

Or so I thought.

We researched Amelia, and one of my team members, Cynthia Stormer, found a small notice posted on a genealogy site by Amelia's son. The notice referenced an Ohio adoption record for his mother. Our first-cousin match, it turned out, had been adopted. She knew who her biological mother was but not her biological father. We built out her maternal line, but it did not connect with any of the trees for other matches with our crime-scene DNA, which meant that most likely the connection was with Amelia's paternal line.

That was bad break number one.

Detective Jeffries reached out to officials in Ohio and asked for Amelia's adoption record, which would contain her birth name and, we hoped, the name of her biological father. But an official told Jeffries that the building that housed those adoption records had burned to the ground.

Bad break number two.

The only helpful information that Amelia could share with us when Detective Jeffries interviewed her was a memory that she had from long ago: her birth surname, she recalled, might possibly be Burns, although she could not be sure.

We also learned that Amelia's son, Tucker, had done DNA testing at AncestryDNA. If Detective Jeffries could persuade Tucker to help by sharing his matches on Ancestry with me, I could poke around the site to identify any of his matches who did not match with his paternal relatives and ask them to upload their DNA profiles to GEDmatch, which would give me additional data points for the speculative tree that I was building. This would help me identify Amelia's father—Tucker's maternal grandfather—which would also help me identify the Clearfield Rapist. First cousins share a set of grandparents, so the Clearfield Rapist had to be the son of one of Amelia's father's siblings.

While Detective Jeffries worked on enlisting Tucker's help, I researched our next best match, a more distant cousin named Madeline.

I located two people related to Madeline (Chester and Bailey), and also identified the most recent common ancestor to these matches, a man named Evan. Theoretically, the next step would be to build down Evan's descendant lines.

But there was *another* problem.

Both Chester and Bailey were from Utah, and both were parents of multiple children. As for the MRCA, Evan had four sister-wives; he practiced plural marriage, and he and his wives collectively had *twenty-five children—many of whom had large families of their own*. Building down all of the MRCA's children's descendant lines would require an extraordinary, almost unfathomable, amount of work and time.

Bad break number three.

I was aware there could be challenges when working with families in Utah, but I had not previously encountered such a daunting number of descendant lines (the number potentially was in the thousands). I could only guess at how long it would take to build down just a fraction of those lines—a period of time measured not in days or weeks but in months and maybe years. One of my team members on this case was herself a Mormon who often worked on cases out of Utah, and she understood how I felt. "Welcome to my world," she said.

Still, it seemed that I had no choice but to at least try to sort through this multitude of descendants. Through Detective Jeffries I requested consensual DNA reference samples from a couple of people on one of the more promising-looking lines, but neither of them was a match with the Clearfield Rapist. Early on, I realized I would have to be very lucky to land on the right line, and if I did not, then the investigation would be hopelessly slowed down. I made the decision to temporarily abandon the research on Evan's family and concentrate instead on sorting out who Amelia's father was, using Tucker's AncestryDNA matches.

Unfortunately, Tucker was reluctant to help us. Through Detective Jeffries, I offered him a deal: I would identify his maternal grandparents for him, which was what he was trying to do, if he would share his AncestryDNA matches with me.

Tucker agreed to the deal. Finally, a good break.

And then, once again, another new technological improvement appeared just in time.

This new tool was called What Are The Odds? (WATO). The tool uses the amount of matching DNA that the person of unknown parentage—in this case, Amelia—has with various persons we have been able to place in a speculative tree. This allows us to compute the odds of where in the tree the unidentified person might fit. This was precisely what I needed to know to sort out who both Amelia and the Clearfield Rapist were.

I came up with a plan: I would focus on Amelia, our initial best match to the Clearfield Rapist's crime-scene DNA. Amelia was likely a first cousin, so if I could find the name of Amelia's father, that would get me closer to identifying the Clearfield Rapist. Unfortunately, Amelia did not have many close matches on FamilyTreeDNA, but her son Tucker *did* have a great many solid maternal-line matches on AncestryDNA. One of the matches was a woman named Norah. Norah matched as a first cousin once removed to Tucker, which would make her Amelia's first cousin. I hunkered down and built out Norah's tree.

And then—there he was: Norah's maternal grandfather.

The grandfather's surname, I learned, was Burns.

Burns! That was the name Amelia had heard could be her birth surname.

I was now ready to use the new What Are The Odds? tool to pinpoint where Amelia belonged on my speculative family tree. But since I did not have any matches to Amelia (who was adopted) on AncestryDNA, I had to come up with a little workaround. Had Amelia been on Ancestry, she would theoretically have had twice as much matching DNA as her son Tucker did with his maternal-line matches. So I entered Tucker's AncestryDNA matches into the speculative tree as Amelia's matches and just doubled the amount of matching DNA.

For example, Tucker matched with Norah at 426 cM. So in the tree, I entered Norah as an 852 cM match with Amelia.

Next, I entered Amelia's speculative tree and her matching information into WATO.

The utility estimated that the highest odds were for Amelia fitting into the tree as the granddaughter of Joseph Burns and his wife.

This couple had three sons—George, John, and Jack—and four daughters—one of whom was Norah's mother. But which brother was Amelia's father?

Amelia was born in 1947. I had estimated that the Clearfield Rapist was born in about 1971. Joseph's sons George and John were born in 1925 and 1927, respectively, but Jack was not born until 1937—making him too young to be Amelia's father. Which meant that, in theory, either George or John Burns was Amelia's father.

Next, I found an obituary for George. He died at the age of forty-two and had no known children. That left the other son, Jack.

But my research into Jack revealed that he had no sons, only daughters.

I went back and researched Joseph's third son, John Burns, and I found the name of his only listed son: Rex. By then, Detective Josh Carlson, a new Clearfield City Police Department officer, had taken over the case from Detective Jeffries. I asked Detective Carlson to dig up Rex's driver's license photo. If Rex resembled the police sketches of the Clearfield Rapist, it would seem we had our man.

However, Rex looked *nothing* like the composite sketches—not even close.

It was a dispiriting moment—we had all been waiting for the dramatic moment of discovery that, it seemed, we were on the verge of. But I did not allow myself to wallow for long. I had enough experience from the other sprawling criminal cases I had worked on to understand that twists and setbacks were simply part of the game. The right question to ask was: *What does this setback tell us about where to look next?*

John was the only one of Joseph's three sons who had a son of his own, and Rex was John's only son. Following the logic of my carefully assembled speculative tree, Rex *had* to be the Clearfield Rapist.

But at least according to the police sketch, he was not. Which could only mean one thing: someone was missing from our tree.

I called Detective Carlson and said, "There *has* to be another man in this family." Someone who, for whatever reason, was not showing up.

I needed Detective Carlson to obtain a DNA sample from Rex. It would not be a consensual, or voluntarily surrendered, sample—we could not risk directly approaching this man, because he was likely a close relative to the actual Clearfield Rapist. Instead, Detective Carlson called for surreptitious DNA retrieval, or what is sometimes referred to as a "trash pull"—meaning Rex would not know that his DNA was being sought (no federal law prohibits this type of DNA collection, though you cannot obtain DNA from someone's body without a search warrant or judicial order). Carlson's officers staked out Rex and discreetly picked up a piece of trash they saw him throw out. They collected several items and ran the DNA obtained from the items through the FBI's extensive criminal database, CODIS.

There was no hit for Rex. Since DNA from the Clearfield Rapist was in CODIS, without question Rex was not the rapist.

This, too, was disappointing. But there was a silver lining.

The Clearfield police chief decided to take the risk of approaching Rex directly and asking him to submit a consensual DNA sample. Rex agreed and sent in a test kit to FamilyTreeDNA, which uploaded his DNA profile to the FamilyTreeDNA database.

Now that we had Rex's DNA, it should have pointed to exactly who was missing from our tree. When the sample finished processing, the results confirmed yet again what we already knew: Rex was not the Clearfield Rapist.

But they also revealed that Rex was the rapist's half sibling.

This was an *enormous* break. We now knew that there was a half brother out there who had not been identified in our research but who existed and who *had* to be the Clearfield Rapist. But how were we going to find him?

We researched Rex's father, John Burns, and learned that he had been a long-haul trucker. That was not the best news, since it meant he could have fathered a child anywhere along whatever trucking routes he was on. Next we reviewed John Burns's obituary, but it did not mention anything about our mysterious half sibling or name any unaccounted for children.

The obituary *did* mention that one of Burns's sons had predeceased him. We dug frantically for any other reference to this deceased son, and we found another obituary.

This obituary said that the deceased son had died at two and a half months old: another seeming dead end. But the obituary went on to report that this deceased son *was survived by a half brother.*

Just like that, we had him—the missing male descendant.

The obituary even listed a name for the half brother: Mark Douglas Burns.

We quickly researched Mark Douglas Burns and made two consequential discoveries.

The first was that he was also a long-haul trucker, and his primary route had been Interstate 80—a transcontinental freeway that crosses through Utah and Wyoming. *All* of the known rape victims lived in apartment complexes along Interstate 80.

The other shocking fact: in 1974, Mark Douglas Burns was convicted of a crime and sentenced to death in North Carolina's gas chamber. His lawyers filed several appeals based on a law that commuted death sentences for crimes committed after a certain date. Burns committed his crime before that date, but his lawyers appealed anyway and a judge vacated the death sentence. Burns served his time and was eventually released from prison and returned to his home in Utah.

The crime that put him on death row?

Rape.

Detective Carlson arranged to bring in Mark Douglas Burns for questioning as soon as he returned home from a trucking run. On September 25, 2019, two years after I was first contacted by Detective Jeffries, officers from the Clearfield City Police Department gathered outside the front door of Burns's pleasant suburban home in Ogden, Utah, their body cameras on. Detective Steve Swenson knocked on the door, and a few seconds later an elderly man in blue jeans, a red T-shirt, and gray socks opened it.

"Mark?" the officer asked.

"Yes?"

"Hi, Detective Swenson, how you doing?"

"I'm well, and yourself?" Burns replied.

"Hey, I need you to come and talk to me for a minute," Swenson said, motioning for Burns to step outside.

"Sure," Burns said.

"We need to take you up to the office with us. I have some questions for you, and I have another investigator who'd like to talk to you."

"About what?"

"Uh, you know, I have no idea."

Detective Swenson frisked Burns, and another investigator went into his home to retrieve his blue Nike tennis shoes from his back bedroom closet, and his house keys from a basket on his bedroom dresser.

"What is this about?" Burns asked again. "You're really handcuffing me?"

"I have to," Detective Swenson said. "I've got no choice."

Police conclusively linked Mark Douglas Burns to eleven sexual assaults between 1991 and 2001. The oldest victim was fifty-two, the youngest eleven. In February 2020, Burns pleaded guilty to seventeen charges—including eight counts of aggravated sexual assault and six more of aggravated kidnapping (the statute of limitations had run on some of his earlier crimes, and he was initially only charged for crimes committed between 2000 and 2001).

"My brain does not function properly," Burns proclaimed during his April 2020 sentencing. "I am a sexual deviant. I am a predator. I had a compulsion that was irresistible. It was unsatisfiable. . . . I never admitted it to anyone."

Burns also expressed a wish that he be given the death penalty. "Pleading guilty and going to prison doesn't fix what I did," he said. "I would ask that the court show me no mercy, because I deserve none."

Burns's courtroom wish was not granted. Instead, Davis County district judge John Morris sentenced Burns to fourteen terms of sixteen years to life, plus three more terms of six years to life, all to be served one after the other—a total sentence of at least 242 years in prison.

But that was not all. During their investigation, police had learned that Burns had not necessarily stopped his crime spree in 2001. In fact, in 2001 he resigned from the trucking company he had worked for and had joined a different company, presumably so he could get a new route, and this opened up the possibility that there were other as yet unlinked crimes. Under questioning, Burns confessed to many other rapes, as well as to his participation in a nearly two-decades-old cold case: the heinous 2001 murder of Sue Ellen Gunderson Higgins in Evanston, Wyoming. He told police he grew "bored" with rapes and moved to Evanston to commit an armed robbery. Burns watched Sue Ellen, twenty-eight years old, pull into her driveway, then knocked on her door posing as a chamber of commerce member who had lost his pen. Inside the home, Burns shot Sue Ellen in the head before stealing some money and credit cards—all while her two-year-old son played in the backyard.

In December 2020 Wyoming judge Joseph Bluemel gave Burns an additional sentence of life in prison for the murder of Sue Ellen Higgins. He also ordered Burns to pay the sum of $7,200 to the family of his victim to cover the cost of Sue Ellen's funeral and the replacement of the blood-drenched carpet in her home.

The Clearfield Rapist case remains one of the most difficult and complicated cases that I have worked on. There were times when it seemed a solution might remain forever out of reach. By then, however, I had learned to trust the DNA. The DNA was like a climbing rope on a very steep mountain: if we kept following it and pulling on it, eventually it would take us to where we needed to be. And, once again, it did.

I was still working on the Clearfield sexual assaults when the Golden State Killer was arrested in April 2018—and when the fallout from the arrest of Joseph DeAngelo shook the genetic genealogy field to its core.

Catching such a notorious serial killer after forty years would have made international news no matter what method was used to find him, but from the start, media coverage of the story was just as breathless about *how* he was found as it was about the fact that he was finally captured. The revelation that law enforcement used popular genetic genealogy websites to identify DeAngelo drew a firestorm of attention to the case.

"How a Genealogy Site Led to the Front Door of the Golden State Killer Suspect," announced *The New York Times*.

Another *Times* article declared, "Want to See My Genes? Get a Warrant."

"What the Golden State Killer Case Means for Your Genetic Privacy," read a CNN headline.

And from *The Washington Post:* "The Ingenious and 'Dystopian' Technique Police Used to Hunt the 'Golden State Killer' Suspect."

Dystopian? The initial media reaction to the arrest suggested we had crossed some fateful ethical line that could never be uncrossed. I was surprised by this reaction, which I believed was overwrought. As I wrote earlier, I have seen how new technology can produce emotional reactions that don't always align with the facts at hand. For instance, it was not as if we invented a new DNA technique to find the killer—I had been using the Methodology developed by DNAAdoption for years in my unknown-parentage cases, without any controversy. The only new development was that we had used the technique to identify a violent criminal suspect rather than an unknown biological parent.

In the weeks and months after DeAngelo's arrest, the early questions developed into a full-blown controversy.

In a 2019 article entitled "The Messy Consequences of the Golden State Killer Case," *The Atlantic* magazine quoted one experienced genealogist as saying, "It was built for finding ancestors. It was built for reuniting families, and now it is being used essentially to get families to put their members in jail."

Several articles suggested we had violated the Fourth Amendment—which guarantees "the right of the people to be secure in their persons, houses, papers, and effects, against unreasonable searches and seizures"—by accessing data on genealogy sites. The blowback against genetic genealogy sites was just as harsh. Critics seized on the fact that site users were not informed that their DNA data could be used by law enforcement.

In May 2019, reporters learned that GEDmatch had helped investigators on another case in a way that violated the site's revised terms of service. These new terms permitted use of the site by law officers *only* in cases involving violent crimes—which it defined as homicide and sexual assault—or in the identification of unknown human remains, and *only* if law enforcement files were identified as such.

In the newly reported case, GEDmatch allowed a DNA-testing lab to upload a file to GEDmatch so that law enforcement could use investigative genetic genealogy to identify a criminal suspect. The crime in question: a man attacking an elderly woman in a church. The attack was bloody but not fatal, nor had the victim been raped. Technically, the assault was not one of the two violent crimes that made it permissible for law enforcement to upload crime-scene DNA to GEDmatch.

GEDmatch co-founder Curtis Rogers explained his decision to take on the case by saying, "Well, look, he didn't kill her but came within inches of it. Okay, I'll let it go this one time." The criticism that followed his decision was not especially widespread, but it was intense enough to lead him to make another major change to GEDmatch's terms of service in May 2018.

Before the criticism, GEDmatch users were automatically enlisted to help law enforcement upon signing up. Rogers eliminated that feature and automatically opted *out* every user in the database. Now users had to deliberately opt in to allow their data to be matched with law enforcement files.

Overnight, the pool of DNA profiles available for matching through GEDmatch dropped from well over a million to exactly *zero*.

Luckily, just before that happened, Gene by Gene, the parent company of FamilyTreeDNA, had changed its terms of service to *allow* the upload of forensic files to its database. That meant that even after GEDmatch opted all its users out of helping law enforcement, we still had a fairly good database to work with. Even so, it seemed clear that the extraordinary window of opportunity that had opened to crime fighters in 2017 with our work on the Lisa Jensen case had now, for the first time, begun to creep closed.

This move by GEDmatch caused controversy in the genealogical community, and a good many people objected to the change. But no matter who complained, the damage was done—a site that was enormously helpful to me in my cold-case work was, suddenly, not. Yes, users had the option of opting in and making their data available to law enforcement matching, and many did—I am told that some 350,000 users have given their permission by "opting in" thus far. But this is still only a fraction of the number of users whose DNA profiles were previously available for matching. Investigative genetic genealogy is a numbers game. However you looked at it, this was a major setback.

Not much later, another controversy erupted. The news site BuzzFeed reported—for the first time—that Bennett Greenspan and his company's site, FamilyTreeDNA, had been working with the FBI on the Golden State Killer case *without* alerting its users. Bennett was heavily criticized for secretly changing the site's terms of service to accommodate law enforcement, and for personally approving the upload of the DNA profile for the Golden State Killer to FamilyTreeDNA at the request of FBI attorney Steve Kramer.

Eventually, Bennett made terms of service changes, too, though not as drastic as those made by GEDmatch: FamilyTreeDNA users in the United States are automatically opted in to law enforcement matching but also are given the opportunity to opt out. The changes also stipulated that law enforcement files would be uploaded to the FamilyTreeDNA database only after a formal review on a case-by-case basis, and only for homicides, sexual assaults, child abductions, or the identification of unidentified human remains.

I had not realized it in my first two years of working with law enforcement, but those years represented a unique time for investigative genetic genealogists like me. The number of people who signed up with the growing genetic genealogy sites such as GEDmatch and FamilyTreeDNA increased the odds of matches with close family members and made the capture of criminals like the Golden State Killer possible, specifically by exposing a vulnerability these criminals did not even know they had, and also could not escape: their genetic makeup.

Suddenly, however, that vulnerability was dramatically reduced, and it remained to be seen if we would ever have as big a pool of potential matches to the DNA of perpetrators of violent crimes again.

But it is not just the changes at FamilyTreeDNA and GEDmatch that impacted the use of IGG. In the aftermath of the Golden State Killer case, the genealogical site MyHeritage also changed its terms of service to prohibit the upload of DNA files for the purpose of solving a crime. The match that was instrumental in identifying the Golden State Killer? I found it on MyHeritage. If I were beginning the search for the Golden State Killer under the current restrictions— assuming no significant new genetic matches suddenly appeared on FamilyTreeDNA or GEDmatch (where they would have to opt in)— I would not be able to identify Joseph James DeAngelo today.

All the early coverage of DeAngelo's arrest made no mention of me by name, since I had asked to remain anonymous. Three things happened, however, that made me reconsider remaining in the background.

In the months after DeAngelo's capture, other genealogists working on different criminal cases stepped forward into the spotlight to discuss their work. If they were not afraid to go public, perhaps I did not need to be, either.

Then my son, Christopher, approached me one day and told me he believed I should finally step forward and acknowledge my role in solving the case.

"People need to know what you did," he said simply.

I was touched by his pride in me, and I drew a lot of strength from it. If Christopher was not afraid of me going public about my involvement in identifying Joseph DeAngelo, then why should I be? Having him by my side, ready to face whatever came next, made all the difference in the world to me.

On top of that, I received a call from Deputy Peter Headley. He had just watched a presentation in which another genealogist seemed to suggest she had solved the Golden State Killer case. In his call, Headley insisted that I go public to set the record straight. I finally told him I was okay with being identified, and he contacted Paul Holes. Paul sent out a tweet on August 22, 2018:

> The genetic genealogist who helped find #GSK has given me permission to divulge her name—Barbara Rae-Venter. Without Barbara's help, we would probably still be building family trees. She gave us structure and her expertise was invaluable.

And that was that. Suddenly reporters were calling. Requests to speak at events and forums poured in. *Nature* magazine named me in their 2019 list of "10 People Who Mattered in Science in 2018." *Time* magazine included me as one of 2019's "100 Most Influential People." In the *Time* piece about me, Paul Holes said, "Rae-Venter has provided law enforcement with its most revolutionary tool since the advent of forensic DNA testing in the 1980s."

This was all extremely flattering and far beyond any reaction I had ever imagined. It was also a bit overwhelming. It felt a little like opening a door and not at all being sure what was waiting on the other side. On one hand, I considered myself a private person with no desire to be famous or even a public figure. I was quite content with the lovely, quiet retired life I had fashioned for myself, and I certainly did not want to disrupt that. On the other hand, part of me wondered if remaining anonymous had been a mistake. So many different people were speaking out and claiming to have identified the Golden State Killer—even people who, as far as I knew, had had nothing to do with the case. And that, to me, was just plain wrong. I felt compelled to set the record straight, even if the resulting spotlight made me uncomfortable.

There was one other reason I decided to finally go public.

I thought back to my time as a young woman breaking into traditionally male fields. I recalled how I was treated differently from, and paid less than, my male colleagues, and I remembered the artificial barriers to advancing beyond a certain point. I thought about how I had spent my life bashing up against those barriers and fighting through them. And I realized that it was incumbent upon me to help other women to do the same, and maybe even have an easier time of it than I had.

Based on earnings data from the 2020 U.S. Census survey, full-time, year-round female employees in all jobs across the country earn eighty-three cents for every dollar earned by men—a 17 percent wage gap. This gap certainly exists in the field of science. According to a study published in the *American Journal of Sociology,* male scientists working for U.S. federal agencies like the National Institutes of Health and the Environmental Protection Agency have earned, as the journal *Nature* put it, "more money than their female counterparts . . . due to hiring practices that circumvent rules intended to ensure equity, and to higher salaries for the types of positions that the agencies hire men to fill."

Women trying to enter the field of law enforcement face a similar cultural bias. In fact, in 2020 only 13 percent of all full-time law enforcement officers in the United States were female.

This needs to be corrected. One of my goals is to see more women enter into the sciences, a discipline long dominated by men. More and more women *have* become scientists over the years, and the gender pay disparity tends to lessen the higher up in a company a woman goes. Still, I would like to see things change *faster and more dramatically.* I want to encourage even more women to become scientists, not because of any small measure of fame they may achieve, but because of *what women can bring to the work:* a different way of thinking and reasoning and seeing the world. It was the sum of my individual traits and experiences as a woman, and even my personal quirks, that allowed me to do what I did. And now I would love to see more women bring their unique perspectives and intelligence to the sciences. The field will be much better off with them in it.

So if my story can inspire a budding young scientist somewhere to pursue her dreams, then my story is a story worth telling.

19

Greek mythology is populated with grotesque monsters—Hydra, Cerberus, centaurs, cyclopes, snake-haired Medusa—but even these mythical monsters were half human, and thus they could be defeated or destroyed.

To make such a monster disappear, however, one cannot push it away. One must draw it closer. Because it is from darkness and shadows that a monster derives its power. So long as it remains mysterious, the monster is free to burrow into our consciousness, knowing full well that our deepest fears will embellish it, make it more horrifying. Only the act of exposing it can strip it of its greatest weapon. To make a monster recede, you must drag it out of the dark, because it will shrivel in the light.

Now the day had come to see the monster shrivel.

After the arrest of Joseph DeAngelo, a daunting question loomed: *What now?* What happens when you catch someone like this and try to subject him to a reckoning? What system could possibly confront the enormity of what this one man had wrought? And what about the dozens of survivors? Would they be forced to relive the horror they endured so long ago?

What would become of Joseph DeAngelo now?

In the days after his capture, no formal charges were filed against him as district attorneys across California scrambled to connect him to rape or murder cold cases in their counties. In that time, the imprisoned DeAngelo "said little," one official noted. He was confined in his own small cell at the Sacramento County Main Jail, given a psychological evaluation, and placed on a suicide watch. No one came to visit him, and no reporters or photographers were allowed access to him.

Then, finally, on April 27, 2018, three days after his arrest, the world got its very first look at the Golden State Killer.

At 1:45 P.M., inside the densely packed courtroom of Sacramento County Superior Court, an officer opened a secured door behind the judge's bench, and a prisoner emerged.

He was sitting in a wheelchair, handcuffed at the wrists to the chair, in a white T-shirt beneath a standard-issue orange V-neck jumpsuit. He was balding, with only traces of white hair around his temples, and his cheeks were ruddy. His head hung listlessly to one side, and his eyes were narrowed to small slits. He appeared sedated, or at least dazed. He did not acknowledge the frantic jumble of camerapersons and photographers jammed together in a corner of the small room, or the dozens of people—some of them victims—crowded together in the rows of seats. He looked down at the ground or up at the judge, his blank expression betraying nothing.

"Is Joseph James DeAngelo your true correct legal name?" presiding Sacramento judge Michael Sweet asked him.

In the barest whisper: "Yes."

"I'm sorry?"

"Yes," he said again, in an only slightly louder voice.

Just four minutes later, DeAngelo's first arraignment hearing was over, and he was wheeled back through the secured door without having entered a plea to the two preliminary charges: the double murders of Brian and Katie Maggiore in 1978. (The case was so complex that it was not a surprise his lawyer delayed entering a plea.) DeAngelo's doddering demeanor and baffled expression never wavered in that time.

For the better part of forty years, this man was just a collection of sketchy, approximate details—likely around five foot ten inches, roughly 180 pounds, possibly a size nine shoe; wore black ski masks during some attacks; enjoyed stealing family items like jewelry and piggy banks. Over the years a thousand reporters wrote stories about him, though none could see him any more clearly than the rest of us.

But now we finally saw him with our own eyes—not a monster after all, but rather, a pathetic old man.

⊲◈⊳

Of course, it was all an act.

Neighbors who had seen DeAngelo shortly before his arrest said he was fit and healthy and agile, and the officers who had surveilled him confirmed this. I was shown videos of DeAngelo in his jail cell after his arrest, videos that would not be released to the public for two more years. They showed DeAngelo walking easily and briskly in his small cell, stretching and doing power push-ups, and even nimbly climbing atop a metal shelf to cover a light fixture with brown paper—an eerie echo of when he draped blankets over lamps and TVs at some of his crime scenes. He did not appear at all feeble or physically compromised. He certainly did not seem to need a wheelchair. The athleticism that had allowed him to elude police by jumping over fences and dashing through woods forty years earlier may have diminished, but it had not disappeared.

Nor had the mental acuity needed to pull off his elaborate crimes. In the videos, DeAngelo seemed determined and purposeful as he cleaned and organized his cell. One video caught him masturbating.

Yet in the courtroom DeAngelo crouched behind a mask of sickly helplessness. It was a cheap and shabby act, and not particularly convincing—the prevailing sentiment was that he was clearly pretending to be in a stupor.

Yes, Joseph DeAngelo was entitled to the full protections of the Constitution, which included a presumption of innocence and a vigorous defense. And no, he was not required to act in any particular way in his courtroom appearance.

Even so, his feigned lethargy struck me as a fresh insult to the surviving victims and the families of those murdered—a refusal to stand up and face his accusers.

DeAngelo's performance aside, the intense first arraignment hearing was just the smallest preview of what his actual trial might look like. The complications such a trial presented were staggering. Diane Howard, the public defender assigned to represent DeAngelo, said she expected to receive hundreds of thousands of pages of files and evidence in discovery, and that was back when there were only two murder charges. What would happen when more murder charges were added? And the dozens of rapes? Would the State of California have to produce millions of pages of evidence? And what about all the crimes for which the statute of limitations had passed? Would they simply be forgotten? What about all the burglaries and home invasions where no DNA had been recovered?

And what about the witnesses? The dozens of detectives, investigators, sheriffs, FBI special agents, police officers, prosecutors, and district attorneys who all had a stake in the outcome? How could crimes that had been committed across several different counties be consolidated into one solid case? Some predicted that such a trial would be not only the longest trial in California history—possibly stretching on for years—but also the costliest, with a potential price tag of $20 million or more.

Yet even if all of that could somehow be managed, would it not be unreasonably cruel to subject the surviving victims, and the families of the dead, to a vivid, months-long re-creation of the Golden State Killer's many gruesome crimes, each retold in granular detail?

It fell to the State of California, and specifically to the lead prosecutor in the case, Sacramento County district attorney Anne Marie Schubert, to confront this legal, technical, logistical, and ethical nightmare, and to find some plausible way to bring the Golden State Killer to justice, once and for all.

∞

When Paul Holes tweeted out my name in August 2018, I was no longer new to the field of investigative genetic genealogy. By then I had

been working on one case or another for nearly four years. I did not
take much time to sit and reflect on the remarkable change in course
my life had taken; frankly, I was just too busy. But when I did think
about it, I felt a deep sense of awe and appreciation. I was grateful
that I had been given a chance to do such meaningful work in my retirement, and I did not take the responsibility that came with it lightly.

In fact, I was so serious about the work that I was doing—and I
found it so rewarding—that I felt compelled to accept each and every
new case that came my way. Knowing I might be able to identify a
suspect in a criminal case after decades of bad breaks and dead ends
for law enforcement made it hard for me to turn down a case, so I
agreed to work on every investigation I was asked to be a part of.

And in the days and weeks after Paul Holes's tweet, there were
many requests. Within six months of going public, I was working on
some *fifty* cold cases.

Eight months after DeAngelo's arrest, I received a call from Major
Tim Horne of the Orange County Sheriff's Office in Hillsborough,
North Carolina.

Tim came from a long line of law enforcement officers. His great-
uncle, his uncle, and his father were all in the business. In his more
than two decades as an investigator, he "did it all," Tim says—crime
scenes, field interviews, homicide cases. He also studied at the presti-
gious National Forensics Academy in Tennessee. Twenty years earlier
he had assumed leadership of a case from Lieutenant Bobby Collins,
the retiring head of Orange County's investigative unit. It was a
uniquely challenging case that reflected the frustration many law officers face while waiting for DNA technology to catch up to the real-
world needs of crime solving.

"I've taken over four major murder investigations in my career and
solved three of them," Tim told me. "This is the only one I haven't
solved."

Tim told me more about the case. On the hot afternoon of September 28, 1998, a landscape worker was clearing away weeds and
scrub pines from a woodsy stretch of land called Industrial Drive
along Interstate 85 in Mebane, North Carolina, a city of some
seventy-two hundred people forty-six miles northwest of Raleigh.

The worker came upon a pile of fallen branches just inside the tree line and below a huge Howard Johnson's billboard towering over I-85. There the worker saw what looked like a white ball a few feet from the pile of branches. He came in for a closer look and saw that it was not a ball.

It was a human skull, bleached bright white by the sun.

The worker called the Orange County Sheriff's Office, and one of the first officers at the scene was Tim Horne.

"I remember it was a miserably hot day, and I was wearing a new pair of gray pants," says Tim. "We searched through all these briars and by the end of the day my pants were ripped to shreds." What he and other responding officers found was deeply disturbing: clothing lying atop a pile of branches—a pair of black-and-white 2XS Sports athletic shoes, white tube socks, and khaki Fox Polo Club shorts.

The clothing was hanging on the skeleton of a small child, later determined to have been a boy.

Tim Horne noted the relevant clues: no blood at the scene, suggesting the boy was killed elsewhere; no knife marks on the bones or bullet holes in the skull, suggesting the child might have been strangled; two twenty-dollar bills and a ten-dollar bill found in the boy's shorts, an unusual amount of money for a child to be carrying; teeth that showed evidence of dental work. A coroner estimated the remains had been there for some four months and ruled the death a homicide. Investigators now faced what one newspaper called "one of the rarest and most daunting mysteries that can confront them— the discovery of an unidentified child's skeletal remains."

The only identification tools available back then would be insect analysis, dental records, clay molds, and missing-children reports. "I wouldn't want to be the one in charge of that case," a local trucker told Raleigh's *News & Observer.* "That boy could have come from Atlanta or D.C.—anywhere." Investigators issued a composite sketch of a dark-haired boy who appeared to be around ten years old, but still the case ran cold and eluded solving for the next twenty years, long after it had picked up a catchy media nickname: The Boy Under the Billboard.

Tim Horne chose to stay with the case all that time. "For us, we just called it the Little Boy case," Tim says. "That's how we saw him: he was the little boy." Over the years, Tim drove past the Howard Johnson's billboard on I-85 hundreds of times, and every single time he thought about the unidentified boy. And he kept the bulky police case file beneath his desk, where it was in his way whenever he swiveled in his chair. "Every day I hit it with my leg," he says. That was deliberate. Tim wanted a constant reminder that his work was not finished.

Tim stayed with the case right up to the year of his retirement, 2018. He postponed his final day by several months, to December 31, 2018, so that he could keep working the case and, perhaps, even solve it before he left. One last shot. Early in November, with not even two months to go before his retirement, Tim phoned me.

"I worked this thing for twenty years and I've only got a few weeks left in my career, and can you find him by end of the year?" Tim asked me. I told him I would try.

I read up on the case and gathered the information at hand. There was a DNA sample that had been extracted from hard tissue in the boy's bones, and there was a long-standing assumption that the boy was likely white or Hispanic. I also learned the detective in charge of the case had previously contacted a well-known DNA-phenotyping company that did some initial analysis on the case but eventually determined that it did not meet their criteria for a case they would work on. Basically, I was starting over with just the DNA profile.

I brewed a café Americano, settled at my dining room table, opened my laptop, and got to work. I received the GEDmatch kit number for the DNA profile and accessed the match information. The first thing I noticed was that the phenotyping company had uploaded the victim's profile to GEDmatch Classic.

But it had *not* uploaded it to the new expansion of the site called GEDmatch Genesis.

Genesis was created to keep up with changes in chip technology: new generations of the chips that were used to create SNP profiles. The revamped chips were designed to provide more sophisticated information about the test taker.

One such improved chip was called a Global Screening Array,

or GSA, chip. GEDmatch Genesis was created to handle data from genealogical companies that had already made the switch to using GSA chips. Genesis made it possible to compare DNA profiles from different testing companies that used either GSA chips or the earlier chips. It began as a beta site (still in the testing stage), but eventually GEDmatch Classic would be merged into Genesis, creating a single GEDmatch database.

But back in 2018, when I began working on the Boy Under the Billboard case, users still had to upload their DNA profiles to both Classic and Genesis. The previous team of genealogists had, for whatever reason, neglected to upload the file to Genesis, and that became my first task. Since I did not have a copy of the victim's DNA profile, I asked the previous lab to upload it to Genesis for me.

This was another of my guardian angel moments. The new upload produced a match that no one had ever seen.

A match at the *first-cousin-once-removed level*.

This was extraordinary. With a match this close, I knew I could solve the case, and solve it quickly. But there was more. I ran the admixture utility on GEDmatch and learned that the Billboard Boy was 50 percent white and 50 percent Asian. The DNA lab that previously had the case had run a haplogroup analysis of the victim's DNA that had determined that the boy's Y-DNA haplogroup was R1b—the most regularly occurring paternal haplogroup in western Europe. This suggested that the boy's father was white and therefore it was his mother who was Asian. That information, coupled with the first-cousin-once-removed match, created a clear path to the boy's identity.

I called Tim on December 26, 2018—just five days before his retirement—and gave him the name of the first-cousin-once-removed match and the names of the match's parents. I told him that if one of these parents had a sibling with a biracial child, the Billboard Boy *had* to be that sibling's son.

We were close. Very close.

Tim promptly left several messages for the match's father, who did not respond. With the help of his girlfriend, Krista Schultz, Tim pored over Facebook and other sources and assembled a list of twenty people in the father's orbit, and called each one. "I called twenty freaking people and not one picked up the phone," says Tim. "What are the chances of that? So I had to leave twenty messages and hope someone called back."

Finally, someone did. Tim was at home in bed, half asleep and half watching TV, when the phone rang. It was a woman from Ohio who said she had married into the first-cousin-once-removed match's family. She told Tim she would call around to find out what she could about the young victim. Eventually she gave him the name of the child's aunt.

Tim reached the aunt by phone and told her about the case.

"You found Bobby," the aunt said simply.

Just like that, there was a name. After twenty years, the Billboard Boy had a name: Bobby.

"I wrote it down on a piece of paper and circled it so many times the ink ate right through the paper," Tim recalls.

The father of the first-cousin-once-removed match finally returned Tim's call and filled him in on the story. He confirmed he had a brother who had married a woman from South Korea and fathered a child named Bobby. He said he had not seen or heard about Bobby in a long time. Bobby's father explained the boy's absence, the man said, by claiming Bobby and his mother had both returned to South Korea.

Bobby, we confirmed through DNA testing, was Robert Adam Whitt, and he had been ten years old when he vanished.

We also learned that Bobby's father was John Russell Whitt. At the time we identified his son, Whitt was serving a long prison sentence for the armed robbery of dozens of victims at ATMs.

But what about Bobby's mother? What had happened to her?

❧❧❧

On May 13, 1998, at 1:30 P.M.—roughly four months before the landscaper came upon Bobby Whitt's body in Mebane, North Carolina— a man was picking up empty aluminum cans to recycle along a frontage road called Casual Drive, just off Interstate 85 in Spartanburg County, South Carolina. The man poked through a pile of debris and saw something shocking:

A woman's legs sticking out behind the pile.

The landscaper got to a phone and called Spartanburg police, who arrived at the scene and found a woman's nude body. The woman was five foot two, weighed around 145 pounds, and looked to be from thirty to forty-five years old. She had curly black hair and brown eyes, and she wore light pink nail polish on her fingers and toes. There was a distinctive four-inch scar on her left forearm, and she was missing nine teeth. The body did not show signs of decay, which police considered a good break.

"Usually these bodies are dumped by the interstate and by the time somebody finds them, they're skeletons," the county coroner told *The Greenville News*. "We're very lucky we have some evidence there."

Investigators guessed the woman was of Asian descent, and they hoped someone who knew her would soon step forward. But no one did. No available evidence helped to identify the body. Months passed, and the case went cold. It remained cold for the next two decades—just like the case of the Billboard Boy, whose body was found four months later some two hundred miles east of where the woman's body was found, along the very same interstate: I-85.

When Tim and I identified young Bobby Whitt in 2018, we also learned the name of his biological mother: Myoung Hwa Cho.

With help from the National Center for Missing and Exploited Children, we determined that Myoung Hwa Cho *was* the Jane Doe found along I-85 in Spartanburg in 1998. We also confirmed that she had been married to John Russell Whitt—Bobby Whitt's father.

Now it was time to hear from John Whitt himself.

When Tim first spoke with Whitt, in a federal prison in Ashland, Kentucky, Whitt denied killing his wife and child, despite the urgings of other family members to come clean. But Tim would not let him off the hook. Tim was now past his final day of work in the office, and into his last month of unused vacation time—technically not yet retired. So he kept working the case. In the course of his many interviews with Whitt, he managed to gain the inmate's confidence.

Then, just a few days before his very last vacation day, Tim pushed Whitt one last time to come clean.

"I said, 'Look, Russ, if you want to wait, fine, but I know he's your child,'" Tim recalls. "'The mother's DNA matches the child, and you were married to her, so I know he's your son.' And he just said, 'You know what, you're right. Come on down, I'll tell you what I know.'"

On January 31, 2019, his final official day on the job, Tim Horne drove six hours to Ashland and took Whitt's full confession.

"He comes in," says Tim, "and he lays down every last detail"—crime-scene conditions, how wounds were inflicted, dates and times. "We get the whole confession, I drive home, go to sleep, wake up, and I'm retired. On my last day in office, I cleared a double homicide."

On August 12, 2019, John Russell Whitt appeared in Orange County court to be charged with the first-degree murder of his son. He was then taken back to his jail cell in Kentucky, where his expected release date on the armed robbery charges was 2037. In January 2020, Whitt pleaded guilty to the murders of both his wife and son, all but closing the case.

Tim Horne, now fully retired, had one last bit of business to handle.

For twenty years he had kept the memory of the Billboard Boy alive, never allowing Bobby to vanish again, this time in an evidence storage room. "I felt the way all the detectives who worked this case felt—that this was my child," Tim says. And now that he knew the boy's name, as well as the identity of his mother, he could at last reunite them and give them a final place to rest. So he volunteered to drive Bobby Whitt's cremated remains to Ohio, where relatives would hold a memorial service for Bobby and his mother.

In mid-May 2019, Tim carried the urn to his 2006 silver Toyota Tundra truck. He opened the back door and carefully set the urn on the seat. "Then I pulled the shoulder strap all the way out and pulled it tight around the urn," he says. "No way he was going to be in the trunk. He rode with me, seatbelted the whole way."

Tim and his girlfriend, Krista, drove 459 miles from Raleigh to Mount Orab, Ohio, mostly on Interstates 77 and 64. Even when they stopped along the way, they didn't leave the urn in the car. "The last thing I was going to have happen was someone breaking into the truck and stealing the urn," says Tim. "So we carried him everywhere in Krista's big purse. Diners, rest stops, everywhere."

Tim even took the urn with him on a visit to a zoo.

In Mount Orab, Bobby was reunited with his mother, Myoung. On May 18, 2009, their family held a formal funeral for them. Not much was known about how or why Myoung came to marry John Russell Whitt, though an old photo exists showing her holding a very young Bobby in front of a decorated Christmas tree and wrapped presents. Her expression suggests joy and contentment. Other details about Myoung and her son emerged: how she was a loving mother and hard worker who often held down two jobs at the same time to care for her son; how Bobby was a typical fun-loving child who loved dinosaurs and *Jurassic Park;* how the little boy was inherently kind and loving, and sometimes gave his toys to friends because they wanted them; and how, as one attendee put it, he "always had a smile on his face and a twinkle in his eye."

The next day, Bobby and Myoung were laid to rest together.

Before that day, all Bobby had by way of a memorial was a small wooden cross—two planks of wood roughly nailed together—leaning crookedly against an old chain-link fence near where his remains were found, with faded and peeling stickers on it that read, simply, "Boy 1998."

Now, as Tim had promised himself and the boy, Bobby had a place, alongside his mother, to finally rest in the peace they deserved.

It was, Tim Horne says, "the first time investigative genetic genealogy had ever been used to solve a murder case in North Carolina."

After twenty years of maddening dead ends for Tim Horne, the DNA helped me solve the Boy Under the Billboard case in less than forty-eight hours.

Believe it or not, that wasn't even the quickest I've ever solved a case. When you have a strong initial match, like a first cousin, you can sometimes crack a case in a matter of hours. The Golden State Killer case was different: our initial match was a third cousin, so it took us sixty-three days. But even that was the blink of an eye compared to the four decades of frustration that preceded them.

I was seeing a trend. Like Paul Holes, Detective Tim Horne was at the very end of a long investigative career, and he turned to me as a last resort—one final chance to solve a case that had haunted him for years. There was a kind of symmetry to this—the limits of traditional law enforcement techniques coming up against the just-emerging promise of investigative genetic genealogy.

Of course, all the cases I solved required a good deal of traditional investigative methods: research, interviews, legwork. But it is also true that these cases might not have ever been solved without the shiny new tool of investigative genetic genealogy, appearing, at least for Paul Holes and Tim Horne, at the very end of a long haul and not a moment too soon.

With each new case, I understood a little better what a momentous time it was for law enforcement—and for devoted pursuers of justice like Paul and Tim.

20

In April 2019, almost a full year after the arrest of Joseph DeAngelo, prosecutors from six California counties gathered in a Sacramento courthouse and announced they would seek the death penalty in the case of the Golden State Killer.

At the time, the governor of California, Gavin Newsom, had declared a moratorium on capital punishment in the state, but the prosecutors were undaunted. With DeAngelo standing nearby in a courtroom cage—in his orange prison uniform and wearing the same dazed expression as at his arraignment a year earlier—the prosecutors cited special circumstances that could merit the death penalty.

Their message: *If DeAngelo's crimes did not deserve the ultimate punishment, what crimes possibly would?*

They ignored the governor's moratorium for a simple reason: it was likely temporary and could be lifted in a year or two. Meanwhile, the trial of Joseph DeAngelo was likely *years* away from even beginning. The case, everyone knew, was incredibly complicated. From his very first known offense—a 1975 break-in and theft of fifty dollars from a piggy bank—to his last known crime—the brutal rape and murder of an eighteen-year-old woman in 1986—the Golden State Killer had committed at least 13 murders, dozens of rapes, and some 160 other violent offenses—possibly the most atrocious series of crimes in U.S. history. In that time he caused unfathomable death, destruction, and damage, and the psychological trauma he inflicted on tens of thousands of citizens could never be calculated. If DeAngelo, who had yet to enter any plea, were to claim innocence, some of those offenses would need to be individually proven in court beyond all reasonable doubt.

There was another concern: the passage of time. DeAngelo was seventy-two when he was arrested, and there was no guarantee that he would survive for the years and years a trial would consume. The prospect of DeAngelo dying before facing a proper reckoning was not welcomed by anyone. Many of the survivors of his crimes, too, were getting on in age, and waiting on a trial risked depriving them of the chance to confront DeAngelo, and to finally see him face justice. Still, if DeAngelo refused to plead guilty, what else could prosecutors do but prepare for a trial?

There was, it turned out, another way.

In June 2020—now more than two years after DeAngelo's arrest— prosecutors announced that they had worked out a deal with the defendant and his attorney. If prosecutors agreed to drop the death penalty, DeAngelo would plead guilty to eighty-eight murder, rape, and other charges, including those rapes on which the statute of limitations had run. For this plea, DeAngelo would be given a life sentence without the possibility of parole.

The deal took months to work out, and there was still a chance DeAngelo might reject it at the last minute, but for the moment it looked like a trial had been avoided, saving millions of dollars and many agonizing months of waiting. A plea hearing was set for June 29, 2020, and it was there that DeAngelo would, in theory, admit his guilt.

After the deal was announced, Anne Marie Schubert, the Sacramento district attorney, invited me to attend the June 29 plea hearing and join the rest of Team Justice there.

It would be my chance to see the Golden State Killer in person.

For me, the important thing was to finally put an end to this case. It had been the first really big case for me—the first time investigative genetic genealogy had ever been used to identify and apprehend a killer on the loose—and I wanted to see it closed and put to rest once and for all, with as successful a conclusion as we could hope for. I had the sense we had accomplished something of real significance, and I knew the world was watching. If all our hard work failed to lead to a conviction and jail time for Joseph DeAngelo, it could have a negative impact on the use of IGG in the future.

DeAngelo's plea hearing would not take place in a courtroom. A courtroom was not practical because of the Covid-19 pandemic, which required such safety measures as not packing too many people into small, contained spaces. Instead, the prosecution rented the great ballroom at Sacramento State University, a sprawling space the size of an airplane hangar. A raised makeshift stage was set up at one end of the ballroom, and hundreds of chairs, placed six feet apart, filled the room. It was an unusual setting for a plea hearing, but then, it was an unusual case unfolding during unusual times.

I drove three hours north from my home in Monterey County, California, to Sacramento, the state's capital, and for only the second time met Paul Holes. He and I had spoken often on the phone, but we had met only once, so it was a treat to finally gather with him and the other members of Team Justice. Investigative genetic genealogy can be solitary work, and our meeting in Sacramento felt something like a reward. I think we all had a sense of accomplishment and pride, but also apprehension: the work of bringing the Golden State Killer to justice was not quite done.

The hearing was by invitation only, and I checked in with the organizers and took my numbered seat in the middle of the ballroom. Everyone wore face masks. The seats filled up quickly, and I could tell that many of the attendees were victims and victims' relatives. Suddenly it hit me: many of them had waited forty years for this turkey to be brought to justice for what he did. *Forty years.* I felt a heaviness in the room, an intensity, and also a sorrow. All around me I could hear people quietly crying and sniffling. I had not expected to feel such heightened emotions, but it was like a vast collective rage swept over the room. This was more than a legal proceeding. This was something holy and sacred. This was a reckoning.

Somberly, the presiding superior court judge, Michael G. Bowman, took his place at the center of the makeshift stage. Designated prosecutors from each county ascended to the left of the stage as their cases were called, district attorneys from Ventura and Contra Costa, from Yolo and Tulare, from Santa Barbara and Alameda and Orange County. On the right side of the stage sat members of the defense, with a space remaining for the defendant himself.

An officer rolled DeAngelo up onstage as he sat slumped in his wheelchair, his mouth hanging open, as if he was catatonic. He wore a bright orange jumpsuit over a white T-shirt, and a clear acrylic face shield. He never looked up but rather stared steadily down at his feet. He appeared even more sickly than at his first public hearing two years earlier. He did not look evil or dangerous. He looked like a frail old man who did not understand what was happening around him.

But, by then, we all knew it was an act.

I felt a sudden sharp pang of anger, followed by revulsion. No longer able to hide from his victims, DeAngelo could not even scrape up the decency to appear at the hearing as himself. Instead he posed as a pathetic caricature of an uncomprehending victim. If he could no longer crouch safely in the dark, he would now disappear into himself and become a cipher yet again.

It was yet another act of cowardice. It made me feel sick.

Judge Bowman called the hearing to order. Case No. 18FE008017—*The People of the State of California v. Joseph James DeAngelo*—was underway. Most plea hearings don't last for more than an hour, and many are sped through and finished quickly. But not this one. It was scheduled to run from 10:00 A.M. to 3:00 P.M., but Judge Bowman allowed it to stretch two hours beyond that. A friend of mine who is a former prosecutor later told me that it is highly unusual for a judge to allow prosecutors to talk at length about their cases; usually, the judge likes to hurry things along. Judge Bowman, however, gave prosecutors all the time they needed to stand before him and recite, in full, the Golden State Killer's vast litany of crimes.

When I first began working on the case, I did a fair amount of research into the killer and his crimes and methods. But that did not come close to preparing me for what we heard in that ballroom. One by one, each prosecutor got up and told the stories of the many victims and survivors from their county, none exaggerated but none censored, either. One survivor, we were told, "witnessed DeAngelo shoot her father twice from a distance of ten feet, [before] DeAngelo turned in her direction and kicked her three times in the face." We learned that after binding another victim with a white nylon cord, DeAngelo raped her and "fired his handgun into the back of her head." He pressed a knife against one victim's left temple so hard that blood trickled down her face and stained her pillow, before threatening her, "If you make one move or sound, I'll stick this knife in you." He apparently used a pipe wrench to smash a woman's face and shatter the teeth she had just spent two thousand dollars having fixed.

On and on it went, a terrible history of boundless evil and depravity. Through it all, DeAngelo sat quietly in his invented stupor. It was not until I heard his crimes recited this way, in the presence of the attacker and his victims, that I felt the true horror of what had happened. It was overwhelming. The elderly women seated next to me were two of his victims, and they sobbed throughout the hearing. When their cases were heard they rose from their seats and stared at DeAngelo, never looking away, never hiding their pain. I felt like a witness to a ritual that was both frightening and powerful, and one that was entirely essential.

Yet hearing about his crimes was only one part of the process.

The other part was hearing him confess to them.

After the charges in each case were read aloud, Judge Bowman turned to DeAngelo and asked him for his plea. With the first charge, the room fell utterly silent as we all strained to hear his response. At first, he just sat there and said nothing. Long seconds passed. The tension in the room was palpable. Was he still toying with everyone, and planning to plead not guilty?

And then, in a weak, almost inaudible voice, he finally spoke a single word:

"Guilty."

Over and over again, as each charge was read, he said it:

"Guilty."

The other crimes attributed to DeAngelo but now beyond the stat-ute of limitations were also recited, and to those, DeAngelo had a different plea, also barely audible, and not even a coherent sentence.

To each one, he said, "I admit."

I admit. I admit. I admit. For the victims of his crimes for which the statute of limitations had run, hearing these words, I could sense, was enormously powerful and emotional—a slight measure of vindi-cation they likely had believed would never come.

Then it was over. An officer spun DeAngelo around and wheeled him off the stage, into a back room, and out of sight again.

I was supposed to do a couple of media interviews after the hear-ing, but I rescheduled them. I was emotionally so drained, so devas-tated by the day, that I didn't think I could carry on a conversation with anyone.

In a way, the hearing validated the hard work we had all put in. It proved that it was absolutely worthwhile. We started with such a tiny genetic match—62 centimorgans—yet we kept going and were able to find some larger matches. And then, sixty-three days after we first uploaded the crime-scene DNA profile to GEDmatch, we were able to identify a suspect. I know that in the context of a forty-year-old cold case, sixty-three days sounds like lightning speed. But it did not feel that way. All of us on Team Justice worked incredibly long hours day after day. Add in all the hours put in by the investigative and law en-forcement sides, and you would be at many, many thousands of hours of work.

One of the takeaways of the day was a deepened appreciation of just how powerful and consequential this new technology was. It was an absolute game changer, and watching Joseph DeAngelo confess to his crimes after forty years as a fugitive from justice strongly con-firmed that. It was now possible to solve previously unsolvable cold cases at a dizzying rate: not just one or two a year, but possibly *hun-dreds* a year.

This would be a watershed moment in the history of American law enforcement—*if* this incredible new tool survived the many ethi-cal challenges to it.

On that day, however, I do not believe anyone in that ballroom could have argued against it, or underplayed its impact on the literally thousands of people affected by the Golden State Killer. Two years earlier, Joseph James DeAngelo had not been a suspect, and likely believed he was perfectly safe in his anonymity.

But on this day he sat before the world, folded into a grotesque façade of bewilderment, unable to face his victims, and destined for the small jail cell that would be his final hiding spot for the rest of his days.

PART FIVE

SEATTLE BABY BOY DOE AND PRECIOUS JANE DOE

JULY 2018

21

Forty minutes before midnight on November 18, 1997, a dark-haired woman in her mid-twenties with a blanket wrapped around her waist walked into a Chevron gas station store on Lake City Way in Seattle, Washington.

The woman went straight to the restroom in the back of the store and locked the door behind her. While she was there, a customer in line for the cashier heard the sound of a baby's cries coming from the restroom. Fourteen minutes later, the woman emerged from the room and left the store.

Early the next morning, a store clerk entered the restroom and found streaks of blood on the floor, toilet, and sink. The clerk was not alarmed by the blood; this was a public restroom, and someone coming in with a cut or bloody nose was not unusual. Another clerk mopped up the blood at 7:00 A.M., and the day proceeded as usual.

It was not until the following day, November 20, around noon, that a third store clerk, Lakota Murray, emptied the trash in the restroom and made a horrifying discovery.

At the bottom of a clear plastic trash liner, covered by debris, Murray found a newborn baby. The baby's placenta and umbilical cord were still attached.

Murray called police at 12:40 P.M. Seattle detectives arrived, examined the infant, and determined that the child was dead. An autopsy later revealed that the child weighed seven pounds, seven ounces, and had been born alive.

At first, the death was reported as the result of natural causes. But, quickly, a medical examiner changed that to homicide. The exact phrasing used on the death certificate was "Full term birth, perinatal death, etiology undetermined." *Perinatal* meant the death occurred around the time of birth. Etiology referred to cause of death.

The unanswered questions: Who had left the newborn child there to die, and why?

The detectives assigned to the case sifted through evidence: a surveillance tape showing the woman entering and leaving the store; the testimony of the customer who had heard a baby crying; and, most important, a placental blood clot smear found with the infant.

A medical examiner preserved the smear and a laboratory produced an STR DNA profile of the newborn's mother. But back in 1998, DNA analysis was still a developing discipline, and the STR profile did not lead to any suspects.

Detectives kept at it, but the case went cold.

It stayed cold for the next twenty years.

In that time, the victim's remains were buried in Seattle's Calvary Catholic Cemetery, in a plot marked by a plaque etched with the figure of Winnie-the-Pooh and the words "We Care." The plaque also featured the only name the victim had: Baby Boy Doe.

One of the people who contacted me in the months after Joseph DeAngelo's arrest was Seattle detective Rolf Norton, who had heard about me from Paul Holes. Rolf filled me in on a homicide case he was handling: Case No. 1997-504314.

The case of Baby Boy Doe.

After two decades with no new clues or leads, detectives had reopened the investigation in 2018, and the Washington State Patrol Crime Laboratory had reextracted DNA from the placental blood clot smear using more advanced technology than was available in 1998. The extract was used to create a new, more complete DNA profile to run through CODIS, the FBI's criminal database, but there was no match.

Next, the Seattle Police Department sent some of the DNA extract to an Oklahoma City lab called DNA Solutions to develop a SNP profile. Finally, the lab sent the SNP profile to Detective Norton to upload to GEDmatch. After a few days, a list of people who shared DNA with Baby Boy Doe's mother was posted on the page for Baby Boy Doe's kit. It was at this point that Detective Norton contacted me and asked for my help. Could these matches somehow lead us to the mother of Baby Boy Doe?

Once again, I said I believed that they could.

The child in this case would be the youngest unidentified homicide victim I had encountered: an infant killed when he was likely just minutes old. An infant who essentially did not exist in any records or even memories—a child never given the chance to live. If I could somehow succeed in identifying his mother, we might be able to finally add this child to his rightful family tree.

I got to work in July 2018. I pulled together a small team of genealogists to help me with the case. The DNA had been isolated from a placental blood clot, which meant that we had the mother's DNA but not the father's.

Among our initial jumble of distant relatives to the mother was a woman named Molly. She was a close match at 513 cM, and she was most likely a first cousin once removed to the mother of Baby Boy Doe.

I started a speculative tree for the mother by building a tree for Molly. I identified a close relative in Molly's tree, Teresa, whom we could test as a reference sample to give us another data point. Because Teresa was such a close relative to Molly, I asked Detective Norton to surreptitiously DNA-test her—a trash pull—so as not to alert her to our investigation, as it was possible that she could be the mother.

Detective Norton's officers surveilled the woman and picked up some chewing gum she tossed away. DNA was taken from the gum, and the resulting extract was used to produce a SNP profile for up-load to GEDmatch. The match results revealed that Teresa was not herself the mother, but she *was* a match with the unidentified mother at 706 cM, suggesting she was likely a first cousin to the mother as well. It was another solid match, and I now had an MRCA, allowing me to build down all the descendant lines in search of the missing mother.

My next step: entering the mother's speculative tree into What Are The Odds? (WATO), along with the match information for Molly and Teresa.

The WATO tool gave me the odds of precisely where on the specu-lative tree the mother likely fit in: in this case, ten-to-one odds that she belonged in one of six possible slots in the tree—slots occupied by six female first cousins.

One of these six cousins was Baby Boy Doe's mother.

But how to determine which one? All I knew was that three of the women were sisters and the other three cousins were each from differ-ent families. To get any further, I had to employ a technique I called the Jonny Perl method.

Jonny Perl, the genealogist who created the wonderful mapping tool DNA Painter, figured out a way to distinguish among cousins when trying to identify an unknown parent. He did this by building back from the spouse of the parent who is a descendant of the MRCA.

I did just that with our matches and came up with the names of the four sets of parents for all six cousins. One parent in each set was a descendant of the MRCA. Now I needed to build back up the ances-tral lines of the spouse of the parent who was the MRCA descendant. What I was looking for was a connection to a match with the uniden-tified mother's DNA matches. Once I found such a connection, I would know I had the right cousin. I did not know how far back I would have to build, but I knew that it would likely be several genera-tions.

It turned out that the father of one of the cousins, whose mother was a descendant of the MRCA, had the surname Warren. Luckily, one of my team members, Lorrie Burns, remembered coming across the name Warren in the huge jumble of our original matches to the mother on GEDmatch. Now I needed to build back in time to see if these two Warrens were related.

I built back two generations and found no connection.

I went back one more, and still nothing.

But four generations back, in each of the two Warrens' trees, I found it: the most recent common ancestor between Warren the original DNA match and Warren the spouse whose ancestral line we had built back.

This was it! Finding the MRCA for the two Warrens told me that the daughter of Warren the spouse *had* to be Baby Boy Doe's mother.

That daughter's name was Christine M. Warren.

Several bits of data pointed to her. Physically, she matched the descriptions provided by witnesses. She resembled the woman in the surveillance video. She also would have been twenty-seven years old when Baby Boy Doe was born, matching estimates of her age in 1997. She had lived in Seattle most of her life and lived there still. And she was a first cousin to Teresa. I presented these findings to Detective Norton, who was now prepared to take the next step: surreptitiously retrieving Christine's DNA and comparing it to their crime-scene DNA.

Detective Norton had to be careful. He did not want to risk confronting Christine Warren before he knew for sure that she was the mother. Instead, he devised a sting.

In November 2020, detectives mailed Christine Warren an invitation to take part in a survey for a fictional flavored-water drink called Sparkling Icy. The invitation included a complimentary gift card. Christine Warren took the bait, filled out a survey, and mailed it to a P.O. box set up by the Seattle PD. First, detectives compared the signature on the survey to the signature in Christine Warren's driver's license records, to make sure they had the correct Christine Warren.

The signatures matched.

Next, in December 2020, they sent the envelope in which the survey was mailed to the Washington State Patrol crime lab. The lab extracted DNA from the envelope seal and the stamp, both of which Warren had licked. An autosomal STR DNA profile, or a short tandem repeat DNA profile (see Glossary, page 247), was created from the extract. This new STR DNA profile was compared to the STR DNA profile created from the placental blood clot smear gathered in 1997. The results came in on December 31, 2020—New Year's Eve.

The two STR DNA profiles were a match.

Beyond any doubt, Christine Warren was Baby Boy Doe's biological mother.

Detective Norton tied up all the incriminating details before, in March 2021, interviewing the suspect. In the interview, Christine Warren admitted to everything. By her telling, the baby's father was agitated by the news that she was unexpectedly pregnant, and for that reason she could not bear the thought of having the child. Instead, she simply "blocked the pregnancy out of her mind," investigators said in a 2021 charging document. "She ignored the fact that she was pregnant."

For the next several months, she received no medical attention, nor did she mention the pregnancy to a single other soul.

Finally, late on November 18, 1997, Warren was riding with a friend in a car when she felt a wave of contractions. She asked the friend to pull over at the Chevron store, covered her stomach with a blanket and walked into the restroom. Calmly, she walked out again fourteen minutes later and went on with her night. She told detectives "the baby dropped into the toilet" and remained there for several minutes. Then she panicked and put the baby in the trashcan and covered him with paper and other debris. "In her mind," detectives explained, "she did not believe the baby was alive." But under questioning she admitted that she never checked and did not know for sure if her child was living.

Police arrested Warren, then fifty years old, set her bail at ten thousand dollars, and later charged her with murder in the second degree—a crime that could send her to prison for as long as eighteen years (as far as I can tell, she has not yet been convicted as of this writing).

My team and I had cracked the mystery of Baby Boy Doe. Still, this was not a resolution anyone wished to celebrate. The details of the case were just too sad. Detective Norton shifted attention to all the dedicated investigators who had worked on the case over the last twenty years, men and women who "created a foundation of evidence that we were able to parlay into a conclusion," as he explained to Seattle's KIRO 7 News. "This was an incredibly sad case in 1997, and it's an incredibly sad case in 2021."

He was right. The death of Baby Boy Doe was senseless and tragic. Even so, identifying his mother and filling out the details of the crime were meaningful. Twenty-three years after his death, the boy was no longer an unidentified phantom, no longer erased from his family tree. He existed, and his short life mattered, and he had not been forgotten.

And when it was finally possible, good people gathered to ensure that justice was done in his honor.

22

Back when I worked mainly as a search angel helping adoptees identify birth relatives, most of my cases originated with a difficult and possibly traumatic family event: the decision of a parent to give up a child.

When I started working on criminal cold cases, that changed. Most of my criminal cases began with a horrible, haunting, often unthinkable tragedy.

Early on the afternoon of August 14, 1977, in a wooded area on Fourth Avenue West in Everett, Washington, some hikers picking blackberries came across the body of a young woman. They scrambled to a telephone and called police. Officers arrived, examined the body, and determined the woman had been deceased for several days. That she had been the victim of foul play was also obvious; she had been shot in the head several times and was unrecognizable. There was no purse or identification card found on the body or nearby.

With no immediate method of identification available, the victim was given a case number—77-8-621—and a label. She was now a Jane Doe.

Just a few days later, however, there was a major break in the homicide investigation. A man called Snohomish County detectives and told them a friend of his, David Roth, had bragged of killing a hitchhiker in Everett. Police searched Roth's car and found a .22-caliber rifle that matched the rounds recovered from Jane Doe's body. In 1979, Roth confessed to the murder and filled in the details. He had spotted the young woman hitchhiking along Bothell Everett Highway on August 9, 1977, and given her a lift. When she refused to have sex with him, Roth strangled her with a bungee cord before shooting her seven times in the head with his rifle.

Investigators asked him: *Do you know the woman's name?* Roth insisted that he did not.

A jury found Roth guilty of first-degree murder, and he was sent to prison for the next twenty-six years. Meanwhile, the investigation into the identity of the Jane Doe went nowhere. Years passed, then decades. Investigators did everything they could with existing technology: a dental exam suggested Jane Doe grew up in a region with good water quality, such as the Pacific Northwest; an artist created a forensic three-dimensional clay model of Jane Doe's head and face; a detective, James Scharf of the Snohomish County Sheriff's Office Cold Case Unit, exhumed her remains, and a forensic anthropologist estimated her likely age to have been between sixteen and nineteen years old.

Beyond these bits of information, nothing of substance emerged. Each attempt to extract usable DNA had failed because the DNA was simply too degraded. The case ran cold for another ten years, with only one change: to attract publicity, Detective Scharf rechristened the victim Precious Jane Doe.

"This young girl was precious to me," he explained. "I knew she had to be precious to her family. So I had to find them. We needed to give her name back to her and return her remains to her family."

Detective Scharf stayed with the case for twelve years. He even included a link to the case in his automatic email signature. In 2017, he learned about promising new developments in genetic genealogy. He contacted a new all-volunteer organization called the DNA Doe Project and asked for their help, and he forwarded the victim's DNA sample to the Doe Project, hopeful that this could be the break he'd been desperately waiting for.

It was not. The SNP file created from the DNA extract from 2008, retrieved from Jane Doe's femur, had a very low call rate (a measure of how many of the 700,000 to 800,000 SNPs that should be present in the file were there) and could not be uploaded to GEDmatch. The detective sent new samples—small pieces of the victim's skull and teeth—to a Virginia laboratory, hoping that this time the lab would succeed in creating a usable DNA extract.

Unfortunately, they could not. The DNA was too degraded. Detective Scharf sent the lab a larger sample, but that did not yield solid DNA, either. It looked like too much time may have passed, blocking any chance to take advantage of the new technology.

All told, the woman's identity had been a mystery for *forty-three years*.

In 2017, Detective Scharf contacted me.

His timing was perfect. I had been working with Professor Ed Green, the scientist who devised a method of extracting autosomal DNA from a single strand of rootless hair. If Snohomish County investigators had preserved any of Precious Jane Doe's hair in 1977, there was a chance Professor Green could create a workable DNA profile. When I learned there *was* a surviving hair sample, I connected Detective Scharf with Professor Green.

In February 2018, the Snohomish County Sheriff's Office sent Professor Green a generous sample of the victim's hair. The sample was about the thickness of a pencil. Still, the hair was more than forty years old. Professor Green, however, was not daunted. It was not the first time he had worked with a very old sample, and he spent nearly all of 2018 attempting to extract enough DNA to sequence and use to create a workable SNP file.

In late 2018, he succeeded, and Precious Jane Doe's DNA file was uploaded to GEDmatch and to FamilyTreeDNA.

Unfortunately, our initial matches included only a handful of distant relatives. A woman named Laura matched Precious Jane Doe's DNA at only 28 centimorgans (a second cousin matches at about 240 cM). Another woman, Kathy, matched at 85 cM, while a man named

Michael was at 86 cM. Without closer matches, it can be extremely difficult to figure out how these lesser matches connect to one another in the speculative tree, which in turn makes it harder to identify an unknown person.

But there was a way to do it.

We had only recently begun using advanced diagramming tools such as Scapple and Lucidchart. These tools make it possible to create a clear graphic visualization of just how the speculative trees built for the matches to the crime-scene DNA might, in the end, all connect. The tools made it much easier to see when, say, the surname of a match's spouse that appeared on one tree also appeared on a second tree—thus connecting the two trees by marriage.

Here is how Scapple worked with the matches for Precious Jane Doe: picture a chart with three clusters of boxes along the bottom. There is one cluster for each of the three closest matches we started with (Kathy, Laura, and Michael) and for whom we have identified a most recent common ancestor. Each box represents an individual who shares DNA with our search subject, Precious Jane Doe. We then transfer the names of the ancestors of the individual matches, all the way up to the MRCA for each cluster to the Scapple.

Then we begin to add names for the *descendants* of the spouse of the MRCA, in hopes of seeing surnames in one descendant line that appear among those in another cluster. Finding these overlapping names will, eventually, show a way to connect all three trees. To find Precious Jane Doe, who we knew was somehow connected to all three trees, we had to find this precise point of intersection.

All of this represented quite a bit of work, but when we began filling in the names of the descendants of the *spouses* of the MRCAs, the hard work paid off.

We discovered that a person in the Laura tree named Mary Wheeler, born way back in 1859, had a daughter named Mary Elizabeth Winans.

Winans was the spouse of Ruben Elder—a name we had seen before. Ruben Elder was a distant cousin to Michael, the match in one of our other two trees.

We now had what we called a connecting couple that allowed us to connect the Michael and Laura trees. Similarly, we were able to find a connecting couple who connected the Kathy and Michael trees.

Looking at our Scapple, we were able to see precisely where all three trees connected.

And, just as all roads lead to Rome, all three trees led to one specific couple: Mary Guinard and Stanley Elder.

Here were the people who connected all three clusters. The matches in all three were related to Precious Jane Doe, therefore identifying this point of convergence allowed us to conclude that Precious Jane Doe *had* to be a descendant of this specific couple. And judging by their years of birth (Mary in 1931, Stanley in 1938, and Precious Jane Doe somewhere between 1955 and 1962), the most likely relationship connecting all three was parent-daughter. This was the only spot on our Scapple diagram where Precious Jane Doe could possibly fit.

There was, however, one little problem.

In the spot in our tree where we expected to find Precious Jane Doe among Mary and Stanley's children, we found only three sons.

No girls, just boys.

Okay, we said, *the girl has to be in there somewhere. Maybe she was given up for adoption. Let's start with contacting the boys.*

Sadly, all three boys had died in a car crash in 1970 that also had killed their father and stepmother. A newspaper article about the crash made no mention of a sister. The biological mother had died in 1995.

How were we going to find this female relative with no trace or mention of her anywhere?

It turned out there *was* a trace of her—on the internet.

Kathy Johnston, one of the members on the small team of genealogists I had assembled to help me on the case, is remarkably skilled in unearthing important names and data from the internet, and she found an obscure genealogy site that featured various family trees. One of those trees, she discovered, was the same as the speculative tree that we had built for Precious Jane Doe—the same, that is, except for one person.

Alongside the three brothers, *there was the missing girl*.

Okay—*now* we had something. We delivered our findings to Detective Scharf, who obtained a copy of the divorce record for her parents. The records confirmed that there had been a biological daughter who was given up for adoption. I sent the name of this biological daughter—Elizabeth Marie Elder—along with the names of her three brothers and an aunt to Detective Scharf.

Still, we had no idea what her adoptive name was, or who her adoptive parents were, and Detective Scharf had no way to identify or contact them.

But with further research, the names we sent Detective Scharf enabled him to locate the missing girl's half sister, whom Detective Scharf reached out to and interviewed.

Luckily for us, the half sister remembered that, long ago, her mother had mentioned a daughter named Elizabeth whom she had given up for adoption. She also recalled that her mother had asked the adoptive parents to keep Elizabeth's first name. If the adoptive parents had obliged her, we now knew we were looking for an Elizabeth.

In June 2020, Detective Scharf asked the Oregon Center for Health Statistics to release the adoptive name of Elizabeth Marie Elder, as well as the names of her adoptive parents. Since Elizabeth and her biological parents had all died, there really was no one's privacy to protect, and no reason to refuse to provide these adoption details.

Yet that is just what the Oregon Center did—refuse Detective Scharf's request.

While Detective Scharf kept pushing for Elizabeth's adoptive name, we acted on another revelation from the half sister: Precious Jane Doe had an older half brother who had also been given up for adoption.

Detective Scharf followed up on small bits of biographical information provided by the half sister and eventually located this new half brother. He contacted the man and learned—once again, luckily for us—that he had previously taken an at-home DNA test. The half brother agreed to upload his DNA profile to GEDmatch, and the match results confirmed that he was indeed a half sibling to Elizabeth Marie.

We were getting closer.

Finally, after a week of prodding, the State of Oregon turned over Elizabeth Marie Elder's adoptive name. She had been renamed Elizabeth Ann Roberts, and she called herself Lisa. More research revealed that Lisa's adoptive mother had died but her adoptive father was still alive. Detective Scharf reached out to him and learned the full story of Lisa.

In 1977, Lisa was a junior at Roseburg High School in Roseburg, Oregon. After a fight with her adoptive parents, she walked out the front door and disappeared. Her parents filed a police report, and the National Crime Information Center listed her as a missing person—though, inexplicably, the report vanished from its system that same day. Lisa did contact her parents one time after leaving, to ask them for five hundred dollars and to say she would consider returning home, as her father begged her to do. Her father sent the requested money to a bank in Everett, Washington, but it was never retrieved. Nor did Lisa ever contact her parents again.

Fifteen days after she ran away, on August 14, 1977, hikers picking blackberries stumbled onto her badly mutilated body. That was when she ceased to be Lisa and instead became an unidentified victim: Precious Jane Doe.

She remained a Jane Doe until I submitted a summary of our DNA research to Detective Scharf, who provided it to the Snohomish County chief medical examiner.

On June 16, 2020—forty-three years after her murder, and fifteen years after her murderer completed serving his time and was released from prison—Precious Jane Doe was officially identified as Elizabeth Ann Roberts.

"She finally has her name back," Snohomish County sheriff Adam Fortney said at the time, "and she can now be returned to her family and loved ones."

In 2020, relatives buried Lisa Roberts's remains in a family plot in northern Oregon, along the banks of the beautiful Columbia River.

My team and I worked on the Precious Jane Doe case for about three years. In that time, I estimate we collectively devoted more than a thousand hours to building out family trees. That may seem like a meager amount of time compared to the forty-three years Lisa Roberts had to wait to get her name back. But still, it was an awful lot of work. The Snohomish County Sheriff's Department congratulated us for finding Lisa's biological parents and credited the identification of Precious Jane Doe to "SNP DNA and Investigative Genetic Genealogy."

A case that baffled dozens of investigators for nearly half a century had been solved in roughly three years using criminology's most powerful new tool. It was another stunning success for the technique in yet another high-profile cold case.

One absolutely crucial component to solving this and other long-cold cases is often overlooked. I am referring to the fierce and relentless dedication of the detectives and their teams who stick with these cases year after year after year. These investigators are the ones who, through tireless devotion, keep the cases alive long enough that someone like me, working with new technology, can finally step in and help solve them. People like Peter Headley and Paul Holes and Josh Carlson and James Scharf and Tim Horne. Tim, for instance, was quick to credit all the other officers, investigators, and detectives who worked the Billboard Boy case before he took it over.

"Every little lead along the way was essential to finally solving the case," Tim says. "And everyone who worked on it before me was just as passionate as I was. I had investigators from other states call me and say, 'This could be my child.' Not 'my case,' not 'my victim'— 'my *child*.' That is the level of dedication we are talking about."

Sometimes it is not a law enforcement officer who keeps a case active, but rather someone like the journalist and writer Michelle McNamara, who—like Paul Holes—simply refused to stop investigating the Golden State Killer. I believe that Michelle, by refusing to allow the case to drop off the radar, deserves a great deal of credit. She kept the case alive so that, in due time, the other members of Team Justice and I were able to use investigative genetic genealogy to finally identify the Golden State Killer.

By the time we closed the Precious Jane Doe case, in 2020, I was nearly into my fifth year as an investigative genetic genealogist. I had worked or was working on at least a hundred different cases and searches, and I had personally spent thousands of hours building family trees. On most of those early cases my team and I worked pro bono, although for some I received a modest fee. Not once in that entire time did I ever consider that what I was doing was drudgery. In fact, it was the opposite. The work always struck me as meaningful and exciting.

When you are deep into a genealogical search, it can be a completely immersive experience. Time disappears, appointments are forgotten. Even those genealogists just starting out in the field fall into this trap and sit glued to their computers for hour after hour, skipping dinners and other social events, secure in the knowledge that building trees and finding new relatives will prove more exciting than any dinner or party could.

To me, investigative genetic genealogy is a little like playing a card game and drawing a winning hand and realizing before anyone else that the game is already over. The thrill is in those precious few moments of realization. Similarly, when I solve a criminal cold case, there is always a wonderful moment when I identify the suspect and, for however long before I share the name with someone else, I am the only person in the world who knows the identity of the perpetrator. That fleeting moment—*that* is the thrill of discovery.

Finding a biological relative or solving a cold case is also an empowering experience. I remember helping one woman whose search for her grandparents stalled after she discovered an adopted family member. I knew she had spent many years looking for them, and I felt motivated to help her find them as quickly as I could. So I stayed up later than usual and worked extra hours and eventually I identified the adoptee's biological grandfather—a major discovery. Of course, that meant I had to spend more hours searching for the biological grandmother. Except I did not see it as *Oh, now I have to do more work to help this woman.*

I saw it as *Oh, now I get to build another tree!*

And at the end of the search, when I finally identified her biological grandparents, I felt elated. This was not even my own family, and yet to know that I could solve in mere hours what the woman had struggled to solve for years filled me with an uncommonly satisfying sense of achievement. There were times when it even felt like I was doing something *magical*.

If, in the course of your own searches, you have experienced this thrilling moment of discovery, perhaps it felt a little like magic to you, too.

PART SIX

HOME

23

The years I have spent in the field of investigative genetic genealogy have been marked by an unusually high level of success and attention. I have also faced my share of resentment as a relative newcomer to the game. But I will be the first to admit that my success has had a lot to do with being in the right place at the right time—and with having the right background to take full advantage of the new DNA tools that appeared just when I needed them.

My progress pretty much parallels the advent of astonishing new genealogical tools that make possible what only a few years ago was thought impossible, or at least too time-consuming to be practical. Whenever I needed a more flexible or powerful option to jostle a stalled case, I turned around and there it was, just waiting for me. Professor Green's incredible breakthrough in extracting autosomal DNA from rootless hair comes to mind, as do tools for analyzing DNA data such as those developed by Rob Warthen and Don Worth (DNAGedcom Client), Jonny Perl and Leah Larkin (DNA Painter and What Are The Odds?), and Evert-Jan Blom (Genetic Affairs).

The ingredient that makes all this technology work is dedication.

A high level of dedication brings with it an understanding of what is and is not valuable to an investigative genetic genealogist, and that is what I would like to share with you now—*if* you are one of the millions of people who have waded into genetic genealogy and enjoyed it enough to stick around.

Before genetic genealogy, there was mainly paper-trail genealogy—traditional family history research that required the assembly of historical records to build a family tree. The introduction of home DNA tests changed all that. By one estimate, some 15 percent of adult Americans—or about thirty million people—have taken a mail-in DNA test, and that number is only expected to grow. Some say the market size will double by 2026, fueled by test takers who primarily are interested in their admixture rather than family history research. Improved admixture reference populations have greatly enhanced the accuracy of admixture estimates for previously underserved groups such as those with roots in Africa and Asia.

Yet while the number of people in the databases may continue to grow, what investigative genetic genealogists most need is for the databases to be more representative of the actual admixture of the U.S. population. Right now there are built-in drawbacks to IGG, including the nature of those who benefit from it and those who do not.

In 2021 *The Atlantic* magazine studied one hundred cold cases solved by IGG and found that only four of them involved a murder victim who was Black. The victims of the Golden State Killer "lived in subdivisions and middle-class neighborhoods," *The Atlantic* noted. Yet "the average American murder victim is a Black man in his 20s, likely living in or around a major city." So far, the magazine reported, "this new technique has been applied primarily to cases with white victims, reflecting biases in the criminal-justice system and in society at large."

There is also a reverse bias in terms of who is getting arrested as a result of IGG. The genealogy databases in general mostly include people with predominantly northern and western European ancestry. Right now, 80 percent of the people in the databases are white, while, according to the 2020 U.S. census, the demographic composition of the nation is 57.8 percent white, 18.7 percent Hispanic, 12.4 percent Black, and 6 percent Asian. As a result, most suspects identified so far have been, for lack of a better phrase, old white guys.

There may be other reasons investigative genetic genealogy is less likely to be used in cases involving Black victims and Black suspects. For one thing, it is simply more difficult to trace the ancestry of Black Americans any further back than the post-Emancipation 1870 U.S. census. You tend to get brick-walled looking for names and useful data from the time of slavery (though this is less likely to happen in the case of those not born into slavery). Records kept by slave owners are mostly handwritten and tend to be spotty, badly preserved, or lost altogether. Some slave ship logs listed Africans not as passengers but as cargo. Family stories can sometimes fill in these gaps, but not always. About one-third of Black Americans are not even sure if their ancestors were enslaved. Still, tracing the heritage of slaves is possible, and places like the Center for Black Genealogy in Chicago are striving to make it easier.

Along with the growth of the databases, DNA technology has consistently and rapidly progressed. Early mitochondrial DNA tests could cost more than eight hundred dollars twenty years ago, but today far more inclusive tests can be purchased for as little as fifty dollars. And the process has become much simpler: an easy cheek swab or spit sample can unlock centuries of family history. *GenealogyIn-Time Magazine* has estimated that more than eleven million people in English-speaking countries are currently active genealogists— amateur or professional—though most of those tend to drift in and out of the field. More than two million people reportedly visit genealogy websites at least once a week.

It has become a busy, crowded field, and all different kinds of people, with all different kinds of skills, are successfully navigating the new technology and building better, more far-reaching trees. In other words, there is not any one type of person who will do better in genetic genealogy than another. But there are specific strengths and insights that *will* make a difference as you pursue genetic genealogy, either as a hobby or as a profession.

One of those keys is *using your background*.

Put simply, *any* background can help. Everything you bring to a search is potentially useful. One of the members of my team has a father who was in military intelligence, and because of that she has an amazing knowledge of military bases in the United States. Quite often in our searches we find someone who has inexplicably hopped from place to place in their lives, and much of the time it is because they grew up in a military family and constantly moved from base to base. So recognizing a potential military connection can be helpful in making sense of geographical data points.

I did not bring this woman onto the team because of this knowledge—she's an incredibly smart person whom I am grateful to know—but her background has proved to be a real asset.

There's a good chance that your own background will be useful to you in your searches, whether it is your particular base of knowledge or your particular way of thinking and seeing. There are many scientists and IT professionals in the field because of their training in logical thinking. There are also many lawyers and former law enforcement professionals. But any profession or specialty can be an asset— carpenter, teacher, doctor, politician, stay-at-home parent. Everything helps. We each bring a unique thought process to our endeavors, so be aware of your particular strengths and skills and mindset, and one day the moment will arrive when you see something no one else does in the daunting sprawl of names, percentages, and connections that is genetic genealogy.

One important trait that anyone can bring to the discipline of tree building is *diligence*.

To build a solid tree, you need solid sourcing. There is a lot of misinformation on all the genealogy sites: misspellings, connections based on guesses, incorrect designations, conflation of people with similar names, and so on. It is simply not good enough to copy names from someone else's tree and move them to your tree. Just one error in a tree that you copy can set you back months. It is important to source every name that you add to a speculative tree—to make sure a connection is truly valid and supported by primary evidence, such as birth, death, and marriage certificates and census and voting records. This can be time-consuming but it is absolutely necessary.

The people who succeed in genetic genealogy are the ones who go that extra step and make absolutely certain any person added to their tree is a person who rightfully belongs there. No shortcuts, no cutting corners. If something does not make sense, do not simply slot someone into the tree; figure out first how to *make* it make sense. Put simply, if you have the wrong people in your tree, you cannot correctly identify an unknown person. The tree you build *has* to be perfect.

Here is an example. I worked on one criminal case where my team identified four brothers as potential suspects. We sent the names of the brothers to a detective on the case. The detective happened to know of one of the men on the list and told me that the man had at least one other brother who for some reason had not appeared in the research on our tree.

I went back and did more research, and what I discovered was that this potential suspect with the missing brother did not even *belong* in our tree. Someone on my team had likely conflated this man and another man with a similar name. A little more cross-checking on our end would have prevented this and kept this one man off the suspect list we sent to investigators. Had the detective not happened to know of this person and his brother, and had I not gone back and discovered the error—another one of my guardian angel moments—investigators would have surreptitiously collected DNA on someone who had *nothing at all to do with the case*. And that would have been, at the least, deeply embarrassing.

The corollary to this is that laziness leads to wasted time, something you should *always* keep in mind. Following the wrong family line in a search can literally derail you for weeks and months and maybe even years. This is an extraordinary penalty for just one wrong name, but that is just the way it works. If you forget that a wrong turn can send you plunging off a cliff, you're likely to be more tolerant of wrong turns. This is one reason why so many genealogists have a background in computer science; in fact, many of the genealogists with DNAAdoption are former IT people. They tend to be linear thinkers who are good at connecting random dots. And they understand, as should all genealogists, the often dire consequences of a wrong turn.

Yet even the best genealogists will sometimes make mistakes and become miserably derailed by a single piece of bad information. It has certainly happened to me, and it is probably one of the most frustrating experiences a genealogist can have. You are sitting there at your computer, building a tree, and things are not falling into place the way you believe they should, and instead of finding common names you are encountering seemingly unrelated people, and a cousin who should be fitting in is not fitting in, and you want to scream at the screen and just give up altogether.

But you cannot. Wasting a lot of time is always going to sting, but you cannot let it scare you away from your task. I have known people who have spent a year or even two years working on the wrong family line, but instead of quitting they persevered and ultimately built out the right tree. Nor did they see those two years as a waste of time, but rather as a necessary step to finding the right path. My advice, therefore, is to be meticulous and avoid chasing rabbits, but also keep in mind that "wasting" time on a wrong family line is just part of the deal. It is going to happen.

In one recent search I used two different websites to do a reverse lookup on an email address for my biggest match in the hope of identifying her. I found a name listed for the owner of the email address, and my team and I built out a tree for this woman. The tree should have connected to the trees we had built for other matches, but, surprisingly, it did not.

Someone was not who they thought they were.

Our next step was to obtain consensual DNA samples from two people who should have matched with this woman, one on her maternal side and one on her paternal side. When we tested them, however, they were not matches, either. Now we had to retrace our steps and do some careful digging: Where, exactly, had we gone wrong?

Eventually, we found the flaw: the reverse-lookup website had conflated the information for two different women with similar names. Our woman's first name was correct but her surname was not. That was enough to strand us at a dead end. Once we had the correct full name of the owner of the email address, we were able to properly build out her tree. Before long, we were able to connect our tree to another, and the case was solved.

Which brings me to the three most disruptive events in genealogy research: affairs, adoptions, and name changes.

If you encounter any of these in the course of your research, things can get pretty murky. The key to working your way through it is trusting the DNA to tell you *when* the disruptive event happened, and *to whom*. Many times you will have all these little wrinkles—you find a tree that should connect to another tree but for some reason does not. This is the DNA telling you to investigate further.

With the Lisa Project, I ran into just such a disruptive event with a woman who was a genetic cousin to Lisa, yet whose tree was not connecting with our other trees. I phoned this woman and asked her if she knew of an adoption in her paternal line, and she flatly declared that there was not one. I was baffled.

After the project concluded, this woman persuaded some members of her immediate family, including both maternal and paternal first cousins, to test. Only then did she discover that her paternal first cousins did not match with her. More research revealed the shocker: her father *had* been adopted, something she had known nothing about.

Once she learned about her father's adoption, she was better able to understand certain behavioral patterns in her family. The adoption, for instance, may have explained why her father never seemed to get along with his parents. The revelation fundamentally changed her understanding of her ancestry. I have seen this happen over and over in our searches—snags in a tree that suggest affairs or adoptions or name changes that are totally unknown to most relatives. Be ready to encounter these disruptive events, and take heart in the knowledge that the more time you spend building trees, the better you will become at recognizing the presence of a disruptive event.

One question I get asked a lot regarding family history research has to do with estimated admixture. Quite often researchers fail to acknowledge the importance of admixture in a search for an unidentified person or suspect. In the Boy Under the Billboard case, admixture was the *key* to quickly solving it. But even in less dramatic situations, determining ethnic background is a huge part of the process, because it can tell you if you are heading in the right direction or not.

I worked a case in which the admixture for the suspect was close to 100 percent sub-Saharan. Yet one of my (former) group members had chased after someone who was white simply because he had the same name as a relative of the match. Unfortunately, all that time and effort was essentially wasted; the admixture should have immediately ruled out that person.

Often, as a mental check, when we are working on a case we include photos of people as we add them to the tree, as well as identifying admixture tags, as a way to confirm that the person is of the correct admixture. However you choose to remind yourself, always stay aware of the admixture percentages—and know that, particularly for Europe, these percentages are most accurate at a broad continental level, rather than at the level of individual countries.

DNA analysis that reveals admixture percentages is only one of an increasing number of advanced tools available to genealogists. If you are serious about genealogy, it is important that you keep up with the constant introduction of new and improved technology that can dramatically increase the speed and accuracy of your research. Some of these tools are basic and easy to access yet often overlooked. For instance, Ancestry has a collection of some twenty-seven *billion* historical records, including immigration records; birth, marriage and death certificates; and census data, all of which I have found extremely helpful because they can track the movement of families over generations. Keep apprised of what kinds of records are available to you and learn the best ways to search through them.

Social media can also be a useful tool, and sometimes even the most useful of all. I know of many cases that were solved because of something that turned up on Facebook or Instagram. I solved one case primarily with a slew of biographical information I found on someone's Facebook page. Become conversant with different social media platforms—Twitter, Pinterest, LinkedIn, Flickr, YouTube, Tik-Tok, Foursquare—and use them when you are researching a relative, and especially when you're trying to confirm if a person belongs in a tree. A photo of someone with their mother in Paris, or wearing a Red Sox cap, or hugging a cousin at a family reunion can be the key that unlocks the solution to your case.

Finally, even though you might not use them, try to keep up with the introduction of new, more advanced DNA tools—utilities like

What Are The Odds? on the site DNA Painter, or Lucidchart—that help you associate things that are not obviously connected. Read articles about these tools and consider the ways you could use them, too.

There is one note of caution I want to sound, and it is directed at those who use genetic genealogy to solve their unknown parentage or otherwise try to find their biological families. My work on unknown-parentage cases has enhanced my understanding of how families work, including my own. When I speak with people about their expectations and hopes regarding finding new family members or biological parents, I always offer the same warning:

You might not find the white picket fence you imagine you will.

I have seen too many people go into a genealogical search with big expectations, only to watch them be shattered by what they actually find. Many times, new family reunions go wonderfully, and adoptees are embraced and accepted into the family. But the opposite can happen as well.

Sometimes your first call to a newfound relative may be your *only* call—your only chance to hear their voice. So be sure that you make that call yourself, rather than have someone else who is helping you make it. Reuniting with biological relatives can be a very delicate process, a situation most people simply are not prepared for. I urge people to make initial contact with a new relative through a letter. Start slowly, because meeting a long-lost relative in person for the first time can be intense, and may not go as planned.

All of this talk about tools and strategies might make you wonder: *Is a good genealogist more of a craftsperson or an artist?*

I think the answer is both. Yes, there is a great deal of craftsmanship involved—methodical, deliberate, blueprint-style building. But there is also an element of artistry. There are some people who are brilliant at seeing connections no one else sees. This is not really something you can teach or learn; it is more a function of someone's innate creativity. I believe all of us are creative in some way, and I believe we can all be craftspeople *and* artists as we build our trees.

There are, of course, dozens of other tips and suggestions for improving your genealogical skills: review your documents to see if there's any date or name or code you missed; tack up records chronologically so you can see a timeline; speak with relatives and collect family lore and research; connect with experts through YouTube and online sites when you need a question answered.

And there is no shortage of books and seminars and webinars that discuss these tips at length. The more research you do, the better you will be. What I have shared are just a few ideas that I find important, based on my experiences.

With that in mind, I would like to share one more concept.

It has to do with something I used to call gremlins, though now the term I prefer, and the term I have used in this book, is guardian angels.

There have been, in the course of many of my searches, occasional lucky breaks that defy explanation. We all need our guardian angels to sneak into our trees and miraculously help us every now and then. I certainly did when I was working on the Lisa Project. At one point we had a large X chromosome match with a close male match, so we knew the male match was related to Lisa through one of his maternal lines. He was a French Canadian, and one of his maternal lines included the name Godbot.

It was an unusual surname, and I could not find a lot of information on the family. One evening, when the internet in my home went out, I drove to my local family history center, where I volunteered on Friday mornings, and sat at the only vacant computer (I literally had never gone there in the evening before). Suddenly, the woman working at the computer next to me made a loud and happy exclamation.

"Yes!" she cried. "I found Lefty Godbot!"

I turned to the woman.

"I'm sorry, you found who?"

"Lefty Godbot, one of my relatives," she answered. "I have been trying to find a picture of him forever!"

I pointed to my computer screen, where she saw the names in the branch of the tree I was researching: Godbots. Many, many Godbots.

"Oh, wow, those are all my cousins!" the woman said. "If you need help with researching this line, there is a whole special Godbot family website you can go to. Everyone is in there with all the most recent births, deaths, and marriages. I'll give you the password."

I sat there thinking, *This didn't just happen, did it?*

Seriously, what were the odds of the only vacant computer being right next to a woman directly related to a French Canadian family I was researching?

That was my guardian angel at work.

Some of you may be saying, *How is it that someone with a background in science believes in something like guardian angels?*

It is a good question. Thinking rationally, I would have to say these occurrences were nothing more than coincidences. But if I turned off my rational mind for a moment, I would say these kinds of things have happened to me way too often to be just coincidences. I have found myself in just the right place at just the right time quite often in my life, and I have made key breakthroughs in genealogical searches thanks to inexplicable bursts of really good fortune. And, over time, I have become more comfortable referring to this timely luck as my guardian angel.

As Albert Einstein purportedly once said, "Coincidence is God's way of remaining anonymous."

24

From the day I first heard from Paul Holes to the day Joseph DeAngelo accepted a plea deal, three years and three months had passed. In that time, both the team seeking to identify him and the team trying to imprison him had been relentless in pushing through countless obstacles to deliver a notorious serial killer to justice.

But even with all that had been accomplished, there remained one more task—one final obligation for those who vowed not to rest until the monster was safely caged away.

The formal sentencing of the Golden State Killer.

Once again, Sacramento district attorney Anne Marie Schubert invited the members of Team Justice, including me, to attend the sentencing. The night before, Anne Marie hosted a pizza party at her home for members of her staff and close colleagues who had worked with her on the prosecution of the Golden State Killer case. The mood was far from celebratory; it was as if we all needed to hear the judge sentence DeAngelo to life in prison, as was his due, before we could finally exhale. That night some folks took bets on whether DeAngelo, who at his plea hearing continued his catatonic playacting, would actually accept the plea deal his lawyers had negotiated. Not everyone was convinced that he would.

The sentencing, inevitably, was quite unusual. Three full days were set aside for those DeAngelo had victimized—they referred to themselves as survivors—to stand up and address DeAngelo directly, at long last airing the grievances they had been unable to let go of for so long. In the same makeshift courtroom in the grand ballroom at Sacramento State University, where DeAngelo had pled guilty or admitted guilt for most of his crimes, he would now face the first phase of the consequences: the wrath of those whose lives he had ruined. As an ironic aside, DeAngelo had attended Sacramento State University as a young man; he graduated in 1972 with a bachelor's degree in criminal justice.

On the first day of the hearing, dozens of survivors and supporters filled the seats in the ballroom, again spaced six feet apart, and waited their turn to speak. Many wore shirts that made statements of their own: one woman spelled out ROT IN HELL in silver sequins on her top.

The testimony began. A woman named Karen Veilleux read a statement on behalf of her sister, Phyllis Henneman, whom the Golden State Killer had attacked in 1976. "I was a normal woman of twenty-two—happy and carefree," the statement declared. "The devil incarnate broke into my home, blindfolded me, tied me up, threatened my life with a knife, and raped me." But, Phyllis continued through her sister Karen, "the roles have now reversed. His victims and their families are now free. And his freedom of forty-plus years is now revoked. . . . I am not what happened to me. I am what I choose to become."

Pete Schultze, the son of a survivor named Wini Schultze, stood up and faced the man who had assaulted his mother. The Golden State Killer "entered our home in Carmichael, California, [when] I was eleven years old," Schultze said, glaring at DeAngelo. "My sister was five and we were sleeping peacefully with our mother. Do you remember me? You woke us up, tied me to the bedpost until my hands turned blue, locked my sister in her room, and performed horrific acts against my mother while she was bound and blindfolded. We have lived with this for forty-four years as a family, and we are here to say my mother is not Jane Doe number twenty-two. We are not just number thirty-seven uncharged offense. We are the family of Wini Schultze, and we have all survived because of her bravery and resolve to do whatever she had to do to save herself and her family."

Kris Pedretti was just a teenager in 1976 when the Golden State Killer changed her life forever. "I was a normal fifteen-year-old kid," she told DeAngelo. "I loved going to school, having sleepovers, and going to church. It was one week away from Christmas. My world was small, predictable, and safe. But by the time that night came to an end, my world changed forever. My safety was shattered as a masked man, DeAngelo, wielding a knife, told me he would kill me if I didn't do what he demanded. He raped me repeatedly, moving me in and out of the house after each time. He made himself comfortable in my home and he stole my family's personal belongings as I lay helpless and sat tied, gagged, blindfolded, and naked in the cold December night. I sang 'Jesus Loves Me' in my head as I waited to die."

Looking hard at her attacker, Pedretti said, "Understand, DeAngelo—there is not a prayer strong enough to save you."

Carol Daly, a former detective who devoted decades to identifying the East Area Rapist, read an impact statement for Kathy Rogers, who survived a 1977 rape by the Golden State Killer.

"I have never thought of myself as a victim, although it is part of my history. . . . I feel my best revenge is to live my life. The monster has been unmasked and is no longer of any consequence. I am leaving him behind. The nightmare has ended. He is the one forever alone in the dark."

On and on it went. Survivor after survivor, mothers and fathers, sons and daughters, friends and supporters—a small army bound by tragedy but united in strength. For three full days, the survivors spoke. Impassively, DeAngelo sat in his familiar wheelchair, his face hidden behind a white Covid mask, and heard the dozens of anguished statements. Whether or not he truly listened to them, no one can know.

The fourth and final day of the hearing, August 21, 2020, was for the sentencing.

On this day, DeAngelo's place on the makeshift stage was aligned not to face the chairs on the floor but rather to face the judge, Michael Bowman, the man who would announce his fate. The eight

California district attorneys were there, and so were DeAngelo's three public defenders. I took my numbered seat on the floor of the vast ballroom.

The air was heavy with tension, as it had been at his plea hearing. One by one the district attorneys rose to restate the charges and speak their final words to the defendant. The Tulare County DA, Tim Ward, noted the technology used to capture the killer and said, "The space for evil like this to operate grows smaller and smaller." Orange County DA Todd Spitzer addressed the horrible injustice of DeAngelo being free for forty years to "be on his boat" and "blow out birthday candles with his family," while his victims' lives had been destroyed. And Anne Marie Schubert, the lead district attorney and final one to speak, assured the survivors that the man who had haunted them for so long would never again be free.

"Paint your children's and your grandchildren's rooms again with hearts and rainbows," she said. "Water-ski again."

And to DeAngelo: "There is honestly little left to say. Your name will fade from the headlines."

Judge Michael Bowman gave the defense a chance to speak. The defense attorneys read brief statements from DeAngelo's family members, including his sister and a niece. "Joe faced many things and I'm sure he couldn't cope with it all," his sister said. "It will never justify what happened." His niece told the court, "There is someone else inside him who I do not know. I'm very sorry to the victims. I can't imagine what they went through."

Then Judge Bowman turned his chair to face DeAngelo and gave him his opportunity to make a statement.

Before that day, the only words the public had heard him utter were "Yes," "I have a lawyer," "Guilty," and "I admit." These words were spoken in whispers. They betrayed nothing of the suspected killer, and satisfied no one who sought some kind of explanation. In fact, in the days after his 2018 arrest, in a police interrogation room vacated by his interviewers but still observed by a camera, the suspect *had* spoken, and *had* addressed his crimes, to himself, and cryptically, but loud enough that his words were heard:

> I did all that. I didn't have the strength to push him out. He made me. He went with me. It was like in my head, I mean, he's a part of me. I didn't want to do those things. I pushed Jerry out and had a happy life. I did all those things. I destroyed all their lives. So now I've got to pay the price.

Here he was blaming an outside force for his savagery: an entity he named Jerry. How much of his monologue reflected reality and how much was just theater was unknowable.

But now, in court, he finally had his chance to state his case.

And then the Golden State Killer rose from his wheelchair—not haltingly or with difficulty, but smoothly and with ease. He pulled off his Covid mask, baring his face, and took a significant pause. Then, at last, he spoke:

"I've listened to all of your statements. Each one of 'em. And I'm truly sorry to everyone I've hurt. Thank you, your honor."

His voice was sturdy, clear, and loud. His stance was straight and balanced. All traces of the feeble old man he had pretended to be were gone. The lie, always assumed, was laid bare.

As for the words he chose to speak, they seemed hollow and pointless—not just to me but, I believe, to every last person in that ballroom. To hear him say "I'm truly sorry" was at once absurd and enraging. And if you knew precisely what he had done—in excruciating detail as most of us did—you could not help but be insulted by such a trifling "apology." I watched DeAngelo throughout the long hearing and I never once saw him abandon his poker face. I never once saw the slightest hint of remorse, or any human emotion, cross his face. He was there, but he was also not there. He suggested not a presence but an absence, as if he were merely a stand-in for the true creature. To see him suddenly rise into the posture of a real human being and speak in a normal manner was utterly surreal.

Things happened quickly once DeAngelo sat back down in his

wheelchair. Judge Bowman clarified for the court that while DeAngelo was given a plea bargain that precluded capital punishment, this did not mean, by any stretch, that he did not *deserve* the death penalty. He also thanked the survivors and said to DeAngelo, "As I've listened to the victims I cannot help but wonder what you are thinking. Are you capable of comprehending the pain and anguish you've caused?"

Then came the formal reading of the sentence. In the end, DeAngelo was given eleven life terms to be served consecutively, plus fifteen concurrent life terms and an additional eight years. Judge Bowman also made clear that DeAngelo had surrendered any right to appeal.

"This is the absolute maximum sentence the court can impose under law," Bowman concluded. "The survivors spoke clearly: the defendant deserves no mercy."

With these words the room erupted in applause: a great collective clamor driven by countless different emotions. A court officer wheeled DeAngelo down the stage ramp and out of sight, a symbolic descent into eternal nothingness. Just like that, it was over. It was *all* over. Except for some minor technical matters that still needed to be resolved, the case of the Golden State Killer was officially closed.

Unofficially, though, it was not closed, and it never would be.

After the sentencing, some survivors expressed the rage they felt hearing DeAngelo speak, while others wondered what prison he would be sent to. It was not enough for them to know the killer would be locked away; they needed to know he would be confined in a truly horrible place, to face endless isolation or the taunts of other inmates, or some other fate befitting his heinous deeds.

It was a long, draining, emotional day. That night, Anne Marie Schubert hosted another event for all the prosecutors and their teams, this one in a mansion by the Sacramento River. The mood at this event was properly celebratory. People gave speeches praising one another, and Anne Marie was commended for doing the impossible: getting eight separate California district attorneys to agree to one plea deal (DAs do not normally play well with one another, I was told). The crushing weight of the case—perhaps the most extensive and costly investigation into perhaps the most destructive serial killer of all time—was lifted, or at least shrugged off for the night. It was as if we all finally felt we were on the other side of an immense obstacle—one that had seemed it might be impossible to overcome.

The next day, I drove three hours south to my home. That evening, I was back working on another cold case. I cannot say I felt fulfilled or even satisfied. But I *was* relieved it was finally all over. Headlines about the Golden State Killer eventually did disappear from front pages, as Anne Marie Schubert had predicted. But the killer did not vanish from newspapers and magazines altogether. Nearly every new story about a cold case cracked by genetic genealogy mentioned the Golden State Killer and the impact of his arrest on law enforcement. His case represented a dividing line between the past and the future, between what came before and what will happen next.

Exactly what this new thing was, no one knew for sure. Was it good? Was it bad? Would it turn us into a dystopian society? Who could say for sure?

On January 26, 2021, the California Department of Corrections and Rehabilitation transferred Joseph DeAngelo from North Kern State Prison, a temporary way station for newer inmates, to the California State Prison in Corcoran, an all-male, maximum-security compound south of Fresno—and just thirty miles or so from where the Golden State Killer's crime spree first began nearly a half century earlier. The California State Prison system once housed Sirhan Sirhan; the Night Stalker, Richard Ramirez; the Dating Game Killer, Rodney Alcala; and Charles Manson; it is currently home to several other high-profile serial killers. As for DeAngelo, he was placed in the Protective Housing Unit, away from the prison's general population.

He was called a monster, a sociopath, the epitome of evil. He poisoned lives and filled minds with fear. Then he was gone, and with him went some of the fear.

Some of it, but not all of it.

25

The Lisa Jensen case in 2015 was the opening of what I earlier described as "a brief but extraordinary window of opportunity"—the moment when crimes long considered unsolvable suddenly became solvable. Our access to the consumer DNA database GEDmatch gave law enforcement a powerful new tool that only grew more potent as people continued signing up with the sites and growing the databases, and as new utilities were created, expanding what was possible for genealogists to accomplish. Late in 2018 FamilyTreeDNA opened its database to the uploading of forensic files, further expanding the field of people available for matching in forensic cases.

When the arrest of the Golden State Killer was made public in 2018, the law enforcement community truly awakened to this stunning new weapon, and the number of cold cases cracked by investigative genetic genealogy began to climb—no longer just a few cases here and there, but now *dozens* of cases, and eventually hundreds of them, all across the country.

In this way, 2018 marked the beginning of the widespread use of investigative genetic genealogy in cold cases and the exponential increase in how many of them were solved.

At the same time, this was also when the public backlash against the use of IGG to solve crimes began. In May 2019, GEDmatch changed its terms of service to automatically opt all users *out* of helping law enforcement upon signing up. The moment that new policy went into effect, the pool of DNA profiles available to law enforcement through GEDmatch went from well over a million to zero. Not much later, MyHeritage joined AncestryDNA and 23andMe in prohibiting law enforcement from using the site. It was as if the fledgling era of opportunity that began in 2015 was just as suddenly beginning to end.

Still, it has not been all bad news. GEDmatch users were given the option to consent to helping law enforcement, and several hundred thousand did, and that number continues to grow. So while the pool of people available to investigative genetic genealogists initially and quickly plummeted beginning in 2019, the pool has grown ever since, thanks to an influx of new users and better awareness of what law enforcement actually does when it employs IGG.

In a way, that golden window of opportunity has opened and closed and opened and closed since 2015, never returning to the numbers we had at first but neither ever shutting so much that IGG ceased to be a powerful and dynamic tool.

That fluctuation will likely continue over the next few years as the field of IGG becomes better understood and, at the same time, better regulated.

Yet while IGG has so far solved many hundreds of previously unsolvable cold cases, in truth the number has been limited by not having access to all the direct-to-consumer databases out there. If, for example, law enforcement could use the two largest existing databases, AncestryDNA and 23andMe, a truly staggering number of cold cases could likely be solved.

I believe the community actually needs to push for *more* access from these companies, until they give their subscribers the option to help law enforcement and permit forensic files to be uploaded to their sites.

Nevertheless, I am aware there are many ways new DNA technology can be misapplied. "Nefarious actors are always going to use what they can for their own benefit," says Richard Weiss of DNAAdoption. "What if your ID card evolves to have a genetic component? Can that genetic information be stolen? Or let's say someone goes through your genetic history and discovers you have a secret child. Can they use that to blackmail you?"

In June 2021, three years after the arrest of Joseph DeAngelo, *Slate* magazine ran an article with a provocative headline:

YOUR CONSUMER DNA TEST COULD GET YOUR DISTANT COUSIN CONVICTED OF A CRIME

The article referenced the Golden State Killer in its first sentence before questioning the ethics of the technique that finally caught him. The case "marked a seismic shift in how investigators use DNA in cold cases," wrote the author. "And yet, lurking in the background were concerns over the lack of regulation regarding police use of genetic genealogy. When cops want to peek inside your family tree, should anything stop them?"

There were many other articles with similar headlines and tones—all of them prompted by the Golden State Killer case. Suddenly it was not the criminals who were "lurking" in the shadows, it was law enforcement officers secretly poking through people's DNA data. This backlash to investigative genetic genealogy created a sense of alarm among the general public. A 2018 *Science* magazine article reported that someone using a DNA database of only 1.3 million people could potentially identify fully *60 percent* of all white Americans, even if those people had not submitted DNA samples to the database.

Three years later, that estimate is up to *90 percent*.

The implication: modern DNA analysis is stripping us of our essential right to privacy. The capture of the Golden State Killer created an ethical quandary that the world is still wrestling with today: Is it okay for law enforcement to use DNA databases to catch criminals? And if so, under what conditions and terms?

Out of necessity, I have given this ethical dilemma quite a bit of thought over the past several years. I fully understand that the work I am doing has implications beyond the field of law enforcement, and I appreciate the need to have a debate about what investigative genetic genealogy will look like in the future.

There are certainly arguments to be made on both sides. Even my friend Professor Ed Green, who has helped me on several criminal cases, has concerns about what the future holds. "The deep ethical issue for me is that, when I decide to upload my DNA data to a genealogy site, I am instantly disempowering any of my relatives who do not want their information on a public site," Ed says. "I have made the decision for them, and now the thing which is most personal to them, their DNA information, is on an open site. There are some really deep questions here."

But as the reporter Josh Zumbrun pointed out in a recent *Wall Street Journal* article, it is probably already too late for anyone "to protect their genetic privacy," as he put it—even those who have not joined any genealogy site. The reason: people who are related share so much DNA that a common ancestor to them will invariably reveal both persons' identities, even if one of them has never taken a DNA test.

In other words, the horse is already out of the barn.

⊶⊷

One argument in favor of IGG is that law enforcement should be able to go anywhere the public goes. This argument, in particular, makes sense to me.

A grocery store is a private enterprise, but just as ordinary citizens are allowed to enter the store, so are law enforcement officials. And if the public is entitled to use a DNA database in the hopes of identifying someone, why should law enforcement not be entitled to do the same?

A counterargument is that investigative genetic genealogy has the potential to be more intrusive in more people's lives, and to require more DNA tests at far greater expense, than a traditional law enforcement investigation. This is not true. In an honors thesis written by a University of Richmond scholar named Hannah Lee titled "The Commercialization of Crime Solving: Ethical Implications of Forensic Genetic Genealogy," Lee notes that "one of the benefits of IGG is that, especially in high-profile cases where the perpetrator is unknown to the victim, it potentially can *reduce* the overall number of such tests that are conducted." In my experience, that's proved true.

Here is a stark example of how it plays out on a case level. This information is part of a presentation the now retired FBI attorney Steve Kramer gives about the Golden State Killer case, and he has allowed me to use it here. Kramer looked at the scope of the traditional investigation into the Golden State Killer prior to the use of investigative genetic genealogy and compared it to what we accomplished with IGG.

"The cost in time, personnel, and money for trying to identify the Golden State Killer prior to the use of IGG was significant," Steve says. "Forty-three years, 15 agencies involved and 650 detectives/agents; 200,000 man hours; $10 million spent; 300 people swabbed for DNA; 5,000 people put under surveillance; 0 suspects."

By contrast, here are the numbers for our IGG investigation: "63 days; 6 people involved; $217 spent; 1 suspect."

❦

Others worry about what is known as "scope creep"—the use of a technique slowly creeping beyond its intended limits and into all facets of our lives. This, the argument goes, could potentially lay waste to our privacy, or even lead to DNA surveillance techniques currently used only in high-profile crimes being applied to all crimes and all suspects all the time.

But there is one obvious and formidable obstacle to scope creep: the fact that investigative genetic genealogy is *really hard*.

What's more, it would be a violation of both FamilyTreeDNA's and GEDmatch's terms of service to upload forensic files for any crime other than a violent crime (as defined in their terms of service).

The successful hunt for the Golden State Killer may have seemed, at the length of just sixty-three days, like a miraculously quick and easy new way of catching criminals. But as I hope I have conveyed, those sixty-three days involved many hundreds of hours of work by the six members of Team Justice. It simply is not conceivable that law enforcement would go to all that trouble and expense to identify, for example, a shoplifter. There are many ghastly crimes that merit such a rich deployment of resources, and as time goes on and technology improves, it is possible that list of approved crimes will grow. But absent automation of tasks such as tree building that are what we call major time sinks (they take forever), IGG will remain an especially complicated and time-consuming method of criminal investigation, just as laboratory DNA testing of forensic samples likely will continue to be expensive (direct-to-consumer testing can be done by robots because the samples are uniform). There is a reason IGG has been used to solve only truly heinous crimes so far: it is a phenomenal new tool, but it is not something you want to wheel out when someone jaywalks.

This is not to say that I am unconcerned about ways IGG can potentially be abused. I *am* concerned. And I do believe there is a need for some kind of code of ethics governing its future use. I may disagree with the most vocal IGG critics out there, but I respect them and their views.

The truth is that, from the very beginning, I have never had any doubt that what I was doing was the right thing to do. The government has always had to perform a balancing act between privacy and safety. A debate just like this one happened after September 11, and other similar debates will happen in the future over other ethical quandaries. That, in fact, is the very essence of democracy: debating the common good. I do know that law enforcement will fight to continue using IGG because of how spectacularly effective it has been. As I am writing this, I believe that more than a thousand cold cases have been solved by authorities working with investigative genetic genealogists—cases that were otherwise likely unsolvable. (Most of these are unidentified-remains cases.)

Personally, I know that my group and I have assisted in solving more than sixty cases.

As a former patent attorney, I also know well that you have to theorize and speculate about the future potential uses of any new technology—that, basically, was my job. But you also have to consider the value this new technology will add to society. In imagining scenarios of rogue investigators and genealogists trampling over our constitutional rights, it is important to not overlook the very real and immediate good that IGG makes possible. If we allow emotions to summon our very worst fears about IGG, then we should also consider the emotional costs of the crimes we are trying to solve.

I have a current case—not a cold case—involving a five-year-old girl.

She was attacked and raped in her bedroom by an invader who came in through her bedroom window and continued his attack even when the child's mother came rushing in. Just describing this crime is sickening, but what makes it worse is knowing that the attacker escaped capture. He left through the window before anyone could stop him, then jumped on his skateboard and took off. And he is still out there, on the loose. It is highly likely he will commit another horrendous and unthinkable assault sometime soon and ruin another little girl's life, if he has not already.

I try to keep my emotions at bay when I apply investigative genetic genealogy to a criminal case, but that is sometimes difficult. Nor would I want to completely block out the human face of the crimes I am trying to solve. I do agree that IGG needs to be debated and ultimately regulated in a smart and practical way, without stripping it of its usefulness in finding criminals. But no matter what happens, I will always look at a crime like the one involving the five-year-old girl and think, *I want to stop that. I want to get that monster off the streets before he hurts another little girl.*

Nothing will ever change that.

26

In November 2021, I was invited to be a panelist at Comic-Con International in San Diego. The panel was called "Spies, Secrets, and Espionage: Technology and Tactics for Deception and Detection," and it featured three speakers. The former chief of disguise in the CIA's Office of Technical Service, Jonna Mendez, spoke about methods of disguise such as elaborate face masks that can be used to evade surveillance. The well-known American magician Jamy Ian Swiss discussed deception and misdirection tactics that can befuddle an enemy, such as the World War II tactic of creating structures that look like tanks in order to give the appearance of having many more of them than were actually deployed.

I handled the detection part.

After the others had finished their presentations, I shared my thoughts about the power of investigative genetic genealogy.

"What we can do with DNA keeps getting more sophisticated," I told the crowd, before referencing a 2020 FBI case I helped to solve based on DNA extracted from a single rootless male pubic hair. And in 2021 a case was solved with an amount of DNA equivalent to that found in just fifteen cells. Then I explained why it did not much matter what criminals did to disguise themselves or deceive their pursuers, given the access I had to an extraordinary amount of evidence that was suddenly more likely to implicate someone than ever before.

"Your body is made up of thirty trillion cells and you shed around five hundred million cells per day," I said. "On your scalp you have about two hundred fifty thousand hairs and shed some fifty to one hundred of them every single day."

In other words, unless a criminal wears an impenetrable hazmat suit 24/7, they will shed evidence I can use to identify them.

And, given enough time, I *will* find them.

Or, as I would tell them, *I know who you are.*

Investigative genetic genealogy is not just a hobby for me. It may have started out that way, but that has not been true for several years now. I generally work on several cases at once, and my usual work hours are early morning to late at night. After seven years of often pro bono work, I now earn a fee for most cases I handle. It's not an exorbitant fee, and I cap my fees for law enforcement. Most important, I continue working on a case until it is solved, either by me or by someone else, and I have never simply stopped working on any criminal case. The FBI estimates there are currently some 250,000 unsolved murders in the United States. I expect the number of cases I handle will never go down, only up.

The cases I work on come to my attention in a variety of ways, usually either by word of mouth or a referral. I am the director of investigative genetic genealogy at Gene by Gene (GXG), the Texas-based parent company of FamilyTreeDNA, and some cases come to me through contracts that GXG has with various law enforcement entities. As an example, GXG has contracted with the Cuyahoga County Prosecutor's Office to work on a number of unsolved sexual assault cases, all of which have been cold for between seven and twenty years.

One by one, my team and I are taking them on.

The Cuyahoga County sexual assault cases involve victims who are living—and still suffering the trauma of their attacks. Emotionally this is different from working on cases with deceased victims. Even though they, too, are cold cases, the Cuyahoga crimes seem more urgent, given that the suspect and/or the victim are still alive. These cases have affected me in a way no others have.

Sexual assault is a massive problem around the world. In the United States, by one estimate, someone is sexually assaulted every seventy-three seconds. Yet according to the Rape, Abuse and Incest National Network (RAINN), the nation's largest anti-sexual-violence organization, only 310 out of every 1,000 sexual assaults in the United States are reported to police. The primary reasons victims do not report their assaults are because they either fear a further, retaliatory attack or they do not believe the police will do anything to help them.

There is a reason why they might believe this: the majority of reported sexual assaults are never solved, mostly due to a ghastly backlog of unexamined DNA rape kits. It is hard to say how many rape kits are languishing in crime labs or storage facilities, but the best guesses put that number in the hundreds of thousands. Despite rapists leaving behind evidence as crucial as their DNA, these cases are simply not being solved or even, or up until recently, addressed at all.

The consequences of this inaction are horrifying. "Each day that passes without the identity of these rapists being known allows them to continue to claim victims . . . and they will," Debbie Smith, a sexual assault survivor and the chief executive officer of Hope Exists After Rape Trauma (H-E-A-R-T), testified before Congress. "Statistics prove that the average rapist claims *eight to twelve victims* before he is caught. How many of [these rapes] could have been prevented?"

The good news is that, over the past few years, things have begun to change. Several U.S. cities have committed to working through their backlogs of untested rape kits. (Sadly, many jurisdictions across the country threw out untested rape kits after the statute of limitations had run on the crimes.) In Ohio, Cuyahoga County used grant money to work through their rape-kit backlog, which has led to thousands of kits being examined and hundreds of serial rapists being caught. One of those rapists alone was linked to seventeen victims.

This push to work through the backlogs coincides with advances in DNA analysis that have made identifying rape suspects easier. In one recent case, a forty-four-year-old man voluntarily submitted a sample of his DNA to a genealogy site. When police reopened a rape cold case and uploaded the rapist's DNA profile to GEDmatch and FamilyTreeDNA, the man's DNA matched the DNA left at the crime scene back in 2007. Further analysis estimated that there was a one in 700 billion chance of the man not being the rapist, and the case was quickly solved. In essence, the rapist unwittingly turned himself in.

More than ever before, DNA-analysis technology offers investigators an incredibly powerful tool that can help restore the citizenry's faith in the ability of police to catch rapists. Whenever I start work on a new case, I always have the same thought: *I want to solve this case. I want to solve all the cases. Give me enough time, and I will solve them all.*

Ultimately, investigative genetic genealogy is not about the thrill of discovery, or algorithms or fancy analytics, or chromosomes or mutations or haplogroups, or even capturing bad guys.

It is about helping people.

People like Lisa Jensen. After learning that she had living relatives, she met her biological grandfather, the last surviving member of her immediate birth family, as well as some of her cousins. She has remained in touch with all of them.

Understandably, Lisa wishes to live her life away from the public's glare. "As a victim in this [incredible] story, I would like to ask that the media respects my privacy," she said in a statement read at a 2017 press conference announcing the discovery of her identity. "Please turn your focus toward the unidentified victims, and other potentially unknown victims in this case, and hopefully their families will also be offered some closure as this investigation continues."

Not long after I identified Lisa's birth mother and Deputy Headley found her given name, I spoke with Lisa on the phone. She told me she had recently been married, and I congratulated her. I knew she had been living with a loving partner and together they had three wonderful children, but Lisa explained that the uncertainty of her identity had made her hesitant to make it official. "When I didn't know who I was, I just didn't want to get married," she explained. "But as soon as I found out who I was, I did it."

It was a quiet and private and beautiful ceremony.

Beneath all the science, there are people. Flesh and blood, vulnerable, striving for answers, hanging on results. Ours is a deeply human business. DNA, after all, is the stuff we are made of, the very stuff of life.

People are why I do what I do.

27

In the final chapter of my father's memoir, *Kiwi Spitfire Ace,* he wrote about the days after Allied Forces liberated the Marlag und Milag Nord, a German prisoner of war complex nineteen miles northeast of Bremen, in April 1945. My father—or J.D., as he was known to his family nearly all his life—was among the freed prisoners and was transported to Brighton, on England's southern coast, where all the New Zealand POWs were housed in an old hotel. Intent on making up for his traumatic two years as a POW, he decided to visit a London pub he knew well from before his imprisonment. It did not go as he expected.

"It was filled with strangers," he wrote. "The world, I discovered, had not stood still while I was away. All my friends from those days were either somewhere in Europe or no longer with us." When he tried a second favorite old haunt, the result was the same: "Not a familiar face to be seen." And when he gave up and joined other former POWs at a club filled with soldiers, he was shocked by the absence of joy or frivolity.

"They were having the greatest difficulty in adjusting to being the way they were before they became prisoners," my father reflected. "The black mood did wear off," but the normality they all craved, he added, would never return. Instead, he wrote, "we gained enough social camouflage so that we at least talked and behaved like everyone else."

It was only once my father returned to New Zealand, and to the isolated *bach,* or beach house, my grandfather built in the beautiful oceanside village of Piha on the coast west of Auckland, that he was finally able to exhale.

"Hardly able to speak with the joy of the moment, I leaned my head against the cool glass and knew with certainty I was home."

When I read, and reread, those passages, I reflected on what it means to be home.

As an immigrant to the United States who arrived in the country at age twenty, I have always wrestled with a feeling that no matter where I am, be it the United States or New Zealand, I am never truly at home. This feeling is similar to what my father described: the sense that familiar places are no longer familiar or even welcoming. New Zealand is my homeland; it is the place where I grew up. But over the years, when I have returned, I have felt a little like my father walking into that London pub—like I did not quite belong. I have spent most of my life, more than fifty years now, in the United States, and I no longer have a feel for contemporary culture in New Zealand. Sometimes I have thought about moving back, but I do not really think I would fit in there anymore.

There are places I do feel comfortable. I have a real fondness for the state of Texas and its citizens. I lived in Texas for almost ten years, first in Galveston, then in Austin for law school, and finally in Dallas, where I had my first job as an attorney. In all my travels, I have found the people of Texas to be perhaps the warmest people in the country. I remember when I first moved from Buffalo, New York, to Galveston right after splitting from my husband. I had left with virtually nothing to my name: no furniture, no kitchen utensils, no bed. The few items I had gathered would take a couple of weeks to arrive in Texas. Prior to my first day of work at the University of Texas Medical Branch, word somehow had filtered out that I was in a difficult spot.

To my great surprise, on my first day at work, when I opened the door to my new office I was greeted by my new colleagues—people I had never met—who together presented me with a collection of home goods: pots, pans, plates, even an army cot to sleep on. I was in tears.

Truly kind and decent people will *always* make you feel at home.

As for Northern California, where I have lived for several decades, I still cannot say it feels like home to me. Part of the reason has to do with me being very much an introvert. I have an adventurous spirit, and I might still hop on a plane at the last minute without a lot of planning. But I am not the most social person, and I suppose I have only become less social, especially since I began devoting my days (and nights) to forensic genealogy. So I think that contributes to my feeling of not quite belonging. And then, of course, there is the isolation due to the pandemic.

Yet there *are* two places where I have experienced an uncanny feeling of being home.

In 2012, I planned a trip to Nova Scotia, one of the beautiful Canadian Maritime Provinces near the coast of Maine. Nova Scotia—Latin for New Scotland—is where, in the early nineteenth century, the Scottish clergyman Norman MacLeod led eight hundred followers out of the Scottish Highlands to a new home in Pictou Harbour, and then to St. Ann's. My great-great-great-grandparents were among those followers, before boarding one of six ships that eventually took them and their descendants, and the Reverend MacLeod, to New Zealand three decades later.

In Nova Scotia I took a three-week full immersion course in Scottish Gaelic at the Gaelic College in St. Ann's, where my ancestors had settled. I wanted to know what it would feel like to step on the very land where my ancestors spent decades of their lives. Thanks to a tip from a local bookseller, I connected with a woman called Bonnie McLeod, who had written a book about the original settlers of St. Ann's and their descendants. I had purchased a copy of her book and studied the map in the front of the book, trying to figure out where my ancestors' property was located.

Bonnie invited me to dinner at her house, and her husband drove to pick me up. As we pulled into their driveway, I asked if he knew which property my great-great-great-grandparents had built their home on.

"You're on it," the husband said.

It turned out that Bonnie's ancestors had purchased the property from one of my ancestors. She and her brother inherited the property and still owned all two hundred acres that my paternal grandmother's MacLeod ancestors received in a land grant nearly two centuries earlier. Bonnie and her husband invited me to spend the night at their new home on the property, and as I gazed out a window at the very view my ancestors had gazed at before me, I got goosebumps. I felt something like a physical pull, grounding me to the land.

The other magical place for me is Scotland.

Years ago I visited the lovely and historic small village of Nethy Bridge in the county of Inverness, in the northernmost part of Scotland. The village, most commonly referred to simply as Nethy, is the place my maternal grandfather, William Edward Grant, and generations of Grants before him were born. It is also where the land is soaked with the blood of those who perished in the Battle of Culloden, the final brutal quashing of the Jacobite army in 1745. I have ancestors who fought and died on both sides of the conflict. I visited Drumossie Moor, a windswept, boggy upland stretch just southeast of Inverness (and the actual site of the Battle of Culloden), and I walked around and experienced its sad, desolate nature, and I tried to imagine all the youthful Scotsmen for whom the moor became a dying ground.

I arrived in Nethy Bridge armed with information from a Scottish census record that showed precisely where my grandfather had been born and lived. The records even indicated that the house had three windows. I also carried with me a small, dark, black-and-white photo of the wee stone house that my ancestors had christened Rymore.

My Scottish guide and I found the house at the end of a gently sloped path. An inscribed wooden plank nailed to the mailbox posts announced, MAINS OF RYMORE. We spoke with some neighbors who told us the present owners (not related to my family) were away on vacation, so I was unable to go inside the home. But I did take the liberty of walking around the grounds and marveling at how small the house was, and yet how perfectly warm and suggestive of home.

Once again, I felt a connection to the land beneath my feet, to the grass and trees and ancient stones. It was a good feeling.

The census records also showed my grandfather's mother had lived in a house named Chapleton just down the road from Rymore in Tulloch. A local farmer pointed us in the right direction and I saw a Chapleton sign affixed to a wooden fence. Behind the fence, yet another wonderfully small but magnificent house, as well as a horseshoe-shaped, red-roofed barn.

The current owners, who were not part of our family, were extremely gracious, and when I explained who I was and why I was there, the wife said, "Oh, there's something you should see inside." To my astonishment, inside the main room I saw an imposing stone mantel that had something carved in its face: A.G. 1878.

The initials and date, I presumed, had been carved by my grandfather's brother, and my great-uncle, Allan Grant—a one-time detective inspector in the London Metropolitan Police, and the forebearer I eventually followed into identifying criminals.

I touched his initials with my fingers, and it felt like touching my history.

"Oh, and there's something else you need to see," the wife suddenly said. "The doors."

She marched us out to the red-roofed barn. It had rained before our visit, apparently heavily, and the ground was quite muddy. I was wearing a pair of slip-on flats, rather than any kind of sturdy boots, and the poor shoes were ruined. But it was worth it. In the barn, we were shown two knotty, wide-planked wooden doors that had once been part of the main house. Both doors were covered with scribblings, made decades before.

I looked closely and saw the scribbled names and dates.

James Cameron, 1941. John Cameron, 1915. Mary Cameron, 1915. And dozens more.

I knew that my grandfather's sister, Jane Edward Grant, had lived at Chapleton before her marriage to Charles Cameron. She died of the flu in 1906. After that, it appeared from the names on the doors, the Cameron family had, at some point, moved into the home.

What an astonishing discovery. It was as if the two old wooden doors were actual records of my family history, as real as a census record but far more evocative. Those two doors were treasures—proof that my ancestors had trod this ground and lived within these walls and dined and danced and struggled in this wonderful place tucked away in the Scottish Highlands.

A place that was my home.

Perhaps we are only ever truly home when we stand on the land on which our ancestors roamed. As a genealogist, I had spent hours tracing my family roots all the way back to these ancestral lands, to the ancient hills and mountains and moors and deserts from which we all have sprung. Why is it that so many of us are drawn to these places, even if, for most of our lives, we were not even aware of our connection to them? What binds us to these lands after centuries of our families being someplace else?

I do not have the answers. Throughout history, men and women have written epic poems and stories and songs about what it means to be home, and about the pull of our homelands. I have written no such poems or songs. But I do feel the pull. In the end, perhaps that is all genetic genealogy is—a tool that helps us achieve what we desire, what we yearn for, at the most primal level:

To belong.

ACKNOWLEDGMENTS

Thank you to my son, Christopher Venter, for being a great kid who grew into an incredible human being. It cannot have been easy having a mother who kept reinventing herself: breast cancer researcher; medical school assistant professor; full-time law student with part-time jobs; patent attorney with frequent travel obligations. I am grateful for having such a wonderful son who made it possible for me to do all of this while also being his mother.

Thanks to my late parents for not clipping my wings when, at seventeen, I decided to leave the nest and fly ever farther away, first to Wellington, then to Sydney, and finally to California, never to permanently return.

Special thanks to Deputy Peter Headley of the San Bernardino Sheriff's Department Crimes Against Children Detail, with whom I worked on the Lisa Jensen and other cases, for referring Stephen Kramer of the Los Angeles field office of the FBI (now retired) to me. This referral led to my working with Steve and the rest of Team Justice (Melissa Parisot, Paul Holes, Kirk Campbell, and Monica Czajkowski) on the case of the Golden State Killer. Thank you, Steve; it was my great honor to work with you and the rest of the team to solve the Golden State Killer case.

Thank you also to all those who shared their stories with me for this book, including Lori Adams, Dr. Peter Speth, Barbara Taylor, Richard Weiss, Professor Richard "Ed" Green, Judy Russell, and Tim Horne. And special thanks to Lisa Jensen for allowing me to share her story.

Thank you as well to the many wonderful folks with whom I have worked on cases over the last several years, including Jim Scharf, Jane Jorgensen, Carol Schweitzer, Amanda Bixler, Rolf Norton, Anthony Johnson, Gena Steward, Lindsey Wade, and Eric Kovanda.

Thank you to the many people from the Monterey Family History Center, along with more than one hundred genetic cousins of Lisa Jensen, who all assisted in identifying Lisa. People who were major contributors include Junel Davidsen; Nancy Averill; Teresa Heyerdahl; John Light; Bonnie Hill; Pam Cote; Paul and Kristi Schofield; Adam Keim; Andrea Ackerman; Kathy Kuzmick; Karen Beck and her late father, Jean DuPont; Mark Brassard; and the late Peg Plummer and Raymond Gelinas.

A special thank-you to the folks at FamilyTreeDNA who made the DNA testing for the Lisa Project doable: Bennett Greenspan, Max Blankfield, and the amazing Janine Cloud. And a shout-out in particular to Bennett for "doing the right thing" to assist with DNA testing for the Golden State Killer case.

Thanks also to the many people who have been there for me over the years, including the late professor Nathan Kaplan, my thesis adviser, and his wife, Goldie; the late Bert Rowland and his widow, Susan Blake; and Pat Cameron and her late husband, D. Bruce Cameron. Bruce, my English 1A professor at the College of San Mateo in spring 1969, was a gifted, inspiring teacher. He and Pat remained my friends over the years. Pat is also one of several friends who read early drafts of *I Know Who You Are* and made comments that were both helpful and encouraging.

Others draft readers include: an old friend from high school days, Thomas Fleming; Brian Swann, a genealogy colleague in the UK; local genealogy colleagues Irene Rossman and Dayna Jacobs; and my daughter-in-law, Julia Adler. Many thanks to all for your input.

My genetic cousin David Abbott and his wife, Jacquie, in the UK were the catalyst for my learning how to do genetic genealogy, and the wonderful folks at DNAAdoption were my teachers: Karin Corbeil and Diane Harman-Hoog. And the incomparable Karen Clifford, my teacher at Monterey Peninsula College, for her four-semester-long family history research course. Thank you all.

And for genetics I have to thank the late Dr. Dan Lindsley. Dr. Lindsley deserves special mention, because when I transferred to the University of California at San Diego as a junior, I had decided over the summer to change my major from French literature to premed— and one of the required premed courses was the upper-division genetics class taught by Dr. Lindsley. He approved my taking the class despite the fact that I had not taken any of the lower-division prerequisites, and in fact had never taken a biology class, not even in high school. Who knows what I might have ended up doing if he had said no?

While I was working as a patent attorney, my inventors kept me up to date on all that was new and spiffy in the biological sciences, but after my retirement from patent law, I no longer had that. To brush up on my genetics for doing investigative genetic genealogy, I took a two-semester online class called Useful Genetics at the University of British Columbia taught by Professor Rosie Redfield. Thank you, Dr. Redfield, for getting me back up to speed.

There are a great many friends, relatives, and colleagues who have been cheerleaders for me as I waded into putting together this autobiography of sorts. It has been inspiring. You know who you are and I thank you all. And among these cheerleaders, I especially wish to recognize two groups. The first is my Ladies Wisdom Circle: Jodi Rickin-Matheson, Debbie Burch, Lisa Reagan, Emily Angotti, Sarah Kelly, Jane Schreiner, Laura Laine, and Kelly Wendorf. Thank you all for helping make it happen. And the second is the Dent community, with special thanks to Steve Broback and Jason Preston.

Thanks to Frank Weimann, my literary agent at Folio Literary Management, for not only brokering a great contract for me but also assisting with finding a superb writer to work with me on this book. And thanks to Alex Tresniowski for his talent in converting my overly detailed descriptions of my work into a compelling story.

And a great many thanks to my editor at Ballantine Books, Mary

Reynics, for those changes, both large and small, that so beautifully crafted my story into a book.

What I do, I do for the victims. May my work, and that of my group, Firebird Forensics, in naming suspects and restoring names to those whose remains were unidentified bring some peace to all who have been touched by violence.

GLOSSARY

ADMIXTURE

Admixture or *bioancestry* refers to a test taker's geographical origins. Markers in the test taker's DNA are compared against markers in DNA collected from reference populations in which the members are believed to all have originated in a particular geographic region. The admixture can be used as a reality check when identifying a suspect. For example, if the admixture for DNA recovered from a crime scene indicates that a suspect's admixture is 60 percent Scandinavian and 40 percent Italian, and the admixture for a potential suspect is lacking in either of those components, it is unlikely that the potential suspect is the perpetrator.

AUTOSOMAL DNA TESTING

Up until 2007, there were two basic direct-to-consumer DNA tests available to the public: one that analyzed mitochondrial DNA, or mtDNA (passed down virtually unchanged from mother to child, but passed to the next generation only by female offspring), and one that analyzed the Y chromosome (Y-DNA, which is passed down virtually unchanged from father to son). Analyzing mtDNA provides information on the direct maternal-line ancestry, while the study of Y-DNA, found only in men, provides information on the direct paternal line.

These two tests are powerful, but limited; they can uncover only a relatively small subset of relatives. However, unlike mtDNA and Y-DNA autosomal DNA changes at each generation through a process called recombination.

In 2007, the genealogy website 23andMe introduced new technology: an autosomal DNA test. Autosomal DNA molecules carry genetic information that appears in the form of a code, which is a combination of four letters representing the four nucleotides, or chemical bases, in DNA: A for adenine, C for cytosine, T for thymine, and G for guanine. When two of these nucleotides combine, they are called a *base pair* (for instance, A always pairs with T and C always pairs with G). As more and more of these base pairs combine into larger strands, you have the building blocks of life.

Each of our genes contains a combination of these four letters that together form a genetic code, so that in a single DNA segment the code will look like AAGGTTA, or AAAGTCTGAC, or any number of series. The collective information in all these segments of code is called the *genome*—the sum of *all* the genetic data in our DNA. This is a staggering amount of genetic information, considering that the human genome contains around *3.2 billion* base pairs. All of this newly available data allows us to discover more and more things about ourselves, including ethnic makeup, medical history, and a bigger array of relatives. An autosomal DNA test provides matching with relatives from all ancestral lines, not just the direct maternal and paternal lines.

AUTOSOMES

An autosome is any chromosome that is not a sex chromosome. Humans have twenty-three pairs of chromosomes, and one of these twenty-three pairs is referred to as the sex chromosomes. (Females have two X chromosomes in their cells, and males have one X and one Y chromosome.) The other twenty-two pairs, numbered one through twenty-two, from the largest to the smallest chromosome, are collectively referred to as autosomes.

CENTIMORGAN (CM)

This is a unit of measurement for how much DNA two people share. The scientific definition relates to the frequency of genetic recombination. The amount of matching DNA is reported for half-identical regions (HIR) of DNA. Blaine Bettinger, a well-known genetic genealogist, has collected information from some fifty-two thousand citizen scientists on the amount of matching DNA for various relationships. As an example, on average, a parent-child match is around 3,500 cM as is that of identical (monozygotic) twins. Full non-twin siblings share around 2,600 cM, whereas half siblings (one parent in common) share around 1,750 cM and first cousins around 860 cM.

CHROMOSOME

This is a threadlike structure located in the nucleus of a cell consisting of genetic material organized into genes. Humans have twenty-three pairs of chromosomes—one pair that is referred to as our sex chromosomes (females have two X chromosomes in their cells, males have one X and one Y chromosome) and the other twenty-two pairs, which collectively are referred to as *autosomes* (any chromosome that is not a sex chromosome). Chromosomes are the highest level of organization of our DNA and proteins.

CODIS

CODIS stands for the Combined DNA Index System, which was created and is operated by the FBI, and which is essentially a vast database of DNA taken from crime scenes and convicted offenders. Law enforcement officers can compare DNA samples from their local crime scenes and match them to existing samples stored in CODIS, greatly aiding in the identification and capture of criminals.

DNA

Present in almost all living organisms, DNA—which stands for deoxyribonucleic acid—is a self-replicating hereditary material present in nearly every cell in the human body. Put simply, DNA carries our genetic information and is the primary constituent of our chromo-somes.

DNA RECOMBINATION

This refers to how the autosomal DNA from each parent of an individual is exchanged (recombined) in the production of sperm and egg cells. Each sperm cell produced by the male and each egg cell produced by the female contains a different random mix of ancestral autosomal DNA. There is also either an X or a Y chromosome in each sperm cell and a recombined X chromosome in each egg cell. Recombination is why one child may have blond hair and blue eyes while her brother has dark hair and hazel eyes.

DNA SEGMENT

A segment is a string or piece of DNA on a chromosome and, more specifically, all the genetic information contained between the start and the end of the segment. By analyzing DNA segments shared by two people (sometimes called matching segments), the number and size of matching segments can be used to determine how closely two people are related. This level of connectivity is measured in centimorgans.

DNA SEGMENT TRIANGULATION

This refers to a method for identifying an unknown person by building speculative family trees for two people who match with the unknown person on the same segment of DNA and all three people match one another on that segment of DNA. That segment of DNA is inherited from an ancestor common to all three people, so the next step is to identify that common ancestor and then identify all the descendants of that common ancestor—the unknown person has to be among those descendants. DNA segment triangulation was developed by the founders of DNAAdoption to assist adoptees in finding their birth relatives. DNAAdoption refers to the technique as the Methodology.

GENE

A gene is the basic physical and functional unit of heredity and carries the information that determines traits such as physical characteristics. Genes are made up of DNA, and each chromosome contains many genes. Each cell in the human body contains about twenty-five thousand to thirty-five thousand genes.

GENEALOGY

Genealogy is the study of the descent of humans or families from their ancestors. The information can be recorded in the form of a family tree showing the ancestors from whom an individual descended (sometimes also referred to as a lineage or pedigree). A family tree is a genealogical document.

GENETIC GENEALOGY

Genetic genealogy (GG) is the use of DNA in family history research to create a family tree based on the results of DNA testing of known relatives.

GENOME

The complete set of all the genetic information in an organism is called the genome. Nearly every cell in a human body contains a copy of the genome.

INVESTIGATIVE GENETIC GENEALOGY

Investigative genetic genealogy (IGG), or forensic genealogy, is the use of DNA testing and other genealogical methods as part of a law enforcement investigation.

MITOCHONDRIAL DNA

The mitochondrion (plural *mitochondria*) is an organelle found in the cytoplasm of a cell. The mitochondria have their own DNA. It is in the form of a double-stranded circle. An organelle ("little organ") is a biological structure in the cell that performs a particular function. For the mitochondria, that function is primarily energy production. Cells with high energy requirements, such as muscle cells, may have many thousands of mitochondria and hence many thousands of copies of the mitochondrial DNA. This is in contrast to nuclear DNA (autosomes and sex chromosomes), for which there is only one copy of each chromosome pair since there is only one nucleus per cell and therefore only one copy of the autosomal DNA per cell.

NCMEC

NCMEC is the acronym for the National Center for Missing and Exploited Children, a Virginia-based nonprofit organization created by Congress in 1984 in response to a series of high-profile child abductions. The organization is dedicated to providing information about and assistance to children who are reported missing or abused.

PHENOTYPE

A phenotype is an observable trait of an individual (such as hair or eye color) and is determined by both genotype and environmental factors.

SNPS (PRONOUNCED "SNIPS")

SNPs are single nucleotide polymorphisms, which are mutations, or variants, that occur in the DNA. For example, if the second G in an AAGGTTA sequence is replaced by an A, the resulting code—AAGATTA—is a variant. If a variant occurs in at least 1 percent of the population, it is called a single nucleotide polymorphism, or SNP. An autosomal DNA test generally examines around 700,000 to 800,000 SNPs, and an algorithm analyzes thousands of DNA profiles by comparing this multitude of SNPs looking for matches. Matching SNPs is how related people are identified; how closely they are related is based on the amount of matching DNA and is measured in centimorgans.

WHAT ARE THE ODDS? (WATO)

WATO is a relatively new analytical tool that uses the amount of shared DNA between an unknown subject and matches (people who share DNA with the unknown subject) to calculate the highest odds for where the unknown subject belongs in the speculative tree built based on the matches' family trees.

Y-STRS

Y-STR is the acronym for a short tandem repeat, or repeated segment of DNA, on the male Y chromosome. A specific combination of Y-STRs is known as a haplotype, while the Y-STRs themselves are known as markers. Y-STR analysis, while limited because the Y chromosome is found only in males, can be useful in providing a surname for a potential suspect by comparing a Y-STR haplotype from the unknown subject against a Y-DNA database.

INDEX

ABOUT THE AUTHOR

BARBARA RAE-VENTER is a New Zealand–born American investigative genetic genealogist, biologist, and retired patent attorney best known for her work helping the FBI and other investigators identify Joseph James DeAngelo as the Golden State Killer. She earned a PhD at the University of California at San Diego and later a law degree at the University of Texas at Austin School of Law. Her investigative work earned her a place on the *Time* 100 list of most influential people and was recognized by the journal *Nature* as one of "10 People Who Mattered in Science in 2018."

ABOUT THE TYPE

This book was set in Sabon, a typeface designed by the well-known German typographer Jan Tschichold (1902–74). Sabon's design is based upon the original letter forms of sixteenth-century French type designer Claude Garamond and was created specifically to be used for three sources: foundry type for hand composition, Linotype, and Monotype. Tschichold named his typeface for the famous Frankfurt typefounder Jacques Sabon (c. 1520–80).